AFRICAN AMERICAN WOMEN AND THE VOTE, 1837–1965

Edited by Ann D. Gordon

with

Bettye Collier-Thomas

John H. Bracey

Arlene Voski Avakian

Joyce Avrech Berkman

AFRICAN AMERICAN WOME

AND THE VOTE, 1837-1965

University of Massachusetts Press *Amherst*

Printed in the United States of America
LC 96-14881
ISBN 1-55849-058-2 (cloth); 1-55849-059-0 (pbk.)
Designed by Mary Mendell
Set in Minion by Keystone Typesetting, Inc.
Printed and bound by Thomson-Shore, Inc.
Library of Congress Cataloging-in-Publication Data
African American women and the vote, 1837-1965 / edited by Ann D.
Gordon with Bettye Collier-Thomas . . . [et al.].
    p.   cm.
Includes bibliographical references.
ISBN 1-55849-058-2 (cloth : alk. paper). — ISBN 1-55849-059-0
(alk. paper)
1. Afro-Americans—Suffrage—History. 2. Women—Suffrage—United
States—History. 3. Suffragists—United States—History. 4. Afro-
American women social reformers—History. 5. Afro-American women—
Political activity—History. I. Gordon, Ann D. (Ann Dexter)
II. Collier-Thomas, Bettye.
JK1924.A47 1997
324.6'23'08996073—dc20   96-1488 CIP
British Library Cataloguing in Publication data are available.

To the Memory of Sidney Kaplan and Helen Harris Bracey

Contents

Acknowledgments

The original benefactors of this volume are the people and institutions who made possible the 1987 conference on Afro-American Women and the Vote, 1837 to 1965, for which these essays were first written. The conference was funded by the University of Massachusetts at Amherst, the Massachusetts Foundation for the Humanities and Public Policy, the Charles H. Revson Foundation, and the University's Alumni Association Board of Directors. The League of Women Voters of Massachusetts cosponsored the event.

For their vision of an outline of African American women's history and knowledge of their field, we thank members of the planning conference who in 1986 developed the historical outline evident still in these essays. They are Sylvia M. Jacobs, Kathryn Kish Sklar, Ellen C. DuBois, Bettina Aptheker, Rosalyn Terborg-Penn, and Bettye Collier-Thomas.

A number of excellent contributions to the conference itself could not be included in this book but deserve notice and thanks nonetheless. Mary Frances Berry launched the event with an address on politics that wove together her command of history and her immediate experience in Washington, D.C. Political practice was again the topic at the end of the conference, in a round-table discussion with Patricia Facey, League of Women Voters; Gracia Hillman, National Coalition on Black Voter Participation; Toni-Michelle Travis, George Mason University; and Saundra Graham, State Representative, Massachusetts. For their enthusiastic and valuable commentaries during the conference, we thank Dorothy Sterling, Ena Farley, Ellen C. Du Bois, and Elaine Smith. For their papers, we also thank Adele Logan Alexander and Sharon Harley.

At the University of Massachusetts, assistance came from the deans of the Faculty of Humanities and Fine Arts and of Social and Behavioral Sciences; the Graduate School; the Chancellor's Office; the Vice-Chancellor for Public Relations and Development; the Office of Third World Affairs; the Department of History; the W. E. B. Du Bois Department of Afro-American Studies; the Women's Studies Program; and University Conference Services.

For assistance in preparing this book we owe special thanks to Edna McGlynn, Colleen O'Neill, Jennifer Boutell, and Tricia Loveland.

The Editors

AFRICAN AMERICAN WOMEN AND THE VOTE, 1837–1965

Introduction

Ann D. Gordon

The essays in this book originated as papers presented at the conference, Afro-American Women and the Vote: From Abolitionism to the Voting Rights Act, held at the University of Massachusetts in the fall of 1987. In the absence of any comprehensive political history of African American women, the conference solicited studies that would lay the groundwork for such a history when presented in chronological order. Formally, the task of synthesizing discrete papers fell to Bettina Aptheker, whose summary also appears in this book. But it was undertaken as well by all participants gathered at Amherst. As they analyzed continuities and common themes in their papers and posed questions for further work, participants began to construct a new narrative history defined by African American women.

The purposes of this exercise included but were not limited to solving problems of scholarship. Many members of the audience and some speakers came to the conference because of their interest in the political empowerment of women. Plans for the event reflected a conviction that histories of struggle for a political voice are pertinent to the exercise of political rights today. Traditions and history about the American Revolution have, for example, always helped to define the identity of white males as citizens. But the later historical experience of other groups who also fought for their citizenship and for political justice is less well known. The conference would try to recover the story and, by establishing African American women's pursuit of political democracy as integral to the nation's history, reinforce their identity as citizens as well.

The conference took place during a revival of political activity in African American communities, as Jesse Jackson geared up for his second campaign for the presidential nomination of the Democratic party. Not only had Jackson inspired a surge of voter registration across the country, he had also given national voice to black political aspirations for the first time since the late 1960s. Moreover, Jackson seemed especially mindful of the leadership role women play in the black community and their particular burdens as impoverished mothers in a society lacking a commitment to human welfare.

While the editors were preparing the papers for publication, political events gave the history new salience. In a striking initiative, 1,603 African American women released a statement of conscience in November 1991, protesting the manipulation of black history and "malicious defamation" of women that marked the confirmation hearings of Judge Clarence Thomas to the bench of the United States Supreme Court. "African-American Women in Defense of Themselves" served as title to their statement and name of their group. Though the phrase harks back to mobilizations of the black community to defend against violent attacks, and the statement expresses fear about rights endangered by a conservative Court, the phrase speaks immediately to the need to defend by self-definition: "No one will speak for us but ourselves."[1]

These essays foreshadowed that phrase. They tell of women who acted on that dictum for a century and a half of American history, and in the telling of those stories the authors act on it as well, retelling African American women's history as they must, "in defense of themselves." Their writing affirms a long tradition of political aspiration for justice, equality, and sovereignty.

The historical essays follow a chronological outline from 1837 to 1965, dates that differ from those generally used to highlight the turning points of political history for white women in the United States. The early date marks the first Anti-Slavery Convention of American Women, an interracial gathering of women held in New York City to define their roles independent of men in the crucial struggles of that era to end slavery in southern states and racial discrimination in northern states. It replaces 1848, the year of the Seneca Falls Woman's Rights Convention at which Elizabeth Cady Stanton and Frederick Douglass teamed up to affirm a woman's right to vote, and the change emphasizes the preeminence of antislavery agitation in the political history of African Americans, including women.

The latter date marks passage of the Voting Rights Act, which reaffirmed the responsibility of the federal government to enforce the right to vote, guaranteed by the Fifteenth and Nineteenth amendments. The Nineteenth Amendment, ratified in 1920, marked the victory of white women's long campaign for the right to vote, and it established a principle about sexual equality, but it failed to overcome, or even challenge, well-established state laws disfranchising black voters. Not until 1965 could the very old promise of universal suffrage become a reality shared by men and women, black and white.

That women now frame their political history anew and supply it with different turning points in order to account for the experience and aspirations of both whites and blacks is indicative of profound change in historical thought over the last thirty years. Simultaneous revivals of women's history and African American history expressed growing resistance to the dominance of white males in defining the past. But the tendency among scholars in both revivals to employ concepts like "women" and "African Americans" without heeding differences of race and gender led, in turn, to a revival of interest in the history of African American women and an ongoing effort to understand how race and gender interacted to distinguish their history.

These modern and historiographical dilemmas about race, gender, and politics are not new. The histories of American people searching for political and social justice uncover countless occasions when similar tensions between self-definition and a status that is imposed surfaced within a movement. When the Anti-Slavery Convention of American Women met in 1837, the group placed an emphasis on their womanhood and a woman's right to speak out and act on public, political questions—specifically to end slavery. Though a few individuals had advanced the notion of a woman's right to vote by 1837, women at the meeting defined politics more loosely as the right to be heard on the great issues of the day, resolving

> that as moral and responsible beings, the women of America are solemnly called upon by the spirit of the age and the signs of the times, fully to discuss the subject of slavery, that they may be prepared to meet the approaching exigency, and be qualified to act as women, and as Christians, on this all-important subject.
>
> . . . that it is the duty of woman, and the province of woman, to plead the cause of the oppressed in our land, and to do all that she can by her

voice, and her pen, and her purse, and the influence of her example, to overthrow the horrible system of American slavery.[2]

All women shared the same duty.

It is of vital importance to understanding the significance of the meeting in 1837 to realize that, in this first attempt to forge a political force of women, participants faced up to the reality of sharp divisions among themselves. They defined womanhood as a universal *ideal,* difficult but necessary to achieve in a racist society. Their remarkable resolutions included this:

> That this Convention do firmly believe that the existence of an unnatural prejudice against our colored population, is one of the chief pillars of American slavery—therefore, that the more we mingle with our oppressed brethren and sisters, the more deeply are we convinced of the sinfulness of that anti-Christian prejudice which is crushing them to the earth in our nominally Free States— . . . and that we deem it a solemn duty of every woman to pray to be delivered from such an unholy feeling, and to act out the principles of Christian equality by associating with them as though the color of the skin was of no more consequence than that of the hair, or the eyes.[3]

There are examples in the historical record, during the months and years immediately following the gathering in New York City, of white women striving to conquer their own prejudice and standing shoulder to shoulder with African American women to resist divisive laws and customs, but their commitment to racial justice distinguished them as radicals even within the vanguard of woman's rights agitation.

By the end of the nineteenth century, this recognition that sisterhood was a social construction requiring great personal and societal change had virtually disappeared from what historians call "the woman's movement." The term itself, like the history it summarizes, ignores the historical contradictions that inhere when "woman" is read to mean white woman. Examples of false universality and inconsistent sisterhood are legion. Consider two letters written to the *Washington Post* in February 1898, while the National American Woman Suffrage Association convened in the capital to celebrate fifty years of claims and agitation for woman suffrage. An open letter to Susan B. Anthony from Helen A. Cook appeared on 19 February. President of the Washington Woman's League, an African American club with several hundred members, Cook avoided the meeting but followed press coverage closely. She was struck by the recurrence at this meeting of an old argument for woman suffrage, dating from the period immediately after the Civil War, that appealed to prejudice, that stressed the "inconsistency of conferring the right to vote . . . upon the newly-emancipated slaves and denying it to the cultivated white women." "Would it not be well," she wrote,

> to signalize the end of the first half century of effort, and the beginning of a new and brighter era by leaving behind the old formula and basing the claims of women wholly on right and justice? . . . I ask you in the name of universal womanhood to rely for ultimate success of a good cause on appeals to the higher nature.[4]

A week later, Charlotte Forten Grimké seconded Cook's letter with direct language of her own.

> These expressions [at suffrage meetings] have for years prevented many of us from attending the conventions held in this city. They have disgusted us. I do not hesitate to say that they can only be characterized as contemptible; for their direct effect is to strengthen a most unjust and cruel prejudice; to increase the burdens which already weigh so heavily upon a deeply wronged people.

She understood very well the complexities underlying terms like "womanhood," electing to remind the suffragists that among their numbers could be found women who fought on the Confederate side to preserve slavery.

> Some of us certainly cannot believe that it would have been just to deny the right of citizenship to the great majority of loyal men of the South—as the negroes certainly were, and are—and confer it upon the disloyal women, who not only did not conceal, but gloried in their disloyalty, however, intellectual and refined they may have been. . . . And while [African American women] appreciate the value of woman's suffrage quite as keenly as other women do, they will never cease to rejoice that their fathers and brothers, and sons and husbands had the right to vote conferred upon them. . . . And we would desire for ourselves no recognition that would involve injustice to such men.[5]

Both Cook and Grimké were linked through their families to the antebellum agitations that joined antislavery with woman's rights through an ideal of universality. They had been touched personally by the political claim raised in 1837 for women to understand and influence public policy and law, but their testimonies in 1898 remind modern readers, as one hopes they reminded contemporaries like Susan B. Anthony, that the key lay not simply in "be[ing] qualified to act as women," in the phrase of the 1837 meeting. The key lay in striving for a day when, in Grimké's phrase, "equal and exact justice be meted out to all."

By 1920 the tradition from which Cook and Grimké spoke had all but vanished from the predominantly white women's groups descended from the abolitionist crusade. "The National Woman's Party has only one object," Alice Paul explained to a leader of the National Association for the Advancement of Colored People, "the passage of an amendment to the National Constitution removing the sex qualification from the franchise regulations. . . . All that our amendment would do would be to see that the franchise conditions for every state were the same for women as for men."[6] In other words, she would let racial inequality persist. It is difficult to find a more cynical attitude toward universal womanhood than this, of promising sexual equality within existing inequalities of race. Black women's struggle to bar states from disfranchising African American men and women was carried on for forty-five more years.

Even before it convened, plans for the conference in 1987 benefited from efforts of scholars in African American and women's history to refine a historical framework and identify concepts indigenous to the history of African American women and the vote. The earliest formulation for a conference asked if the suffrage movements of black and white women could be compared. Having established that racism seriously jeopardized cooperation between them, could historians look at grass-roots support for the vote among both black and white women to learn more about ideas and organizations underlying their commitment to the cause? When an editor of the *Papers of Elizabeth Cady Stanton and Susan B. Anthony* discussed the idea with the director of the Mary McLeod Bethune Museum and Archives, they concluded that historians were not ready for comparison; historians of neither group had sufficiently developed their subject to get beneath leadership, national conventions, or the best-known pronouncements.

The question shifted in the second formulation: Could the history of the suffrage movement among black women be recovered? Because the topic had not previously been treated as a whole, a conference would bring together historians not otherwise collaborating to create a mosaic of historical examples out of dispersed and unconnected studies. A preliminary proposal was drawn up in the winter of 1986 and circulated first among faculty at the University of Massachusetts and then to six prominent outside historians. It suggested turning points in the political history and identified topics for consideration in each era, anticipating that this tentative framework would be revised during the course of the conference. At a two-day planning session in October 1986, scholars found themselves prepared to revise it on the spot, in what amounted to an intense historical seminar. Rosalyn Terborg-Penn's opening essay in this book discusses in detail the plan that evolved and its relationship to earlier historiography. The new formulation lessened dependence on chronological and topical structures borrowed from the history of white women, and it asked a more open-ended question: What is the political history of black women?

It remained to suggest a chronology, one that indicated where critical changes probably occurred in political activity, and invite historians to fill it in and, when necessary, revise it. If an era began with the Anti-Slavery Convention of American Women, it seemed to end during Reconstruction, about 1869, when slaves had won their freedom and their citizenship. Abolitionism no longer bound together an interracial alliance in the North. Contributors to the session on "Coalitions of Gender and Race" were asked, in particular, to define how northern women came to seek a political voice in this era and what experience of coalitions they gained.

Though 1869 seemed an appropriate conclusion to an era in the North, a new era in the South started earlier, and the session "Personhood and Citizenship; The Struggle of Afro-American Women" spanned the years from 1865 to 1898. During those decades, with nominal protection from the courts, women joined (perhaps led) the struggle to attain legal rights, to make real their freedom from slavery and define their new citizenship. An important key to understanding the history is learning the extent to which women pursued gender-specific ideals of citizenship. This era "ended" with judicial validation of Jim Crow laws in 1898.

Two sessions recognized the growing importance of organized activity among African American women throughout the country at the end of the nineteenth century. In the first, "Defining for Themselves: Creating a Black Political Base," the essays focused on organizations that coordinated national campaigns against lynching and for temperance, woman suffrage, and better education in the years between 1890 and 1920. Though concurrent with new organizing among white middle- and working-class women, this burst of activity in the African American community needed an independent examination, one that could allow for similar organizations to arise from radically different social and political needs.

The second of these two sessions, "Defining for Themselves: Consolidating the Struggle," explored the mass experience of African American women during years of intense racism and political experimentation, from 1900 to 1935, when women played important roles in developing new political structures and strategies to move their community forward.

Finally, in "Movin' On Up: Afro-American Women's Search for New Forms of Political Power," participants looked at women's importance to the resurgence of black political power and at how the new movement for enfranchisement between 1930 and 1965 contributed to the rise of African American feminism.

Through this framework the authors of these essays have begun to construct a history that defines citizenship from the perspective of women who fought long and hard to gain minimal legal recognition of rights deemed "natural" by the founders of the United States. Thus the essays undermine all history that has ignored historic limitations on rights, fabricated a universal experience from stories of the privileged, or turned a deaf ear to the ideals that African American women have defined as significant for themselves, their families, their race, and their nation.

Proceedings from a conference often fail to convey the energy, excitement, and intellectual fireworks that occurred. In this case that difficulty is compounded by our inability to include the commentaries or transcribe discussion. In offering the papers from this event we want to draw attention to the new and imaginative reconstructions and reinterpretations they contain. As the research of these scholars continues and the published results make their way into the arena of historical debate, we will soon realize that we will no longer be able to teach the old "truths" of American, African American, and women's history. A lot of what we thought was solid ground is being taken out from under our feet in every time period, in every area of focus. We can resist new knowledge and approaches and try to hold fast to what we have learned and taught previously. Or we can read these essays as guideposts to a much more interesting and complex view of the history of the United States than we had ever imagined.

Notes

1   "African American Women in Defense of Themselves," *New York Times*, 17 November 1991. Nine participants in the 1987 conference signed the statement.

2   Dorothy Sterling, ed., *Turning the World Upside Down: The Anti-Slavery Convention of American Women, Held in New York City, May 9–12, 1837* (New York: Coalition of Publishers for Employment, 1987), 12–13.

3   Ibid., 19.

4   Helen A. Cook, "A Letter to Miss Anthony," *Washington Post,* 19 February 1898, in *Papers of Elizabeth Cady Stanton and Susan B. Anthony,* ed. Patricia G. Holland and Ann D. Gordon (Wilmington, Del.: Scholarly Resources, 1991, microfilm), reel 38, frame 276.

5   Charlotte F. Grimké, letter to the editor, *Washington Post,* 24 February 1898, in Susan B. Anthony Scrapbook, 1892–1901, Susan B. Anthony Papers, Manuscripts Division, Library of Congress.

6   Alice Paul to Mary White Ovington, 31 March 1919, Papers of the National Association for the Advancement of Colored People, Library of Congress, cited in Paula Giddings, *When and Where I Enter: The Impact of Black Women on Race and Sex in America* (New York: William Morrow, 1984), 163. See also Nancy F. Cott, *The Grounding of Modern Feminism* (New Haven: Yale University Press, 1987), 68–70, 307–9; and Kathryn Kish Sklar, "The Debate between Florence Kelley and Alice Paul over the ERA, 1921–1923," paper prepared for the Sixth Berkshire Conference in the History of Women, 1984.

African American

Women and the Vote:

An Overview

Rosalyn Terborg-Penn

The right to vote is a privilege only recently exercised by the majority of African American women in the United States. Nonetheless, it is a right many of them fought to achieve, beginning in the antebellum period of United States history. Often behind the scenes or ignored in the history of the woman suffrage and black suffrage movements, the African American female was significant in both. Passage of the Nineteenth Amendment, which enfranchised all American women, was due in part to the efforts of African American women. In addition, the struggle to maintain the ballot continued for more than a generation after passage of the woman suffrage amendment in 1920, as the majority of enfranchised black women were robbed of their hard-won ballots by the success of white political supremacy in the South. A victory in the struggle came with the 1965 Voting Rights Act, when the majority of black men and women, disfranchised in communities all over the South, regained their lost right to the ballot.

Three aims propelled the authors of essays in this book. The first speaks to the need in scholarship on black women to understand the impulse for political power in terms of the black community and its experiences. The second looks to provide historians with models for analyzing the political component of women's culture in the United States, specifically as these models relate to the experiences of African American women. And the third seeks to stimulate discussion about the status of African American female citizenship during the late 1980s.

The essays cover the time period from 1837 to 1965, spanning the political activity of five generations of African American women. Our historical sojourn begins with the turbulent times when the first national convention of female abolitionists met. Although only a handful of black women participated in politically motivated organizations during the antebellum period, the abolitionist movement represented a significant coalition of reformers—females and males, blacks and whites—who sought the eradication of slavery. We end our sojourn with a positive time, the year the Voting Rights Act passed in Congress, after another coalition of reformers used various political strategies to bring political equity to African Americans. During our journey, we meet a large number of black women involved in this struggle, whose political involvement grew steadily over time and culminated in a political victory. Collectively the essays capture the illusive history of African American women's political travails and triumphs.

Methodology

How do we go about reconstructing the history of African American women's involvement in the mainstream woman suffrage movement and specifically their own struggle to vote? As a student of the black role in the woman suffrage movement, I began the process in the early 1970s initiating research for my dissertation at Howard University. In the 1977 study that resulted, "Afro-Americans in the Struggle for Woman Suffrage," I recovered scores of blacks, both men and women, who had publicly supported the woman suffrage movement. Yet most of these individuals had been lost in contemporary studies of the movement.[1] During the 1970s, the myths were pervasive that, historically, black women were uninterested in feminist politics and that black men opposed feminist issues. Finding data that disproved these myths encouraged me to search further, investigating traditional and nontraditional sources for evidence to demonstrate that many nineteenth- and twentieth-century blacks were suffragists.[2]

When I began my research, there were very few published works analyzing even the mainstream of the woman suffrage movement. Biased accounts of the movement, written by white women who had been suffragists, were available and familiar to scholars of women's history. Often when blacks were mentioned in this literature they were described either as opponents of the inclusion of women during the controversy over the Fifteenth Amendment and opponents of the Nineteenth Amendment or as subjects of antisuffrage arguments, made mainly by white southern suffragists who sought to exclude black women from state suffrage referenda. In my research I found none of the anti–woman's rights speeches or newspaper articles black men had been accused of writing. I did find dynamic black women feminists, not merely black female victims.

Two studies were helpful in the early 1970s. One was Eleanor Flexner's *Century of Struggle,* in which several African American women were included. Yet Flexner concluded that African American women, when given the choice between fighting racism or sexism, opted to fight against racism. I speculated that black women could indeed fight both institutions at the same time and continued my search for other historical analyses. The second study, Aileen Kraditor's *Ideas of the Woman Suffrage Movement, 1890–1920,* confirmed my suspicions by delving into the anti–black woman suffrage argument among white southern suffragists and their northern supporters and noting that some black suffragists protested the racism in the woman suffrage movement. Although Kraditor's study covered the white leadership in the movement and only those active during the last thirty years of it, I theorized that black men and black women had remained in the woman suffrage movement for more than seventy years of the struggle, fighting both racism and sexism simultaneously.[3]

To prove this thesis, I began with African Americans' history rather than white women's history. My most helpful secondary sources for the antebellum period were the books and articles written by Benjamin Quarles, who as early as 1940 had published an essay about Frederick Douglass and other black men in the abolitionist movement who had supported women's rights.[4] I also read manuscripts, newspapers, journals, organizational proceedings, and biographies by and about nineteenth-century and early-twentieth-century African Americans, many of whom were abolitionists or civil rights activists as well as woman suffragists.

The recovery of the names of black reformers was important. The six volumes of the *History of Woman Suffrage* gave the names of several men and women unknown as African Americans to historians of white women's history. In addition, sources contemporary to the woman suffrage movement were helpful, including the Susan B. Anthony Papers, *The Life and Work of Susan B. Anthony,* and the periodicals *Revolution* and *Woman's Journal.*[5] The major problem I found in using histories of the woman suffrage movement was that the names of blacks began to disappear by the turn of the century, especially after the publication of the fourth volume of the *History of Woman Suffrage*. In addition, some of the statements published in this history were contradictory and needed to be investigated further.

Barriers also prevented searching for quantifiable data about black suffragists during the twentieth century. Although voter statistics had been kept that reflected both race and gender, few data were available about black women. Blacks were not separated by gender, and women were not separated by race. Helen Woodbury had found a similar problem in 1896, when she analyzed the impact of woman suffrage upon Colorado, one of the few states to grant women the right to vote in the nineteenth century.[6]

Elinor Lerner faced the problem again in researching her 1981 dissertation about the role of the ethnic vote during the woman suffrage campaigns in New York City. Although she discussed the black vote, finding some areas where blacks resided to be prosuffrage and some to be antisuffrage, Lerner did not provide a voter analysis for black neighborhoods, as she did for several European ethnic communities. One of the reasons she noted was the difficulty in distinguishing the black from the white vote in specific neighborhoods.[7]

In the early 1980s I reflected upon the methods I used to research my dissertation, as I set out to write the history I am now doing on the African American women involved in the woman suffrage movement. The issue was whether to take a black nationalist perspective or a woman-centered perspective. I concluded that I needed both, because too many variables influencing the political experiences of African American women involved both race and gender.

In researching my revised study, I looked at additional primary sources that treated African American women in the suffrage movement, and I read the scholarship about woman suffrage published since I completed my dissertation. Among the studies most helpful to me were Ellen Carol DuBois, *Feminism and Suffrage: The Emergence of an Independent Women's Movement in America, 1848–1869;* Bettina Aptheker, *Woman's Legacy: Essays on Race, Sex, and Class in American History;* and Elisabeth Griffith, *In Her Own Right: The Life of Elizabeth Cady Stanton.*[8]

DuBois's feminist analysis of the radical white suffragists of the post–Civil War era provided insight for characterizing the politics of black woman suffragists. Aptheker, who often disagreed with DuBois's interpretation of the radical feminists and their relationship to blacks, wrote about the link between abolitionists and suffrage as well as the Fifteenth Amendment controversy. Her analysis is a Marxist-feminist approach to the suffrage issues with a black perspective, the first analysis to appear since my dissertation that took a different approach from mine to the roles of blacks in the movement. Finally, Griffith's biography of Elizabeth Cady Stanton included discussions about Stanton not only in her role as an abolitionist and suffragist but also in her relationships with selected black and white reformers. Although Griffith admitted that her analysis was pro-Stanton, her evidence enabled me to see why I interpreted this pioneer woman suffragist as a racist.

New sources combined with the old supported my original thesis that black women, in their struggle for the right to vote, fought racism and sexism simultaneously. By the last decade of the nineteenth century and continuing through to the end of the struggle for the Nineteenth Amendment, a large number of African American women took leadership positions in local and regional woman suffrage activities. During these years black women's support for woman suffrage often paralleled, yet developed differently from, that of white suffragists. Although there were similar strategies and coalitions between blacks and whites, experiences between the two racial groups differed over time. The existence of an anti–black woman suffrage rationale and strategy among many whites, including women, and the discrimination black women found at the polls reinforced differences between African American and white woman suffragists. Despite the fact that black male leaders publicly supported woman suffrage, black women still carried the burdens imposed by a sexist society, limiting their political visibility. As a result, the struggle for suffrage among black women was similar to but different from that of both white women and black men.

African American women's struggle for political equity since the ratification of the Nineteenth Amendment is characterized similarly by tension between their race and their gender. The coalition between black and white suffragists fell apart shortly after the passage of the amendment. Racism among white women seeking an equal rights amendment prevented them from relating to the plight of black women voters experiencing disfranchisement. African American women in the political arena quickly strengthened their coalitions with black men to fight the loss of political equity among both groups. For the most part, the political efforts of black women in the Republican party, and later in the Democratic party, appear peripheral because scholars who have written about this period focus primarily on male political activity. In studies about the drive for voting rights in the South during the 1960s, male leadership has been the focus. Grass-roots women are seen, however, through the visual records of the movement. The advent of videotaping for television provided an unintended historical medium for examining the presence of African American women in political activities. However, aside from Fannie Lou Hamer, most of these women remain anonymous and the historical analysis of their roles neglected.[9]

Overview

The history of the woman suffrage movement and women's subsequent political struggles raises questions about how blacks, both men and women, fit into the quest for universal suffrage from the antebellum era through the post–Nineteenth Amendment period in United States history. This overview sets the stage for the historical reconstruction in the essays that follow, wherein lost African American women suffragists are recovered and their goals, ideas, and coalitions placed within the framework of the wider political goals of Americans during the mid twentieth century.

The expansion of suffrage during the antebellum years was a phenomenon experienced by white males, not women and black men. White manhood suffrage, not universal suffrage, was symbolic of the growing democratic process. African Americans of both sexes supported and argued for universal suffrage because, like white women, they were denied political rights. In placing African American women within the framework of antebellum reform movements, we find a preponderance of male leaders, both black and white. Students of the abolitionist movement and of other early-nineteenth-century reforms know that white women often worked behind the scenes in petitioning governments and in fund raising. They know less, however, about African American women in these movements. Seldom do we hear about women like Charlotte Forten, Sr., who, Dorothy Sterling noted, was overshadowed by her husband, James Forten, Sr.[10] Although black and white female reformers shared the invisibility of gender, mainstream scholars who have discussed the work of the abolitionists emphasize the white man, may include black men and white women, but omit significant reference to black women, thereby perpetuating their invisibility.[11] Questions must be raised about the whereabouts of African American women in this era and how they fit into the movement.

Universal suffrage was the goal of woman suffrage advocates until the post–Civil War years. During the late 1860s, a split in the movement developed over strategy. The debate that ensued divided suffrage advocates for twenty years. Although most suffragists followed the "Negro suffrage" wing, many women supported the "woman suffrage first" side of the controversy, with men and women of both races found in both camps.[12]

Questions remain: Where did African American women suffragists fit into this controversy? Why were so few black female voices heard? Perhaps ambivalence among black women who felt torn between both sides of the argument may also have made it difficult for them to articulate their sentiments. However, during the twenty years after the schism, more African American women affiliated with the suffragists who had supported the Fifteenth Amendment than those who had opposed it.

Against this background, authors of the first essays explore the "Coalitions of Gender and Race" forged by black women between 1837 and 1869. They discuss the political experiences of African American women from the time of the first meetings of the interracial Female Anti-Slavery Society through the split between abolitionists and feminists over the suffrage agenda after the Civil War.

Throughout the twenty years of the split in their ranks, suffragists used two different strategies to gain the ballot. For a brief period, the more radical members of the National Woman Suffrage Association held that women should focus their efforts upon challenging the Fourteenth Amendment by attempting to vote. For a while they focused upon state referenda, but they eventually worked toward a constitutional amendment to enfranchise women. The members of the more conservative American Woman Suffrage Association, who had supported the Fifteenth Amendment and universal suffrage, focused on state legislatures in attempts to obtain woman suffrage at state levels. Blacks participated in both organizations, and their strategies and coalitions in the years from 1870 into the 1890s need examination. For this era the recovery of lost black women suffragists is significant, because at this time black women's clubs with unique goals and concerns began to emerge. As a result, black women suffragists moved in two directions, identifying with the mainstream white women suffrage organizations, on the one hand, while on the other hand developing their own agendas.

For the most part, we assume that the masses of African American women were outside of the organizational framework of reformers and political activists of the time. Emerging from slavery with few benefits other than abstract freedom, many black women living in the South were forced to deal with both physical and economic survival on a day-to-day basis. Concern with civil rights at times overshadowed concerns about political rights. Are these assumptions correct, or did arenas of political activism among newly freed women in the South exist? Questions emerge about how African American women fared with the courts. Were they able to use the few civil rights laws that began to surface during the Reconstruction years? How did they fare during the post-

Reconstruction backlash that swept the nation, leaving a laissez-faire policy about race relations in local southern governments to prevail?

"Personhood and Citizenship: The Struggle of Afro-American Women, 1865 to 1890" is the second theme these scholars explore. Here historians examine the first struggle of African American women to make real their emancipation from slavery, in an era characterized both by southern grass-roots participation in electoral politics and by nationwide court validation of Jim Crow legislation.

At the same time, the mainly white and middle-class women in the national woman suffrage movement developed plans for gaining enfranchisement. The state suffrage strategy worked best in the West, while in the East and in the South, white men, for the most part, remained resolutely opposed to woman suffrage. By the 1890s only four states offered full suffrage to women. Between the 1870s and the 1910s, women gained limited suffrage in an additional ten states. Throughout this period, African American women participated in grow-ing numbers in the movement, yet the probability of their achieving suffrage was far less than that for either black men or white women. Despite the fact that most African American men in the South had been disfranchised during the 1890s, those who lived in all regions outside the South could still vote, and black politicians nationwide used a variety of strategies designed to reenfranchise black males. As for black women, in the states where women had won full or partial voting rights the black female population was small, and the over-whelming number of women who gained the ballot were white. Nonetheless, African American women suffragists and black suffrage associations continued to grow as black, not white, suffragists utilized tactics in support of universal suffrage. The question is—why?

During the 1890s, in the middle of the second generation of woman suffrage, a third strategy developed among mainstream suffragists as some form of literacy requirement was legislated in eight states. Among woman suffrage advocates, this trend was known as "educated suffrage" and was obviously meant to limit the black and foreign voters. Some suffragists, therefore, adopted the scheme of trying to convince the white male electorate that the ballot should be extended to the middle-class, educated white women of the nation. Some historians maintain that this tactic impeded the cause, because it served to alienate potential supporters from the working class. Not until the First World War, they note, were suffragists able to realize that the immigrant and working-class voters were not threats, as had been predicted. Other historians find that, in spite of support among working-class men and women in cities long before the First World War, the scheme of the conservative, middle-class white suffragists was to play down the socialist, immigrant, and working-class voters in an attempt to recruit more middle-class, native-born, white male support.[13]

At this point questions about gender, class, race, and region must be raised when analyzing issues of female suffrage. As for African American women, did they identify themselves by class or by race? Was region a factor in how they set their political priorities? Authors of the essays address the theme, "Defining for Themselves: Creating a Black Political Base." They examine political associations developed by African American women from 1890 to 1920, with attention to specific areas of the nation where their political strategies included coalitions with groups outside of their race or gender.

As African American women mobilized during this period, especially in the South, it was not surprising to find mainstream white women suffrage leaders remaining unmoved by the attempts of southern whites to cancel out the black vote entirely and writing black women out of state or federal proposals for woman suffrage amendments. However, the efforts of white supremacists to exclude black women from suffrage amendments only stimulated black men to join their women in the push for a Nineteenth Amendment, which would exclude no women. During the last eight years before ratification of the federal amendment, coalitions of black men and black women on national and local levels fought white supremacy.

Throughout the existence of the movement, suffrage advocates of both races identified the absence of civil and political rights as barriers to the progress of women. They also argued that female reformers could better solve the problems of their society if they were armed with the ballot. This view was especially popular among suffragists during the abolitionist and progressive eras. At these times during the suffrage movement, societal ills were addressed, including intemperance, political corruption, inadequate economic and educational opportunities for women, and, by the twentieth century, crime and limited consumer protection. Black female suffragists argued all of these issues, even after middle-class white suffragists had abandoned many of them. But white suffragists did not include racial discrimination and the plight of disfranchised black women in their priorities for social reform. Unlike the African American suffragists and reformers of the day, whites often avoided the race question or opposed the inclusion of black women in their woman suffrage arguments. Questions remain here also: Was political expediency, or racism, or a combination of the two, the reason white suffragists abandoned black suffragists? Why did African American women continue to connect progressive era reform to the woman suffrage movement after mainstream suffragists abandoned such strategies?

Although opposition to woman suffrage failed to check the growth of the national movement, attempts to keep black women disfranchised continued until both houses of Congress passed the federal amendment in June 1919. By the time the Nineteenth Amendment was ratified in August 1920, nine more states had granted woman suffrage through legislative enactment, including two southern states—Tennessee and Kentucky—where large numbers of black women were enfranchised, for a period at least, equally with white women.

As for the enfranchisement of African American women, it is important to realize that they might not have gained the right to vote with white women without a struggle. Paula Baker theorizes that woman suffrage itself might not have come automatically with urbanization, industrialization, and changes in the nature of electoral politics, unless an effective lobby to include women were established.[14] Similarly, at local and national levels, black women struggled to remain visible to assure that they would be included as voters. Just how this visibility was achieved is the question.

When African American women became voters, they lobbied for political candidates, several of whom were women. In addition, black women organized voter education groups in their own communities, ran for a variety of offices, and fought attempts by southern racists to keep them from the polls. In spite of these efforts to implement their political rights, black women in the South were disfranchised in less than a decade after the Nineteenth Amendment enfranchised them in 1920, and black women outside the South lost the political clout they had acquired. As many black female suffragists anticipated, white women voters ignored their plight. Having encouraged black women to join the movement in order to bring black male voters into the woman suffrage camp, white suffragists then abandoned disfranchised black women. Similarly, middle-class white suffragists abandoned working-class women as they turned to achieving the equal rights amendment as their single goal in the 1920s. As a result, the coalitions established during the push for the Nineteenth Amendment dissolved. Politically conscious women outside of the mainstream became disillusioned with the goals and strategies of the new middle-class feminist leadership.[15]

In the meantime, there was a growing awareness among black women leaders of the international nature of racism and its effects upon women of color throughout the world. As a result, during the 1920s some African American women reached out to their sisters in Africa and the African diaspora in an attempt to sensitize them to their common struggle against racism, poverty, and political neglect. Others addressed the economic plight that scourged African Americans even before the 1929 stock market crash precipitated a depression among mainstream Americans. Using their own secular and religious institutions, black women advanced political strategies to thwart the tide of racism against them. At this juncture we may ask if class effected the political strategies of African American women. Who were the leaders of the masses of black women?

Self-determination persists as a theme of this history into the first third of the twentieth century, and the essays about "Consolidating the Struggle, 1900 to 1935" explore issues that made woman suffrage merely one seam in the fabric of women's political struggle. Scholars examine the experiences of those concerned with the masses of black women in an era of racism and political experimentation.

The thirty years after the ratification of the Nineteenth Amendment have been called decades of discontent for feminists in the United States. Joan M. Jensen and Lois Scharf found that women were discontented during these years because, despite the many achievements of individuals, women faced contradictions and paradoxes in the economic structure, the political institutions, and the social ideology characteristic of American life. These contradictions stifled the women's movements that had prevailed prior to the 1920s.[16]

For African American women, discontent was compounded by disillusionment. The mainstream of the women's movement had failed to seek common ground for political action between blacks and whites. Race, which often determined class, took priority over gender during the decades of discontent. Nonetheless, the African American women leaders of the suffrage era continued to work on their own political agendas, often in coalitions with men in organizations like the Urban League and the National Association for the Advancement of Colored People or in coalitions with white women in organizations like the Young Women's Christian Association. Some, like Mary McLeod Bethune and the women of the National Council of Negro Women, made inroads into the segregated political arena of the American mainstream. Others, like Charlotta Bass, who in 1952 became the first woman of any race to run for the vice-presidency on a national party ticket—the Progressive party—formed coalitions with predominantly white groups outside of the mainstream to focus on issues such as peace and United States foreign policy.

In the meantime, the daughters and granddaughters of black woman suffragists would become the leaders of the civil rights movement that revolutionized America from the mid 1950s until the early 1970s. Here again we see African American women behind the scenes in groups such as the Southern Christian Leadership Conference and the Student Nonviolent Coordinating Committee, where they were often overlooked by chroniclers, who wrote about black men asserting their manhood after years of emasculation. As this new movement for enfranchisement culminated with the passage of the 1965 Voting Rights Act, a resurgence of black feminism also occurred. Once again, however, African American women in the early years of the new feminist movement, like Pauli Murray, Shirley Chisholm, and Aileen Hernandez, remained invisible. What became even more upsetting to the African American women who protested discrimination because of gender was the negative response of some black men who felt threatened by feminism. Their response prompted civil rights activist Frances Beale to write her classic 1968 essay, "Double Jeopardy: To Be Black and Female."[17] Why would African American men of the 1960s, unlike their fore-fathers, feel threatened by feminism?

It is within these contexts that the final essays treat the theme "Movin' On Up: Afro-American Women's Search for New Forms of Political Power, 1930–1965." The authors examine the resurgence of black political power to find the role of women within it.

Words from the late Supreme Court justice Thurgood Marshall about celebrating the bicentennial of the American Constitution seem fitting to conclude this overview. Addressing a group in May 1987, Justice Marshall talked about how defective the Constitution was at its inception 200 years ago. Arguing that the present-day Constitution was not the vision of those who debated it in 1787, Marshall noted that indeed "slavery has been abolished and the right to vote has been granted blacks and women, but the credit does not belong to the framers. It belongs to those who refused to acquiesce in outdated notions of 'liberty,' 'justice,' and 'equality' and who strived to better them." He observed further that the framers of the Constitution would not have accepted "a Supreme Court to which had been appointed a woman and the descendant of an African slave." Marshall spoke of an evolving Constitution, the dynamics of which we should celebrate.[18]

Perhaps it is the nature of the American Constitution that makes politics and law dynamic, hence amenable to change. Although the changes often bring the most vulnerable among us travail, at times the dynamism brings triumph. It is the possibility for triumph in change that has allowed African American women to continue the struggle for political equity in America.

Notes

1   See Rosalyn Terborg-Penn, "Afro-Americans in the Struggle for Woman Suffrage" (Ph.D. diss., Howard University, 1977), appendixes.

2   Commenting about my findings in a review of *The Afro-American Woman* (see n. 12 below), Bess Beatty said: "[Terborg-Penn] seems predisposed, however, to conclude that white women almost always discriminated, but black men were relatively equalitarian. Black post–Civil War newspapers are replete with evidence that many black men con- demned women's rights and endorsed proscriptive stereotypes, evidence that Terborg- Penn generally ignores in reaching her conclusion" (*Journal of Southern History* 45 (May 1979): 304–5). I found no such sources in any of the post–Civil War black newspapers, despite my conscious attempts to locate them.

3   Eleanor Flexner, *Century of Struggle: The Woman's Rights Movement in the United States* (New York: Atheneum, 1973); Aileen S. Kraditor, *The Ideas of the Woman Suffrage Move- ment, 1890–1920* (Garden City, N.Y.: Anchor/Doubleday, 1971).

4   Benjamin Quarles, "Frederick Douglass and the Woman's Rights Movement," *Journal of Negro History* 25 (January 1940): 35–44.

5   Elizabeth Cady Stanton et al., eds., *History of Woman Suffrage*, 6 vols. (1881–1922; rpt., New York: Arno Press, 1969); Susan B. Anthony Papers, Manuscript Division, Library of Congress; Ida Husted Harper, *Life and Work of Susan B. Anthony*, 3 vols. (Indianapolis: Hollenbeck Press, 1898, 1908).

6   Helen Laura Sumner Woodbury, *Equal Suffrage: The Results of an Investigation in Colo- rado, Made for the Collegiate Equal Suffrage League of New York State* (New York: Harper and Brothers, 1909), 70.

7   Elinor Lerner, "Immigrant and Working Class Involvement in the New York City Woman Suffrage Movement, 1905–1917: A Study in Progressive Era Politics" (Ph.D. diss., University of California-Berkeley, 1981), 172, 391.

8   Ellen Carol DuBois, *Feminism and Suffrage: The Emergence of an Independent Women's Movement in America, 1848–1869* (Ithaca, N.Y.: Cornell University Press, 1978); Bettina Aptheker, *Woman's Legacy: Essays on Race, Sex, and Class in American History* (Amherst: University of Massachusetts Press, 1982); Elisabeth Griffith, *In Her Own Right: The Life of Elizabeth Cady Stanton* (New York: Oxford University Press, 1984).

9   An exception to the male-focused studies of the movement is Vicki L. Crawford, Jac- queline Anne Rouse, and Barbara Woods, eds., *Women in the Civil Rights Movement: Trailblazers and Torchbearers, 1941–1965* (Brooklyn, N.Y.: Carlson Publishing, 1990). For visual evidence of black women participating in the movement, see the video based on Juan Williams's *Eyes on the Prize: America's Civil Rights Years, 1954–1965* (New York: Viking, 1987).

10 Dorothy Sterling, ed., *We Are Your Sisters: Black Women in the Nineteenth Century* (New York: W. W. Norton, 1984), 119.

11 See, for example, James M. McPherson, *The Struggle for Equality: Abolitionists and the Negro in the Civil War and Reconstruction* (Princeton, N.J.: Princeton University Press, 1964). This is one of the best accounts of the work of the abolitionists in that it does include black men and white women.

12 See Rosalyn Terborg-Penn, "Discrimination against Afro-American Women in the

Woman's Movement, 1830–1920," in *The Afro-American Woman: Struggles and Images*, ed. Sharon Harley and Rosalyn Terborg-Penn (Port Washington, N.Y.: Kennikat Press, 1978), 17–27.

13 William L. O'Neill, *Everyone Was Brave: The Rise and Fall of Feminism in America* (Chicago: Quadrangle Books, 1969), 71–72, 74–75; Kraditor, *Ideas of the Woman Suffrage Movement*, 126–28; Lerner, "Immigrant and Working Class Involvement," 8–10; Sherna Gluck, ed., *From Parlor to Prison: Five American Suffragists Talk about Their Lives* (New York: Vintage/Random House, 1976), 16; Ellen Carol DuBois, "Working Women, Class Relations, and Suffrage Militance," *Journal of American History* 74 (1987):34–58.

14 Paula Baker, "The Domestication of Politics: Women and American Political Society, 1780–1920," *American Historical Review* 89 (June 1984): 639.

15 Rosalyn Terborg-Penn, "Discontented Black Feminists: Prelude and Postscript to the Passage of the Nineteenth Amendment," in *Decades of Discontent: The Women's Movement, 1920–1940*, ed. Lois Scharf and Joan M. Jensen (Westport, Conn.: Greenwood Press, 1983), 264–67; Nancy F. Cott, "Across the Great Divide: Women in Politics Before and After 1920," in *Women, Politics, and Change*, ed. Louise A. Tilly and Patricia Gurin (New York: Russell Sage Foundation, 1990).

16 Scharf and Jensen, *Decades of Discontent*, 3–4.

17 Frances Beale, "Double Jeopardy: To Be Black and Female," in *The Black Woman: An Anthology*, ed. Toni Cade (New York: New American Library, 1970), 90–100.

18 *Washington Post*, 7 May 1987, A1.

Architects of a Vision:

Black Women and Their

Antebellum Quest for Poli-

tical and Social Equality

Willi Coleman

Whether struggling within the clutches of "the evil institution" or mounting efforts as free persons, the ideas of mutual aid and collective action led African Americans to more specific forms of political action. Among free people in the northeastern United States, who experienced lives of comparative rather than complete freedom, self-help and racial uplift had become driving forces of community life and activity well before the end of the eighteenth century. Living free in cities such as Philadelphia, New York, and Boston forced men and women to strain against a plethora of legal constraints and social restrictions designed to maintain their status as members of an "accursed race." As the decades wore on, successful attempts at self-help gave rise to a generation open to various forms of social protest to address their concerns. What was nurtured and continued to evolve in the process was a belief in black leadership and a sense of race consciousness necessary for organized political action. Black females formed a crucial flank at every stage of this struggle as they themselves moved forward through overlapping phases of individual and group action. Starting with mutual aid societies, continuing through literary and antislavery groups and beyond, they helped to reshape and broaden the very concept of political action.

Before the last decade of the eighteenth century, free black women demonstrated their interest in organizations dedicated to self-help and mutual relief. By creating their own groups as well as joining with black men, they pooled resources to "look after their sick, care for their poor and bury their dead." Although class differences, along with color and religious affiliations, may have impacted the membership of a few groups, economic conditions combined with the impulse toward self-help were mighty equalizers.[1] In spite of the overwhelming problems that led to the creation of self-help groups, the task was approached with a sense of pride and belief in the power to make changes. Such a tone was evident in the constitution of one of Philadelphia's women's beneficial societies.

> Reflecting on the vicissitudes of life to which the female part of the community are continually exposed, . . . and stimulated by the desire of improving our condition [we] do conclude that the most efficient method of securing ourselves from the extreme exigencies to which we are liable to be reduced, is by uniting ourselves in a body for the purpose of raising a fund for the relief of its members.[2]

Though the language of this society suggests the presence of women who were literate, other groups in the city with the same goals were less florid in their language. The Daughters of Africa, some 200 strong, serving primarily as washerwomen and servants, were able to disperse "to Ann Hacket . . . the sume, of four dollars for the burial of her child." Within the following six months they also paid the funeral expenses for one of their members and to "Sally Pratte ten dollars for the loss of hir housband [her husband]."[3]

Similar organizations were evident in New York among the Abyssinian Benevolent Daughters of Esther. Although almost all ages were welcomed, certain people were found unacceptable, and their rejection tells us much about issues of concern to the community. The Benevolent Daughters were willing to accept seventy-five cents quarterly dues from females ranging in age from sixteen to fifty, but no admittance was possible for those "addicted to inebriety or having a plurality of husbands." Women were not alone in responding to the "evils of strong drink"; men were equally likely to address the issue of intemperance. Indeed, alcohol struck such a discordant note within the black community that, by 1835, Boston had become the headquarters for New England's Black Temperance Societies.

With the vast majority of women required to assume financial responsibility for themselves or contribute to family income, beneficial societies served practical as well as social needs. In 1838 alone, women of Philadelphia were responsible for nearly two-thirds of the $20,000 paid in claims to worthy individuals.

Such fervor suggests that women were more likely than men to join mutual aid societies. The appeal of such groups to laundresses and domestic servants may be obvious; what may be obscured is the practical need filled in the lives of women who have been historically regarded as well off. Neither birth nor marriage into a family of literate, free, or famous blacks placed one beyond "the ragged edge of solvency."[4] After the publication of his autobiography, fear of being returned to slavery sent the runaway slave Frederick Douglass to Great Britain for nearly two years. Describing the impact of this and other separations on the family he left behind, his daughter, Rosetta Douglass Sprague, wrote, "mother with four children, the eldest in her sixth year . . . sustained her little family by binding shoes." Unlike her husband, Anna Murray Douglass was legally free and illiterate. She was accustomed to taking care of herself and had been instrumental in Douglass's flight to freedom. It was her skill at being "a help meet rather than a burden" that made it possible for Douglass to return home "with not a debt contracted during his absence."[5]

While spared the drudgery of employment as household servants or washer-women, so-called middle-class black females, married and single, were very much working women. Their efforts helped to sustain their households.[6] For women as well as men, superior education was not in itself insurance against the ravages of ill health, death, or family crisis. Sarah Mapps Douglass, of no relation to Frederick Douglass, and Susan Paul were not simply teachers but outspoken pioneers in African American education. Their backgrounds, coupled with extensive involvement in the antislavery movement, had made each well known within both the black and white communities. However, association with the wealthy, the radicals, and the well known represented but one aspect of these women's lives. Sarah Mapps Douglass, when in her seventies, wrote from Philadelphia to a friend, "I suffer greatly from rheumatism. . . . Yet I go to school every day because my bread depends on it." Sarah's story was echoed in Boston by Susan Paul, who had assumed responsibility for her large extended family. Paul not only taught school but was "diligently employed in sewing for their support." In spite of her efforts, the care of an aging mother and orphaned nieces and nephews proved too much. In a state of "pitiable anxiety and perplexity," she solicited loans and gratefully accepted help from friends of both races.[7]

By the 1830s, black resistance to slavery and lack of civil and social rights had evolved to a second stage. As if to accompany the rumor and reality of the Denmark Vesey conspiracy plot of 1822 and the bloody Nat Turner uprising in Virginia five years later, activities within the free black community reflected a more radical and action-oriented mood. In formats ranging from the publication of the first weekly black newspaper to the appearance of the fiery antislavery pamphlet *David Walker's Appeal,* resistance dialogue emerged.[8] As the Negro convention movement became the vehicle for local, state, and nationwide gatherings, a larger public forum was opened for addressing the most important issues affecting the race. The meetings focused not only on solving economic and social problems of those who were free but also on abolishing slavery and debating the impact of white leadership within that struggle.[9]

It was, then, within this new environment that African American women began to articulate an aspect of black self-determination that had been all but ignored. While most women continued to accept and support male leadership in the setting of a social and political agenda, some women began to question it. The seeds of a challenge to male leadership had shown themselves over a decade earlier in the most stable and male-controlled institution within the black community. By 1820 at least two women had begun to lobby and then defy church leadership in order to pursue their personal dreams as preachers. Jarena Lee and Zilpha Elaw demanded a new reading of the Scriptures, insisting that God had not reserved the role of preaching for men only. Pitting themselves against those who believed "the scriptures did not call for women preachers" and against family obligations described as "the excesses of natures ties," the two women ultimately ascended to the pulpit. Succeeding beyond their own expectations, Lee and Elaw pursued their mission not only throughout the northeastern and southern parts of the United States but into India and Europe as well.[10]

By 1831 the issue of gender equality had expanded beyond religion to include the secular world in general and that of social action specifically. Fueled with the same Christian zeal that propelled Zilpha Elaw and Jarena Lee, Maria Stewart felt called upon to address the earthly problems of her people. Intruding herself into the public arena reserved for men, she wrote essays and made speeches attacking slavery and outlined an agenda for the acquisition of civil rights. In a style resembling that of some of the more radical men of the day and predating others, Stewart urged blacks to economic and educational self-sufficiency. But "boycott[ing] white business . . . and [suing] for your rights" were not the only weapons she was willing to unleash. Faced with the still simmering reaction to the recent Nat Turner insurrection, Stewart refused to back away from the suggestion of physical confrontation. The "rich and powerful men . . . of . . . foul America" were warned that "many powerful sons and daughters will shortly arise, who will . . . have their rights; and if refused . . .

will spread horror and devastation around." Preaching a gospel of social change that was both broad-based and multilayered, Stewart addressed a variety of concerns. Black men as well as white women were taken to task for their short-comings. Those "gentlemen of color . . . blessed with wit and talent, friends and fortune," who had not done enough to "alleviate the woes of their brethren in bondage" caused Stewart's "blood to boil." White women who "transacted business" were taken to task because they hesitated in giving "Black girls with the most satisfactory references . . . an equal opportunity with others."[11]

In September of 1833, Maria Stewart delivered her final speech on behalf of "the mighty work of reformation." Although her time in the public arena lasted less than three years, extraordinary feats had been accomplished. In her zeal to right the wrongs done to her people, Stewart had become the first American-born woman of any color to lecture publicly on political issues. But that is not the extent of her work as a pioneer. She preceded a long line of African Americans, including Frederick Douglass, Sojourner Truth, Frances Harper, and Henry Highland Garnet, for whom language would serve as a mighty weapon for social change. Stewart was never more prophetic, political, or radical than when reenvisioning the world of black women. Having chosen to fight for equality for her people, one who began as "a chaste keeper at home . . . possessing a meek and quiet spirit" evolved to inquire: "How long shall the fair daughters of Africa be compelled to bury their minds and talents beneath a load of iron pots and kettles?"[12] The more profound challenge may not have been to the external and larger community of others but to those whose condition she shared.

But in nineteenth-century America, not even the fervor of religious calling could long sustain a woman daring to seek the public arena. Maria Stewart had begun as a beacon light of progressivism, warning others, "Be no longer astonished . . . that God at this eventful period should raise up your own females . . . in public and private, to assist those who are endeavoring to stop the strong current of prejudice that flows . . . against us." Encountering contempt "in the eyes of many," Stewart retreated. Steeped in piousness and submission, her farewell speech reflected the ideals expected of "true women" of the day:

> those ideas of greatness which are held forth to us, are vain delusions . . . airy visions which we shall never realize. All that man say or do can never elevate us. . . . drop all political discussion in our behalf. A spirit of animosity is already risen, and unless it is quenched, a fire will burst forth and devour us.[13]

Retreating from the life of a public lecturer, Maria Stewart confined herself to women's organizations. But the image of the African American female sharing leadership with black men in shaping the political consciousness of the race had begun to unfold. The tug and pull between constructing a philosophy of freedom and equality and practicing the reality were soon to be taken up by others.

A series of state conferences, begun as early as 1817 and held throughout the Northeast, had by 1830 traveled a circuitous route to national organization. In addition to more than fifteen state meetings, twelve national conferences successfully assembled in the three decades preceding the Civil War. Debating issues that ranged from colonization in Africa to the impact of temperance, black men designed their own forum and developed their own leadership bent on constructing a united theoretical and practical vanguard. As always, the participation of women was expected and desired, but only within those roles clearly designated appropriately female. Men of the race, as "representatives of the oppressed," were urged to "take the oath of freedom . . . to swear eternal enmity to oppression and leave conservatism behind." Revolving within a sphere that was supportive in nature, women created means of accommodating the new mood of militancy. The flood of words pushing men to victory was balanced with action equally traditional and perhaps more crucial, for black women "pledge[d] themselves to furnish means," more tangible in nature. The story of the financial assistance provided by women has been all but lost except for lines of gratitude in organizational minutes. By including donations with their letters of good wishes, women involved themselves in the mundane but crucial matter of finances. On occasion, their generosity ensured the publication of convention proceedings.[14]

In general, black men emulated the attitudes of their white counterparts toward issues of leadership and gender. The public arena, and especially that of politics, was masculine by law, religion, and custom. With the notable exception of men like Frederick Douglass, Martin Delany, men of both the Purvis and Forten families, and Henry Highland Garnet, few men thought that the treatment of women had any philosophical or political relationship to the broader struggle for social and political equality.[15] Although discussions about "woman's place" tended to cause less disruption among black reformers than among whites, equal female participation on the convention floor was viewed as an encroachment on "manhood rights."

At the closing of the 1848 Colored National Convention, delegates listened to a lone woman's impassioned discourse on women's rights. It was an audience unconvinced that women needed "the Elective Franchise, the right of property in the marriage," or involvement in "making laws." But included among final conference resolutions was a pledge to invite women to "hereafter take part in our deliberations." The auspicious beginning did not indicate that women had cleared all the hurdles. A year later, at Ohio's state convention, women still sought clarification of their position, even though many of the same delegates were present. Among resolutions forwarded for consideration by the convention was the following: "Whereas we the ladies have been invited to attend the Convention, and have been deprived of a voice, which we the ladies deem wrong and shameful. Therefore . . . we will attend no more after tonight, unless the privilege is granted." Four years later, in commenting on a convention in New York, Frederick Douglass noted, "We had one lady delegate . . . Mrs. Jeffery of Geneva, strange to say we had good sense to make no fuss about it." The Negro convention movement never developed a concrete philosophy to which males were expected to adhere or upon which women could rely. When the question of active participation arose, it was settled by each group for that particular meeting only. A year after Douglass expressed his pride in the progress that had been made, a convention expelled a woman "for no reason [other] than her sex."[16] There is much significance, however, in the fact that women were willing and able to plead their own cause for equality within the earliest attempts to create a unified and mass political agenda among African Americans.

Black females did not concentrate the major part of their energies on efforts to integrate spheres claimed by men. They chose instead to radicalize, and were themselves radicalized within, their own organizations. In spite of class differences, the tight cocoon of gender and race similarity provided a base that nurtured leadership and harbored the kernels of progressive ideas. It was an allegiance bound by equal portions of devotion to race and an insistence that women must "awake, arise and distinguish yourselves." By 1830 women's organizations had become a common phenomenon within the African American community. The organizations began to reflect and, on occasion, anticipate the new determination that slavery must be abolished at all costs. The new mood of militancy was officially ushered in with the first meeting of the American Anti-Slavery Society in 1833, a year after black women of Salem, Massachusetts, had come together to form their own female antislavery society. The constitution of the Female Anti-Slavery Society of Salem, dated 22 February 1832, makes theirs the flagship of the societies that sprang up among women of both races shortly thereafter. What began in Massachusetts was, in a few years, replicated in Rhode Island, Connecticut, New York, and throughout the Northeast.[17]

The formal agenda of women's antislavery societies did not differ markedly between the races. In addition to the crucial task of fund raising, both groups attempted to stem the tide of slavery and educate their communities with petition drives and schemes to replace slave-produced goods with those made by free hands. But for African American women, the antislavery sentiment was a fact of daily life. It was a perspective that fueled their organizations and propelled them across established lines of race, gender, and social custom. It was, for example, Boston's Afri American Female Intelligence Society that sponsored Maria Stewart's "promiscuous" ascent to the public platform. Although not officially designated as an antislavery organization and with obvious awareness of who the speaker was, they paved the way for the first female political attack on slavery. Though members of female literary societies defined their purposes as "uplifting the morals of the community" and the "encouragement and promotion of polite literature," those goals were merely the base for a wide range of activities. Polite literature invariably included the reading, writing, and discussion of antislavery selections, and raising money to feed and clothe fugitive slaves comprised good works.[18]

Among the African American women dedicated to abolition and racial progress were Sarah Mapps Douglass, the Forten women, Mary Shadd Cary, and Susan Paul, all born into free families of modest to comfortable means and all grown up within environments where antislavery and the quest for civil rights were the guiding principles of family life. In their lives, femininity and womanhood took on added dimensions. Mothers and other womenfolk modeled behavior and nurtured younger women into roles of active female participation, while family life exposed them to purposeful and militant males. In this instance, nineteenth-century marriage and family life served to widen rather than restrict the world in which women were expected to live. These were families whose daughters were as likely as sons to be educated, to travel, and to exercise decision-making powers over their own as well as family income.[19]

Although married to Robert Douglass, the founder of Philadelphia's first African Presbyterian Church, Grace Douglass followed the religious tradition of her own family and attended Quaker services. In addition to caring for her family, she operated a millinery store out of her home and helped "the many poor distressed . . . of our color." Resisting the temptations of conspicuous consumption, Grace Douglass shaped her social life around the principle of fewer "morocco shoes . . . fine muslin dress" and less "entertaining with . . . the best wine and the best cake." Her husband's friends were advised that they, too, would always have something for the poor if they would "try my plan for one year." For at least three decades before the Civil War, Douglass and her daughter Sarah were leaders and active participants in a variety of Philadelphia's women's organizations. Living up to a belief held by many black abolitionists that the time had passed for "occupying the very same position in relation to our Anti-Slavery Friends, as . . . to the pro-slavery community," the Douglass women, along with the four women of the Forten clan, integrated Philadelphia's Female Anti-Slavery Society.[20] Five years later the same group of stalwarts, joined by a few other black women, traveled to New York to attend the 1837 Anti-Slavery Convention of American Women. Returning from that gathering as vice-president of the organization, Grace Douglass was prepared for the conventions of 1838 and 1839, held in Philadelphia. Both Grace and her daughter Sarah were elected to office at subsequent gatherings. But their success was only part of the picture. At the 1838 convention, women were greeted by a mob of Philadelphia's citizens prepared to register their outrage at a racially mixed gathering. Braving bricks and jeering crowds, the women were forced to find new accommodations after their meeting site was leveled by fire.[21]

The threat of physical repercussions from those hostile to abolition was coupled with discord from within. Commitment to antislavery did not, in the eyes of many, elevate the Negro to a level of social equality, and the specter of "racial intermingling" haunted the movement. The leader of New York's female society, "in a very sinful state of wicked prejudices about color," steadfastly refused black members. Taking a somewhat different turn, the women of Fall River, Massachusetts, were willing to tolerate African American women as visitors, but the group nearly disbanded over the prospect of "putting them on an equal footing with ourselves" by accepting blacks as members. The fact that the problem of racial prejudice was placed on the agenda at the convention in 1838 indicates that these were not isolated incidents. A resolution reminded members of "the duty of abolitionists to identify themselves with . . . oppressed Americans, by . . . receiving them as we do our white fellow citizens." The response to such bold possibilities caused so much dissension that the president of the Pennsylvania Abolition Society advised that the resolution be expunged from the minutes. In spite of efforts on the part of sincere white women and the boldness of black women who dared to speak out, the philosophical incongruity and moral weakness of the "monster prejudice" remained a part of women's interracial interactions.[22]

The other passion that occupied Sarah Douglass's life was educating the youth of the race. With a superior mind and a classical education, she spent over forty years in the schools of New York and Philadelphia. Between 1852 and 1858, Douglass expanded her interest in science by attending classes at the

Female Medical College of Pennsylvania and Pennsylvania Medical University. Ignoring those in her own community who insisted that the mere discussion of anatomy was "inconsistent with the delicacy of woman's character," Douglass gathered women in her home to teach a series of lectures on "womanly health and the origins of life."[23]

Friends of the Douglass women, the Fortens were equally active in reform movements. Headed by James and Charlotte Forten, the family included two sons, Robert and James, Jr., and three daughters, Margaretta, Harriet, and Sarah. As early as 1797, James Forten agitated for the abolition of slavery, against forced colonization, and for equal civil rights; he and his family involved themselves in the establishment and financing of at least six separate abolitionist organizations. In addition to running a household continually open to both black and white leaders of the antislavery movement, Charlotte Forten had, along with her daughters, helped to found Philadelphia's Female Anti-Slavery Society. Begun in 1833, the organization lasted for close to forty years, eventually including a third generation of Forten women. Their influence was notable. Margaretta Forten, a teacher, helped to draw up the organizational charter and served on the educational committee, while her sister Sarah was a member of the governing board. In addition to coordinating antislavery petition drives, sponsoring fund raisers, and supporting a black school, they also elected to give aid and support to the predominantly black Philadelphia Vigilant Committee. The Vigilant Committee, headed by Harriet's husband, not only hid those who had "bid adieu to whips and chains" but also found jobs for some, and passage, food, and clothes for others headed for Canada. It was work that skidded around the edges of legality, courted violent reactions from proslavers, and required vast amounts of money. In his book on the black abolitionist movement, Benjamin Quarles suggests that "the need for funds" was the first on the list of problems that had to be solved. It was women with their fairs and bazaars who helped to meet that need.[24]

Both Harriet and Sarah married into another politically active family, the Purvises, and continued their activities, including those requiring travel. Harriet added occasional lectures on women's rights and an interest in the free produce movement to her agenda. Replicating her mother's life, her home became a way station for both weary leaders of the abolitionist movement and fugitive slaves. While the former were being entertained in an "uncommonly rich and elegant" style, runaways were secreted in a room reachable only by a trapdoor. This environment also nurtured a niece, Charlotte Forten, Jr. Left without a mother at an early age, this second Charlotte's life was shaped not solely by the insults from which she could not be protected or by interactions with her famous father and uncle. Hers was a world in which women's daily lives included conversing "almost entirely about prejudice," attending abolitionist lectures and fairs, and deliberately walking past the site where a runaway slave was being held "completely surrounded by soldiers with bayonets fixed." A young girl's life was profoundly affected by the world opened up to her through her aunts and an extended family of female friends. Among the latter was abolitionist and women's rights lecturer Sarah Parker Remond who, in 1859, carried the antislavery message to England, Scotland, and Ireland. Young Charlotte Forten continued the family's work and tradition by going south during the last stages of the Civil War as a teacher for the freedmen. The diary that she kept from May 1854 to May 1864 is one of the few documents giving insight into the development of a black female social activist from adolescence to adulthood.[25]

The tradition of women as an active force, both continuing and broadening the reformist tendencies in a family, was replicated by other African American women. The same pattern is evident in the life of Mary Shadd who, in 1851, emigrated alone to Canada. Her father, a shoemaker in Delaware and Pennsylvania, was a founding member of the American Anti-Slavery Society and the national Negro convention movement, serving as president of the meeting in 1833. His wife Harriet ran a house filled with thirteen children and a series of "black transients" making their way to freedom. Settled in West Chester, Pennsylvania, the Shadd family turned their home into a way station on the Underground Railroad. While supporting herself as a teacher, Mary Shadd had, prior to leaving for Canada, published a pamphlet analyzing the impact of politics and economics on African Americans. The positive review her work received from both Martin Delany and Frederick Douglass undoubtedly fueled the flames for her next idea.[26]

Once in Canada, in search of a way to promote her idea, Mary Shadd became, in the words of William Still, "the first colored woman on the American continent to establish and edit a weekly newspaper." The significance of Mary Shadd's paper, the *Provincial Freeman*, rests not simply in the fact that it can be listed as a first. More importantly, Shadd was in charge of a vehicle for keeping blacks in both Canada and the United States "informed on those issues which affect them." In 1854 those issues, in the mind of the *Provincial Freeman*'s editor, included local as well as international events and, most important, the antislavery movement. Articles on the emigration movement, scathing essays on the debilitating effect of white abolitionists, and less than complimentary reports on black leaders she found wanting bore the unmistakable Mary Shadd touch.

Her pleasure at seeing "quite a large number of females . . . at political gatherings" ensured reports on their activities. After teaching first her younger sister and then her brother the skills needed for publishing, Mary Shadd, in the summer of 1854, returned to the United States. Expanding her voice beyond the editorial page and hoping to gain new subscribers, she began one of several lecture tours in Canada and the States. Mary made speeches before antislavery, women's rights, and social gatherings in Indiana, Ohio, and Chicago.[27] Reaching Philadelphia in October of 1855, she presented herself for admittance to the gentlemen assembled for the Colored National Convention. In the heated debate that followed, Frederick Douglass was among those to point out an inconsistency in rejecting female participants. Having gained entry, she then

> succeeded in making one of the most convincing and telling speeches in favor of Canadian emigration. . . . She at first had ten minutes granted her as had the other members. At their expiration, ten more were granted. . . . the House was crowded and breathless in its attention to her masterly exposition of our present condition, and the advantages open to colored men.[28]

On this occasion, the Shadd family had come full circle. The sense of racial consciousness evident in their household in the third decade of the nineteenth century had been ingested by the younger generation. When Abraham Shadd accepted the presidency of a fledgling organization "convened . . . as representatives of the free people of color of eight of the States of the Union," his eldest child, Mary, was ten. President Shadd and the other gentlemen faced a formidable agenda, including antislavery, colonization in Africa, education for the masses, and moral elevation of the people. By 1855 that organization had an established history as the Negro convention movement, but the Shadd in its midst was now a woman. She had come not as a leader but to insist on equality within a group whose agenda remained essentially the same.[29]

In addition to working within and helping to create antislavery and other organizations, there were other means, both sporadic and planned, of resistance to "the evil institution." Pitting themselves against judicial court systems and laws blessed by the Supreme Court, free women counted physical force among the tools at their disposal. None was better known for the use of force than Harriet Tubman, who rescued members of her own family and dozens of other people as well. From her start in 1845, she was still practicing her own brand of liberation on the eve of the Civil War. Her trips into the slave states brought her notoriety, but Tubman was also known for her daring exploits on behalf of fugitive slaves who had made their way to free territory. One of her last rescues took place between 1859 and 1860 in Troy, New York. While the fate of a "fugitive from justice" was being deliberated, he was taken from his guards by force by a crowd of men and women of both races. The names of "several other colored women" who were there are lost to history, but Harriet Tubman's participation was well documented.

> She seized one officer and pulled him down, then another, and tore him away from the man. . . . keeping her arms about the slave, she cried to her friends, "Drag us out." . . . [S]he tore off her sun-bonnet and tied it on the head of the fugitive. . . . amid the surging mass of people the slave was no longer recognized. Harriet's outer clothes were torn from her, and even her stout shoes . . . yet she never relinquished her hold on the man, till she had dragged him to the river, where he was tumbled into a boat.[30]

Nearly the same scenario had taken place in Boston in 1836. Two women, being held in a courthouse as suspected fugitives, were simply taken from the building by a mob. Outraged that "prisoners have been forcibly rescued, at noonday, from our highest court," Boston's newspapers demanded punishment for the rioters and protection of the "rights and property . . . of our southern brethren." Although none of the group was ever apprehended, news publications on both sides of the issue noted the presence of women. An antislavery newspaper proclaimed, "the rush was made, and the liberated prisoners were born out by the colored females in attendance." Horrified at the lawlessness of such behavior, another report noted, "A colored woman of great size who scrubbed floors for a living . . . threw her arms around the neck of one officer immobilizing him."[31]

With the weight of the Fugitive Slave Act on their side, slaveowners were relentless in pursuing their "property." A woman lived in virtual terror that she or her children would be scooped up in the streets or that "her husband . . . must leave her to insure his own safety." Knowing that they could not depend upon "legislators of the dominant race" moved women to become their own means of protection. One unsuspecting slave catcher, surprising his prey in her own home, was physically ejected by a group of her female friends. Once outside, he found himself faced with another group of "mostly women and children." Amid a hail of stones, he stopped only once in his headlong flight, "seeing them streaming after him terribly in earnest." In spite of editorials in white newspapers labeling such behavior a "danger to the state" and black publications that incomprehensibly "beg[ged] their husbands to keep them at home and find some better occupation for them," women continued to involve themselves in riotous rescues.[32]

There was another, more appropriately female source of resistance entailing far less danger. Since maintaining her family's supplies of food and clothing was at the core of the nineteenth-century definition of woman's role, boycotting slave-produced goods provided a means of resistance well within the female sphere of influence. That this was a "woman's issue," and no less political, was made very clear by Frances Ellen Watkins Harper. Harper, an abolitionist and suffragist, incorporated the free produce message into her antislavery lectures. Writing to a friend that she "believe[d] in that kind of Abolition," she chose "Free labor dress, [even] if it is coarser." Originating with the Quakers, the principle of abstaining from the use of slave-produced goods had evolved into an identifiable antislavery tool outside of that community by 1826. Over the next twenty years, more than two dozen societies sprang up in nine states, most of them in New England. By the 1830s, with an emphasis on diverting money from the pockets of slaveholders, the movement had followed a circuitous route into the African American community. New York and Philadelphia had functioning female societies by 1831. One of the most active societies was formed when Philadelphia's Bethel Church called together over 500 black men and women to form the Colored Free Produce Society of Pennsylvania. Their original meeting was followed by the opening of a free produce store next to the church and the organization of another association apparently open only to women. In accord with the traditional division of labor, male support was most evident at conventions where delegates were urged to "use the utmost exertions . . . in recommending to coloured capitalists, the establishment of [free labor] stores." Newspaper articles urged abstinence from any items produced by the sweat of the slaves' brow.[33]

Women's work for the movement relied on traditional activities such as fairs, food sales, church displays, and picnics that imbued the use of sugar, rice, coffee, and tobacco with new meaning. A typical free produce event might include the lure of foods grown and harvested only by free hands. Those sponsoring the affair were outfitted in dresses made of "free produce cotton." Being able to purchase garments which had provided much needed work for free black women or tobacco grown by blacks in Canada gave the use of ordinary goods significance well beyond the ordinary.[34]

Although the movement has been declared "an empty gesture," an insignificant force against slavery because of the difficulties involved in procuring, manufacturing, and marketing free produce, that is not the complete story.[35] The impact that it had on, and the opportunities it opened for, those with limited access to other vehicles of protest may be measurable. That it formed a part of a wider circle of protest activities cannot be doubted.

It is, then, within the decades before the Civil War that African American women envisioned a universe in which they were not relegated to a sphere of powerlessness. In moving to make that world a reality, they empowered and reinvented themselves as political activists. Relying on traditional tactics and moving into new arenas, they helped to lay the foundation for activists of succeeding generations.

Notes

1   James B. Browning, "The Beginnings of Insurance Enterprise among Negroes," *Journal of Negro History* 22 (October 1937): 417, 422–23, 428, 429; Leonard P. Curry, *The Free Black in Urban America, 1800–1850: The Shadow of the Dream* (Chicago: University of Chicago Press, 1981), 197–200; Rosalyn Terborg-Penn, "Black Male Perspectives on the Nineteenth-Century Woman," in *The Afro-American Woman: Struggles and Images*, ed. Sharon Harley and Rosalyn Terborg-Penn (Port Washington, N.Y.: Kennikat Press, 1978), 29; Emma Jones Lapsansky, "South Street Philadelphia, 1762–1854: A Haven for Those Low in the World" (Ph.D. diss., University of Pennsylvania, 1975), 231, 240–45, 265.

2   Gary B. Nash, *Forging Freedom: The Formation of Philadelphia's Black Community, 1720–1840* (Cambridge, Mass.: Harvard University Press, 1988), 98, 210–11.

3   Daughters of Africa Society Order Book, Historical Society of Pennsylvania, in Dorothy Sterling, ed., *We Are Your Sisters: Black Women in the Nineteenth Century* (New York: W. W. Norton, 1984), 105–7.

4   Facts on Beneficial Societies, 1823–1838, in Minutes of Pennsylvania Abolition Society, Historical Society of Pennsylvania; Curry, *Free Black*, 199–201; Sterling, *We Are Your Sisters*, 184.

5   Emma Jones Lapsansky, "Friends, Wives, and Strivings: Networks and Community Values among Nineteenth-Century Philadelphia Afroamerican Elites," *Pennsylvania Magazine of History and Biography* 108 (January 1984): 8–9; Rosetta Douglass Sprague, "Anna Murray Douglass—My Mother as I Recall Her," *Journal of Negro History* 8 (January 1923): 96, 100; Frederick Douglass, *The Life and Times of Frederick Douglass: Written By Himself* (1898; rpt., New York: Bonanza Books, 1962), 232–58.

6   Nash, *Forging Freedom*, 152, 251–53; Sharon Harley and Rosalyn Terborg-Penn, "Northern Black Female Workers: The Jacksonian Era," in Harley and Terborg-Penn, *Afro-American Woman*, 10–11.

7   Sarah Douglass to Charles Weld, 1 June 1876, Weld–Grimké Papers, Clements Library, University of Michigan, in Sterling, *We Are Your Sisters*, 133; Lydia Maria Child to Jonathan Phillips, 23 January 1838, William Phillips, Jr., Collection, Salisbury, Conn., in ibid., 184–86; James Oliver Horton, "Generations of Protest: Black Families and Social Reform in Ante-Bellum Boston," *New England Quarterly* 49 (Juen 1976): 247–48.

8   Herbert Aptheker, *One Continual Cry: David Walker's Appeal to the Colored Citizens of the World, 1829–1830* (New York: Published for the A.I.M.S. by Humanities Press, 1965), 27–28, 36–37; also see Dorothy Burnett Porter, comp., *Negro Protest Pamphlets: A Compendium* (New York: Arno Press, 1969).

9   Howard Holman Bell, *A Survey of the Negro Convention Movement, 1830–1861* (New York: Arno Press, 1969), 62; Douglass, *Life and Times*, 228–30; Martin Robison Delany, *The Condition, Elevation, Emigration, and Destiny of the Colored People of the United States* (1852; rpt., New York: Arno Press, 1968), 10, 27.

10 William L. Andrews, ed., *Sisters of the Spirit: Three Black Women's Autobiographies of the Nineteenth Century* (Bloomington: Indiana University Press, 1986), ix, 6, 36, 76, 90–93.

11 *Meditations from the Pen of Mrs. Maria W. Stewart* (Washington, D.C., 1879), 27, 32–33, 55, 71–72; Marilyn Richardson, ed., *Maria W. Stewart, America's First Black Woman Political Writer: Essays and Speeches* (Bloomington: Indiana University Press, 1987), 10.

12 Richardson, *Maria Stewart*, 14, 26, 70; Stewart, *Meditations*, 32.

13 Stewart, *Meditations*, 77; Richardson, *Maria Stewart*, 72–73, 27; Barbara Welter, "The Cult of True Womanhood," in *Dimity Convictions: The American Woman in the Nineteenth Century*, ed. Barbara Welter (Columbus: Ohio University Press, 1975); Benjamin Quarles, *Black Abolitionists* (New York: Oxford University Press, 1969), 224–25.

14 Constitution of the Citizens' Union of the Commonwealth of Pennsylvania, 1848, in Philip S. Foner and George E. Walker, eds., *Proceedings of the Black State Conventions, 1840–1865* (Philadelphia: Temple University Press, 1979); Ohio, 1851, in ibid., 266; Ohio, 1856, in ibid., 307; California, 1856, in ibid., 2:150, 154–55.

15 Dorothy Sterling, *The Making of an Afro-American: Martin Robison Delany, 1812–1885* (Garden City, N.Y.: Doubleday, 1971), 112.

16 Proceedings of the Colored National Convention Held at Cleveland, Ohio, in Howard Holman Bell, comp., *Proceedings of the National Negro Conventions, 1830–1864* (New York: Arno Press, 1969), 11, 17; Ohio, 1849, in Foner and Walker, *State Conventions*, 1:227; Philip S. Foner, *Frederick Douglass on Women's Rights* (Westport, Conn.: Greenwood Press, 1979), 23; *Troy Daily Times*, 6 September 1855.

17 Quarles, *Black Abolitionists*, 9–18; *Liberator*, 17 November 1832 and 16 February 1833, in Sterling, *We Are Your Sisters*, 113, 108–9.

18 Porter, *Negro Protest Pamphlets*, 561, 564, 569; Sterling, *We Are Your Sisters*, 107–12.

19 Janice Sumler Lewis, "The Forten–Purvis Women of Philadelphia and the American Antislavery Crusade," *Journal of Negro History* 66 (Winter 1981–82): 281–88; Horton, "Generations of Protest," 247, 254–55; Lapsansky, "Friends, Wives, and Strivings," 8, 13, 16; Janice Sumler Lewis, "The Fortens of Philadelphia" (Ph.D. diss., Georgetown University, 1978), 80; Jim Bearden and Linda Jean Butler, *Shadd: The Life and Times of Mary Shadd Cary* (Toronto: NC Press, 1977), 15–19, 26.

20 Anne Bustill Smith, "The Bustill Family," *Journal of Negro History* 10 (October 1925), 643; Grace B. Douglass to John Gloucester, 28 February 1819, in Sterling, *We Are Your Sisters*, 103–4; Delany, *Colored People*, 10, 27; Leon Litwack, "The Abolitionist Dilemma: The Anti-Slavery Movement and the Northern Negro," *New England Quarterly* 34 (March 1961): 62–64.

21 Sterling, *We Are Your Sisters*, 114–17; Dorothy Sterling, introduction to *Turning the World Upside Down: The Anti-Slavery Convention of American Women, May 9–12, 1837* (New York: Feminist Press at the City University of New York, 1987), 5; for equally violent reaction in Boston, see Alma Lutz, *Crusade for Freedom: Women of the Anti-Slavery Movement* (Boston: Beacon Press, 1968), 56–62.

22   Quarles, *Black Abolitionists*, 38–39; Leon F. Litwack, *North of Slavery: The Negro Question in the Free States, 1790–1860* (Chicago: University of Chicago Press, 1969), 221–22; Proceedings of the Anti-Slavery Convention of American Women (1838), in Sterling, *We Are Your Sisters*, 115–16; Curry, *Free Black*, 225.

23   *Weekly Anglo-African*, 23 July 1859, quoted in Sterling, *We Are Your Sisters*, 129.

24   Lewis, "Fortens of Philadelphia," 18, 46–60; Charlotte L. Forten, *The Journal of Charlotte L. Forten*, ed. Ray Allen Billington (New York: Collier Books, 1961), 12–19; Lewis, "Forten–Purvis Women," 284–85; Quarles, *Black Abolitionists*, 143–67.

25   Sterling, *We Are Your Sisters*, 121; Forten, *Journal*, 20, 44–46, 99, 102, 114, 118, 124; for information on Remond, see Ruth Bogin, "Sarah Parker Remond: Black Abolitionist from Salem," in *Essex Institute Historical Collections* 110 (April 1974): 120–50; Lewis, "Forten–Purvis Women," 284–85; see also *Two Black Teachers during the Civil War: Mary S. Peake and Charlotte Forten* (New York: Arno Press, 1969).

26   Quarles, *Black Abolitionist*, 149; Bearden and Butler, *Shadd*, 15; see also C. Peter Ripley, ed., *The Black Abolitionist Papers* (Chapel Hill: University of North Carolina Press, 1986), 2:184–92.

27   Still quoted in Alexander L. Murray, "The *Provincial Freeman*: A New Source for the History of the Negro in Canada," *Ontario Historical Society: Papers and Records* 51–52 (1959–60): 26; Bearden and Butler, *Shadd*, 138–39, 155–62, 182–87; Mary Shadd was tracing the steps of her own father in attempting to put her paper on a firmer financial footing. In 1833 Abraham Shadd had served as an "agent" for a reformist publication, the *Emancipator*. It was his responsibility to "obtain subscriptions and collect arrearages" (Quarles, *Black Abolitionists*, 33).

28   Proceedings of the Colored National Convention, Philadelphia, 1855, in Bell, *National Negro Conventions*, 10; Frederick Douglass's paper, 9 November 1855, in Sterling, *We Are Your Sisters*, 170–71.

29   Bell, *National Negro Conventions*, 28–31.

30   Earl Conrad's biography of Tubman lists the date as 27 April 1860, whereas Dorothy Sterling places the dramatic rescue in 1859. See Earl Conrad, *Harriet Tubman* (New York: Paul S. Eriksson, 1974), 131; Sarah H. Bradford, *Harriet, the Moses of Her People* (New York, 1886), quoted in Sterling, *We Are Your Sisters*, 222–23.

31   Leonard W. Levy, "The 'Abolition Riot': Boston's First Slave Rescue," *New England Quarterly* 25 (March 1952), 88–89; Quarles, *Black Abolitionists*, 205.

32   Mary Frances Berry, *Black Resistance/White Law: A History of Constitutional Racism in America* (New York: Meredith Corporation, 1971), 72–77; Linda Brent, *Incidents in the Life of a Slave Girl* (1861); rpt., New York: Harcourt Brace Jovanovich, 1973), 196–99; "Reminiscences," *Woman's Era* (Boston), August 1894, excerpted in Sterling, *We Are Your Sisters*, 222.

33   Sterling, *We Are Your Sisters*, 160; Ruth Ketring Nuermberger, *The Free Produce Movement: A Quaker Protest against Slavery* (New York: AMS Press, 1942), 13, 116–18; Quarles, *Black Abolitionists*, 74–75.

34   Carol C. V. George, *Segregated Sabbaths: Richard Allen and the Rise of Independent Black Churches, 1760–1840* (New York, 1973), 131–32; Nuermberger, *Free Produce*, 61.

35   Norman B. Wilkinson, "The Philadelphia Free Produce Attack upon Slavery," *Pennsylvania Magazine of History and Biography* 66 (July 1942): 294–313.

Frances Ellen Watkins

Harper Abolitionist and

Feminist Reformer 1825–1911

Bettye Collier-Thomas

Of the Negro race in the United States since 1620, there have appeared but four women whose careers stand out so far, so high and so clearly above all others of their sex, that they can with strict propriety and upon well established grounds be denominated great. These are Phillis Wheatley, Sojourner Truth, Frances Ellen Watkins Harper and Amanda Smith.[1]

Few women, black or white, have sustained public careers that earned the level of respect and fame enjoyed by Frances Ellen Watkins Harper. She was a person of great presence, considerable charisma, and an outstanding speaker. During her lifetime, she won national recognition as a lecturer, writer, and activist through her participation in all the prominent reform movements of the nineteenth century. Harper was the single most important black woman leader to figure in both the abolitionist and feminist reform movements. Her feminist leadership included work in the suffrage and temperance movements. As a participant in the abolitionist, suffrage, temperance, peace, civil and woman's rights movements, between 1854 and 1890 she was one of the few African American women present at conferences and meetings dominated by the black male leadership and, prior to 1890, with few exceptions, was the only woman of her race to consistently hold positions of leadership in the national organizations controlled by white female reformers.

Sojourner Truth, Harriet Tubman, Amanda Smith, Ida Wells-Barnett, Mary Church Terrell, and Frances E. W. Harper were all widely known in the nineteenth century. Sojourner Truth, the veteran antislavery and woman's rights worker, was most active as a public figure during the period from 1850 to 1870. Harriet Tubman, celebrated for her role as an abolitionist and Union spy, settled after the Civil War in Auburn, New York, where she was concerned with more local causes. Amanda Smith, surfacing as a public figure during the late 1850s, became famous after the war for her work as an evangelist and temperance worker. Wells-Barnett and Terrell were among the leaders of the post–Civil War generation whose public careers were launched in the 1890s. Among this group of eminent women, Harper, whose primary concern was moral and social reform, was the only one to have a public career that spanned all of the major periods and movements of the nineteenth century.

Harper's impact upon the issues and events of her time has not been adequately measured. As a lecturer of national repute who moved in and spoke to all levels of society, and as a writer whose works were read by the elite and by the masses, black and white, Harper had a major influence in shaping public opinion on reform issues during the antebellum and postbellum periods. Harper was set apart from most African Americans because of her literacy and because of her sensitivity to issues of race, class, and gender. As a black woman who argued for human rights, she brought attention to the plight of black people and women, particularly black women.

Despite her important career as an abolitionist and feminist leader, Harper has been best known as an author. Her first volume of poetry, *Forest Leaves,* was published in 1845. *Poems on Miscellaneous Subjects,* published in 1854, had by 1871 gone through twenty editions and sold more than 10,000 copies. Her short stories, essays, and poetry appeared in African American and mainstream newspapers and periodicals. In 1892 she published *Iola Leroy; or, Shadows Uplifted,* for many years acclaimed as the first novel written by an African American woman.[2] Until Paul Laurence Dunbar, she was the most acclaimed and prolific black poet in America.

Harper's national reputation was built upon a skillful integration of her intellectual, oratorical, poetical, and prose writing skills. Although her reputation as a reformer was well established, after her death she was evaluated chiefly as a poet and, at best, adjudged to be a minor one. Widely known as a lecturer and writer, she drew considerable praise during her lifetime for her essays and poetry, which mirror the underlying concerns that motivated her extraordinarily diverse activities. Harper's poems focused upon issues of slavery and racial discrimination and reflected the broad spectrum of African American life. They were skillfully intertwined in her public addresses. Her concern was not to create "art for art's sake" but to write poems that would liberate her people. Thus, while she understood the criteria for achieving technical excellence and poetic grace, these were not her primary goals. Even so, black and white contemporaries frequently praised her work and noted that, following Phillis Wheatley, she was the first African American woman to attract widespread attention for her poetic production. Harper was cited by John Dixon Long, in *Pictures of Slavery*, as one of the few southern poets and was mentioned along with Edgar Allan Poe, Amelia B. Welby, and Nathan C. Brooks as "among the best."

Because Harper's writings and lectures were in the protest tradition and because she had access to a broad-based, primarily American, audience, she became the first major popularizer of African American protest poetry. This type of poetry, one of the by-products of the abolitionist movement, found a major exponent in Frances Harper after 1840. A clear strain of racial and gender consciousness is found in most of Harper's lectures and writings. Her insistence that African American writers incorporate race into their writings, her role as a pioneer in new African American literary forms, and the sheer impact of her writings upon aspiring black writers and the general population demonstrate her importance as a major literary figure whose life and work form a key, though frequently overlooked, link to the Harlem Renaissance. Joan R. Sherman, in *Invisible Poets: African Americans of the Nineteenth Century* (1974), among the first of the recent literary critics to reevaluate Harper's work, states that, "In short, Mrs. Harper's total output is the most valuable single poetic record we have of the mind and heart of a race whose fortunes shaped the tumultuous years of her career, 1850–1900."

Few African Americans have been able to finance and sustain careers as reformers and advocates of unpopular causes. Primarily dependent on one source of income, usually derived from a job, most were unable to spend months traveling on behalf of the movements they supported. Harper, however, was able to gain a measure of financial independence through the fees she received for public appearances and from the sale of her literature. As a lecturer, in the postwar years, she was often paid less than others, such as Anna Dickinson, a white lecturer with whom she was often compared, and black male leaders of equal (and lesser) stature. However, early in her career, Harper decided to print her public address and her verse in paperback and to sell these self-published works for less than a dollar, usually a minimum of twenty-five cents, at her public appearances. She also took advantage of numerous invitations to publish in African American and mainstream newspapers and periodicals. Taken together, these opportunities provided Harper with sufficient remuneration to maintain herself and her daughter in a comfortable, but not extravagant, life style. She purchased real estate and stock in Ohio, Pennsylvania, and Maine; made generous donations to individuals, organizations, and social causes; and traveled extensively throughout the United States and occasionally abroad. In later life, when her escalating racial consciousness and feminism circumscribed opportunity, she remained financially independent but lived on a more restricted income.

Born free in Baltimore, Maryland, in 1824, Frances Watkins was an only child. Orphaned at an early age, she was raised in the home of William J. Watkins, Sr., her uncle. Watkins, a well-known disciplinarian, mathematician, and grammarian, was hailed as the most learned African American in Maryland, where for over twenty years he kept one of the largest schools in the state, the Watkins Academy. In his position as an educator and United Methodist minister, Watkins devoted considerable energies to the abolitionist movement as an organizer, lecturer, and writer. He was well known among the black social and political elite and maintained a close relationship with white abolitionists such as William Lloyd Garrison. Frances Watkins received one of the best educations available to an African American during the antebellum period; the Watkins Academy and the favorable climate of the Watkins home allowed her to meet and talk with distinguished writers, abolitionists, and religious figures who visited her uncle.

At an early age, Frances Watkins was sent to live in the home of a well-to-do Baltimore family, where, like many free black children, she served an apprenticeship. The skills she acquired as a seamstress were sufficient to allow her later appointment to teaching positions in other parts of the country. It was also during this time that she took advantage of the bookshop run by this family to further her study of poetry. Her first volume of poetry, *Forest Leaves,* was published during her apprenticeship.

In 1850 Frances Watkins left Baltimore to teach sewing at the Union Seminary School in Columbus, Ohio, where she became the first female instructor. This school, originated by the African Methodist Episcopal church, was the precursor to Wilberforce College, the first institution of higher learning to be established by African Americans in the United States. Dissatisfied with her job and wanting to return to the East, in 1852 she accepted a teaching position in Little York, Pennsylvania, where her contact with fugitive slaves and concern about the precarious existence of free blacks diminished her interest in teaching. In 1853 Watkins was particularly concerned that Maryland had enacted a law restricting northern free blacks from entering the state upon penalty of imprisonment and enslavement. A free black man violated this statute, was sold to Georgia, became a fugitive, and died from exposure and illness. Outraged by this incident, Frances wrote to a friend, "Upon this grave I pledged myself to the Anti-Slavery Cause." She resigned her teaching position and sought employment in the antislavery movement.

Frances Watkins initially moved to Philadelphia where she resided with William and Letitia Still, celebrated black abolitionists whose home served as a station for the Underground Railroad. However, her attempts to find an appropriate role in the movement were unsuccessful. Impatient and anxious to begin work after several weeks of inactivity, she traveled to Boston and New Bedford where she was invited to lecture on the subject of "Education and the Elevation of the Colored Race." By September 1854 Frances Watkins was engaged as a lecturer for the Maine Anti-Slavery Society. Within two years of her employment as an antislavery lecturer she had gained a national reputation for her oratorical and writing skills.

From 1854 to 1860 Watkins traveled extensively throughout the eastern states and the Midwest, speaking on the evils of slavery. Her eloquence and intelligence astounded audiences, who were shocked that a black and a woman could speak and reason so well. She often shared the platform with William Lloyd Garrison, Frederick Douglass, Lucy Stone, Lucretia Mott, Wendell Phillips, John Greenleaf Whittier, and other well-known figures, with whom she would later work on other reforms. During this period her audiences were predominantly white. After the Civil War, her work involved her more directly with the African American population.

Watkins entered the abolitionist movement at a crucial moment. The passage of the Fugitive Slave Act had escalated intersectional strife, with militant abolitionists openly assisting fugitives and preventing their return to their masters. She supported such efforts, invoking God's law as the highest authority, superseding the Constitution, which was man's law. She criticized the passage of the law by northerners who, she claimed, while clothing themselves in the clichés of justice and liberty had, for the sake of political convenience, succumbed to the pressures of the proslavery advocates. She emphasized that, while northern states such as Pennsylvania, New Jersey, New York, Massachusetts, and Vermont had abolished slavery and were viewed as bastions of freedom, in the streets of their cities fugitives were hunted and in their courts the rights of slaveholders took precedence over freedom. Even the personal liberty bills, passed in states such as Vermont, did not apply to slaves.

Watkins proclaimed that there was no free soil in America. She argued that as a free person she and other African Americans traveling in the North deserved to receive equal treatment with whites. Citing the discrimination she encountered in her antislavery work, she singled out Pennsylvania as being "the meanest of all as far as the treatment of colored people is concerned." She told of the insults she received on railroad cars and how on one occasion she refused the request of a conductor and passengers to move to the platform or sit in a corner. At the end of the ride the conductor refused her money, whereupon Watkins responded by throwing it on the floor and leaving.

Watkins embraced a number of strategies that she felt would help bring an end to slavery. Since slavery had an economic base rooted primarily in the production and sale of cotton and its products, the boycott of slave produce could be an effective weapon against the institution.

As a supporter of the Garrisonian abolitionists' philosophy, she believed in civil disobedience. This tenet, as well as other well-honed Garrisonian themes, permeated her lectures. She emphasized the immorality of the Fugitive Slave Act, stressing that the Supreme Court and the Constitution were utilized as a part of the process to keep African Americans enslaved. For her there was little justice in America; the Supreme Court's decision in the Dred Scott case was proof of this. Stressing this point in one of her speeches, she said, "I stand at the threshold of the Supreme Court and ask for justice, simple justice. Upon my tortured heart is thrown the mocking words, 'You are a negro; you have no rights which white men are bound to respect.'" In summarizing her stance on slavery, a lecture patron observed that "She preached the whole gospel of liberty, and would 'let the Union slide' and [allow] the Constitution to be torn into shreds, rather than that one of God's poor should be proscribed."

Although a militant abolitionist, Watkins's radicalism was shielded and made palatable by her shrewd rhetoric, her physical attractiveness, and her delicate femininity. White journalists and intellectuals constantly commented on her uniqueness as a female, particularly a black one, and this fascination tended to obscure her radical message. Watkins never verbally or directly advocated retribution or violence as a means for ending slavery, but in 1859 she openly supported John Brown's attempt to launch a military operation against Virginia slaveholders. Watkins's philosophy regarding resistance movements was not original. Clearly, she had imbibed some of her uncle's beliefs. William J.

Watkins, Sr., prior to his death in 1858, had become increasingly militant in his support of resistance movements and finally concluded that he must emigrate to Canada to find a measure of freedom. At the time of the Harper's Ferry insurrection, Frances Watkins's cousin William J. Watkins, Jr., was one of several abolitionists, including Frederick Douglass, said to have been informed beforehand of Brown's intentions.

Frances Watkins supported the efforts of John Brown and corresponded with him, his wife, and his imprisoned comrades, offering them solace and sending material aid in the form of money to Brown's wife and food and clothing to the prisoners. Weeks after the Harper's Ferry incident, she wrote to Brown that, although it was not possible to visit him in the Virginia prison, no "bolts or bars" could prevent her from sending him her "sympathy." Speaking for the many black girls purchased for use as sex objects and for black mothers whose children were wrenched from their breasts to be sold as property, Watkins told Brown, "I thank you, that you have been brave enough to reach out your hands to the crushed and blighted of my race. You have rocked the bloody Bastille." During the two weeks prior to Brown's execution, Frances Watkins stayed with his wife in Philadelphia at the home of William Still. Several months after his death, she pleaded for continued agitation against slavery but stopped short of calling for an escalation of armed resistance against the planters. She did, however, along with the Garrisonian abolitionists, support a dissolution of the Union.

Amid the tense discussions of the state of the Union, Watkins indicated concerns about the state of her life. Given the conventions of the times, as a single woman in her midthirties she was an anomaly. Although there is no extant public criticism of her, she evidenced her concern. In a letter reporting her political activities, she said that she felt herself "an old maid going about the country meddling with the slaveholder's business." Less than a year later, in the fall of 1860, she married Fenton Harper, a widower and resident of Ohio. Investing her savings in a farm near Columbus, for four years she divided her time between housekeeping chores and antislavery activities, which she confined primarily to writing. In 1864 she was widowed. One child, a daughter named Mary, was born to that union.

During the four years of her marriage Harper wrote extensively. Her letters to William Still and the press and her articles reflect her concerns about the war and the status of African Americans. Writing to her old friend Still, she hoped for the emancipation of the slaves and thought General Fremont's proclamation freeing the slaves of the rebels in Missouri a positive move. Impatient with President Lincoln and the Republicans, like many abolitionists Harper wanted the government to proclaim slavery a major cause of the war and to take swift steps to remove "the festering curse." Prior to issuing the Emancipation Proclamation, Lincoln explored various plans to achieve emancipation by compensation to owners for their slaves and by colonization of African Americans in Central America or in some other place such as Canada or Africa. Responding to such schemes, Harper declared that under Lincoln the nation had lost its "moral power" and its "mental perception." The colonization plan was just one indication of the moral and ethical bankruptcy of the Lincoln administration.

Harper believed that Lincoln's colonization plan would fail, because it was neither logical nor feasible to transport four million people, a significant proportion of the American laboring population, to another country. Moreover, it was her feeling that African Americans would be a very significant factor in the rebuilding of the nation after the war. With the understanding that the Civil War would bring an end to slavery, Harper publicly demanded that the freedmen be given more than "bare freedom," that they be given complete citizenship. She concluded that, "when the colored man drops the bullet, he must have placed in his hands the ballot."

In May 1864, immediately following the death of her husband, Harper returned to the lecture platform. Invited to speak to integrated audiences in several Indiana towns, she chose as her subject "The Mission of the War." In this oration, she reviewed the nature and impact of slavery and the slavocracy, the government's proslavery war policies and measures, and postwar reconstruction. She spoke of the future of the nation as being inextricably intertwined with the destiny of the African American and made clear that black people expected national recognition as free persons and citizens. So powerful was her lecture that one journalist commented, "Seldom have we heard a more cogent, forcible and eloquent lecture upon any subject, especially from a woman." Moreover, he concluded, her ability to comprehend and articulate political philosophy was "remarkable in any woman, no matter what her color."

In November 1864, five months prior to the conclusion of the war, Maryland granted freedom to its slaves. Frances Harper rejoiced that she could again visit her native state without fear of arrest. Returning for a celebration of "Maryland's Freedom," she spoke about the lessons of the war. Asserting that the battle had begun not at Bull Run but with the arrival of the first Dutch slave ship, she reiterated that historically African Americans were oppressed by the Constitution and the government and that one of the lessons of the war was that "Simple justice is the right of every race." Harper continued to be critical of President Lincoln for what she viewed as his ambivalence toward African Americans and his failure to publicly articulate the actual cause of the war, namely slavery. Ignoring Lincoln, she praised Vice-President Andrew Johnson for his support and involvement in helping to defeat the South.

After the war, Harper saw the need to expand her reform activities to include woman's rights and temperance. At the very beginning of her abolitionist career, Harper exhibited a keen awareness of the problems confronted by women, in particular black women. In her early speeches and writings she frequently chose examples of slave women to illustrate the plight of African Americans. In doing so, by inference, she pointed out the duality of their position as slaves and as women with vulnerabilities not shared by black males and white females. White feminist reformers and black men frequently subsumed black women in the espousal of their causes, without addressing the important issue of their status as black women. Harper spoke not as an African American and not as a woman but always as an African American woman who recognized that for most Americans race was the key definer of her existence. However, she knew that both issues were of equal importance and that as a public person fully committed to the equality of black people and women it was imperative that she represent both causes.

Building upon her reputation and notoriety as an abolitionist, and utilizing the contacts she had established in the antislavery movement, Harper made the transition from abolitionist to woman's rights advocate. She became one of the best-known African American women participants in the movement. Harper attended meetings, held membership, and served as an officer in a variety of reform organizations. Between 1870 and 1900 she affiliated with and held office in the Association for the Advancement of Women (AAW), the Woman's Christian Temperance Union (WCTU), the Universal Peace Union, the American Woman Suffrage Association (AWSA), and the International Council of Women (ICW). She was the first black woman to speak at the AAW's Woman's Congress and one of a few to appear on the programs of the National Council of Women (NCW), the WCTU, and the ICW. In 1896 she participated in the founding of the National Association of Colored Women (NACW), of which she was elected a vice-president.

During the antebellum period, woman's rights had been part of the larger reform movement, which embraced abolition, temperance, and other issues. Following the war, white feminists tended to focus less on woman's rights and more on woman suffrage. Many former abolitionists, in seeking support for the Fourteenth and Fifteenth amendments, saw the expediency of placing woman suffrage on hold in light of the more urgent issue of Negro suffrage. Limiting the suffrage to black males, however, engendered anger and bitterness among some white suffragist leaders who felt that if a choice had to be made educated white females were more deserving of the vote than illiterate black males. Further, the suffragists appealed to black women to join them in seeking the vote for women first.

On the issue of which should be first, woman or Negro suffrage, the old abolitionist coalition, which included a racial and gender mix of key reform leaders, collapsed. Harper agreed with Frederick Douglass, an ardent supporter of woman's rights and friend of Elizabeth Cady Stanton and Susan B. Anthony, that black males must have the vote and that the plight of black women was more related to their race than to their gender. Taking a broad historical view of the role of race in American society, she argued that emancipation had not eliminated race as the major determinant of one's status. "When it was a question of race I let the lesser question of sex go. But the white women all go for sex letting the race occupy a minor position." Harper pointed out that "Being black means that every white, including every working class woman, can discriminate against you."

African Americans, particularly black women, were in a difficult position. Though they sought equality as women, the slave experience had reinforced the belief that race held a higher priority than gender. When this issue surfaced at the meeting of the American Equal Rights Association (AERA) in May 1869, Elizabeth Cady Stanton, Frances Gage, and Sojourner Truth emphasized their support for universal suffrage, a position taken by most reformers. However, they indicated that if there were no other choice they favored enfranchising women, including black women, over black men. Sojourner Truth, like Harper one of the few African American women present at the meeting, believed that if black men were enfranchised first they would "become masters over the women, and it will be just as bad as it was before." Of course, Sojourner regretted having to make a choice and continued to emphasize that her first choice was for universal suffrage.

In 1868 Stanton's and Anthony's alliance with George Train, an antiblack, wealthy Democrat, and their support of "educated suffrage" suggested that African Americans might be abandoned, with black women indirectly used as a wedge against black men. Train agreed to finance the *Revolution,* a publication sponsored by Stanton and Anthony. Among other things, the *Revolution* served as an organ to articulate sentiments adverse to the passage of the Fifteenth Amendment. Disparaging references were made to black men, who frequently were depicted as being inferior and prone to commit criminal acts. Harper felt that the efforts of some suffragist leaders to create such images of black men and to imply that white women without the ballot were more susceptible to rape by ignorant black males left black women open to continued sexual exploitation and black men more vulnerable to lynching.

The national woman suffrage leadership split over the black suffrage issue. In 1869, following the AERA meeting, two woman suffrage associations were created, the National Woman Suffrage Association (NWSA) and the American Woman Suffrage Association. Frances Harper, consistent with her antebellum abolitionist philosophy, chose to affiliate with AWSA, an organization which reflected her concern that the struggle for woman suffrage be couched in the larger arena of women's reform activities. Unlike the NWSA, headed by Stanton and Anthony, the AWSA included male and female officers and eschewed the view that only women's experiences could define woman's conscience. In 1890, when Negro suffrage was under attack and after other differences were reconciled, the two associations merged to form the National American Woman Suffrage Association (NAWSA).

During the years 1870 to 1900, many of Harper's views and activities were set within the mainstream of the woman's reform movement.[3] Within this sphere, movements for temperance, social purity, and the suppression of vice—throwbacks to the antebellum activities and experiences of women—gained even greater importance than suffrage. Embracing these issues, Harper became one of the few African American women involved in the woman's club movement of the 1870s and 1880s. This movement began in 1868 with the founding of Sorosis in New York City. Not wishing to address woman's rights issues, in 1873 Sorosis sponsored a Woman's Congress, which created the Association for the Advancement of Women, an independent association. The Woman's Congress sponsored annually by the AAW was the principal forum in which woman's rights issues were addressed for many years.

By 1888 a number of national organizations were formed to address a variety of issues. To harness the growing power of national women's groups and to develop a more powerful voice for woman's rights issues and woman suffrage, Frances Willard and Elizabeth Stanton organized in 1888 the National Council of Women and held an International Council of Women meeting, which led to the development of an organization by that name. In 1891 clubs with local and regional memberships were organized into a national organization, the General Federation of Women's Clubs (GFWC). All of these national associations of women, and the International Council of Women, were separate entities with a specific focus; however, they frequently had interlocking directorates and featured many of the same women on their programs. By focusing women who ordinarily would not be involved in woman suffrage on woman's rights issues, Willard and Stanton were able to build support for woman suffrage indirectly. Willard, the president of the WCTU, forced the issue in her organization.

Until the 1896 founding of the National Association of Colored Women, there was no national organization through which African American women could articulate their specific concerns. The postwar generation of African American women castigated the white feminist leadership for failing to speak on behalf of African Americans and refused to attend or participate in the deliberations of the major women's gatherings. Harper, the most visible and active African American in the movement until 1890, frequently disagreed with the white feminist leadership, but her experience in the abolitionist movement taught her that one could be more productive working within a movement than on the outside.

Frequently referred to as *the* principal representative of "colored women," Harper was conspicuous by her presence and often by her participation in the deliberations on behalf of women and African Americans. Her voice and that of several others provided a distinctive view which incorporated concerns of race and gender. This was extremely important during a time when the prevailing perception was that white women as feminist leaders spoke for women and that black men as race leaders spoke for African Americans. Though both groups incorporated some of the concerns of black women, neither fully addressed the range of issues so important to African American women. Thus it was important to have women like Harper as spokespersons. In gatherings of predominantly white females, she constantly underscored the problem of race. She reminded white feminists of the power conferred upon them because of their color and their access to the central rulers, white men. Frequently, as the only African American woman to be recognized and to speak in predominantly black male gatherings, she interjected the issue of gender.

How was Harper viewed, and what was the nature of her relationship to white feminist reformers and leaders in the woman's club movement? To what extent did these women seek to involve African American women in their movement? To what extent did these early women's clubs address issues of concern to African American women? These questions are essential to understanding the evolution of the black woman's club movement, as well as to defining the stance taken by the new generation of black female leaders who surfaced in the 1890s. By 1890 Harper, at sixty-six years of age, had spent almost forty years working in the key reform movements of the nineteenth century. Like most African American leaders of her day, she had maintained a professional relationship with reformers like Elizabeth Cady Stanton, Lucretia Mott, Lucy Stone, and Frances Willard. Race, not gender, however, prevented her from developing close personal relationships with most of these leaders and from advancing to the highest levels of leadership in their organizations. Many of the white feminist reformers knew each other well. They moved and networked with each other and with persons representative of the social, economic, and political elites of the day. Many of these women were married to influential men and had brothers and fathers who occupied positions of power and wealth. Few black women, if any, had this kind of access to wealth and power.

Because Harper was articulate and her work and talents were highly respected by both black and white reformers, she was frequently invited to speak at meetings of the major reform associations. Though some white feminist reformers favored African American women like Sojourner Truth and Amanda Smith, for various reasons they were not as accessible as Harper. Truth, at least twenty years older than Harper, by 1870 was in semiretirement and not as mobile as Harper. Amanda Smith traveled and worked in Europe, India, and Africa between 1870 and 1890. Some African American feminist reformers, like Sarah Parker Remond, had emigrated to Europe. Following the AERA fight over Negro suffrage, a number of black women lost respect for leaders like Stanton and chose not to affiliate with or work in the woman's movement. By the 1890s, incidents of segregation and discrimination within the club movement and the failure of white feminists, like Frances Willard, to repudiate lynching caused some black women to question the value of their attending such meetings.

Frederick Douglass and Frances Harper, as integrationists, constantly urged African American women to attend and to make their voices heard in the meetings of the major reform organizations. In 1888 Harper implored younger women to attend the fortieth jubilee celebration of the 1848 Seneca Falls convention. She stated that "the most gifted and noted women" of the various reform movements would be in attendance and that "the question arises have we, the colored women, no part nor lot in this matter?" In 1895, on the day of his death, Douglass attended and spoke at the NCW meeting. He remarked to Mary Church Terrell, a rising star of the younger generation, that he was pleased to see her in attendance and deplored the lack of interest in such gatherings among African American women. Black women, like Josephine St.

Pierre Ruffin, were interested in attending and being active participants in the meetings of the NCW, NWSA, WCTU, and GFWC; however, they demanded their participation be as equals and that issues of importance to them as African Americans be fully addressed and supported. They rejected tokenism, patronization, and in some cases blatant racism. It is to this end that they formed separate local organizations and in 1896 organized the National Association of Colored Women.

The 1890s brought to the fore a cadre of African American women leaders, many of whom had been born either on the eve of, during, or immediately after the Civil War. Ida Wells-Barnett, Mary Church Terrell, and Victoria Earle Matthews were born between 1861 and 1863. Fannie Barrier Williams and Josephine St. Pierre Ruffin were born before the war in 1855 and 1842, respectively. These women, representative of the black female leadership that predominated at the turn of the century, for the most part represented an educated and social elite among African Americans. They viewed Harper as their elder, and though they held her in high regard, they favored a more direct frontal attack on racism in the woman's movement. Wells-Barnett, Ruffin, and Matthews openly attacked Frances Willard and the WCTU for being "apologists" for lynching. They questioned the bonds of sisterhood in the NWSA which would not permit white suffragists to address issues of discrimination against black women and their families on public transportation and in other areas of American life. They confronted the General Federation of Women's Clubs' unwritten policy involving the inclusion of black women's clubs as member organizations. For years, Harper had raised some of the same questions in her speeches and writings; however, during the years 1870 to 1890 she was a lone voice. In the 1890s these younger voices not only provided the chorus but escalated the response.

It was Harper's address, "The Colored Women of America," delivered at the 1877 AAW Woman's Congress, that defined the issues and in effect set the protest agenda that would be adopted by Terrell and other NACW leaders in the late 1890s. This widely reprinted speech was a comprehensive analysis of the history, status, and concerns of black women. If there was any doubt about her feminist concerns, this speech dispelled them. Less interested in her allusions to white racism, white feminists were intrigued by her analysis of the treatment of black women by black men. For many it confirmed their predictions and justified their earlier arguments that woman suffrage should precede Negro suffrage. Harper pointed out that after the war African American women experienced a major change in their condition; however, when black men gained the vote in 1870, they acquired advantages over the women. She stressed that, "In the new condition of things, the colored man vaulted into power, the colored woman was left behind to serve." Harper asserted that in fact the overall societal emphasis on "the subjection of women" was not lost on black men. Seeking their manhood rights, some men believed that physical force was necessary to maintain their power. Harper related that in the South she was told by many men that "You must whip them or leave them."

Although Harper related the postwar problems black males and females encountered in trying to establish normal relationships, the overall theme of her speech to the Woman's Congress was the "perseverance, courage and heroism" of black women. Emphasizing how slave masters exploited black women as sexual objects, she pointed out the many ways in which black women had resisted their captors and seducers. Demonstrating how racism effectively shut black women out of white charitable institutions, she described their extensive organizational work, particularly their fund raising to build schools, churches, orphanages, and homes for the aged and women. Harper gave examples of women supporting their families with and without husbands, and she discussed their struggle to move into the professions.

Along with her feminist commitments, Harper became affiliated with the Woman's Christian Temperance Union, an organization founded in 1874. Temperance was not a new issue. As an antebellum reform cause, however, it had been overshadowed by the abolitionist movement. The WCTU, the first national temperance organization of women, under the leadership of Frances Willard became one of the most powerful women's associations in the nation. Temperance was among the most prominent of the social reform causes. Like many African Americans, Harper felt that, while temperance was an interracial issue affecting many persons, it was of unique significance to African Americans, particularly black women. It is not clear exactly when Harper became involved with the WCTU. At some point in the early 1880s she attended a local, predominantly white union meeting in Philadelphia, accepted an invitation to become a member, and later was made city and state superintendent of the Department of Work among Colored People in Pennsylvania. At the 1883 WCTU national convention she was elected superintendent of the Department of Colored Work in the North, replacing Jane M. Kinney of Michigan. Work among African Americans became a separate department in 1881.

The WCTU, similar to the Sons of Temperance, Good Templars, and many other postwar reform organizations, was frequently questioned about its policy regarding black membership as well as its efforts to organize among African Americans, American Indians, and white ethnics, who were identified as "foreigners." In working with the black masses, the WCTU believed that white workers could be equally as if not more effective than African Americans. For years, Sallie F. Chapin, an heir to the Charleston, South Carolina, slavocracy, served in a dual capacity as superintendent of Southern Work and superintendent of the Department of Colored Work in the South. Although officially Harper was assigned to work with black women in the North, she also worked with black woman in the South, because temperance, like her other interests, became an integral part of her reform work. From 1865 to 1880, however, Harper traveled extensively in the South, lecturing and living among black people. During this period, her lectures and writings focused heavily upon the plight of southern blacks. She firmly believed that talented northern blacks should give greater consideration to participation in efforts to organize the freedmen. Since she was dependent mainly upon lecture fees and the sale of publications for her livelihood, she chose not to limit her work to any given geographical area. The title of WCTU superintendent carried no remuneration. Local unions frequently were unable to defray her traveling and living expenses. This was a problem, as Harper continued to point out that African Americans were too poor to underwrite her expenses and lecture fees.

Harper's work in the temperance movement is significant for a number of reasons. It provides an additional model for examining the relationship and functioning of a black leader in a major white reform organization during the nineteenth century. To date the most salient example has been Frederick Douglass's involvement with William Lloyd Garrison and the American Anti-Slavery Society. Harper represents one of the few examples of a nineteenth-century African American leader who was able to move beyond issues exclusively related to the cause of black advancement to become prominent in broader and predominantly white social movements. Harper, at different times, had held offices in white organizations and worked with whites on behalf of suffrage and peace, but her tenure and involvement in the WCTU for over thirty years, in a key leadership position for over a decade, provide an opportunity to explore the ways in which white female reformers related to an African American woman, particularly one who was educated, cultured, attractive, outspoken, persistent, and uncompromising in most of her views. In many ways Harper was the equal of Elizabeth Cady Stanton, Lucretia Mott, Frances Willard, and others who rose to leadership in the various women's reform organizations. How these women viewed and evaluated Harper or the extent to which they were silent or restricted in their comments about her is revealing.

In the postbellum period white women appeared to be more comfortable with Sojourner Truth and Amanda Smith than with Frances Harper. They viewed Truth and Smith as highly spiritual, unlettered women whose work was valuable and whose presence at some meetings helped to demonstrate the acceptance of black women by white women. They did not see Truth and Smith, former slaves, as women of culture and breeding. They could be ornaments in the white world but not social equals. Harper, a third-generation freeborn woman with dignified bearing, quiet elegance, refined manner, brilliant articulation, acute intelligence, and exceptional attractiveness, was in some ways disturbing to these women. Unlike any other African American woman of her day, she had moved beyond mere participation, attending and giving papers at the national meetings of important reform organizations. Harper held positions of leadership which allowed her to see the internal operations of the organizations and penetrate their inner circles. White women sensed that she was every bit their intellectual and social equal and that if she had been white she could have ascended to the presidency of one of the national women's organizations. White men frequently commented that she was remarkable for a woman, not an African American woman. That she was elected and appointed to the executive boards of the AAW, AWSA, WCTU, Woman's International Temperance Society, and the Universal Peace Union is revealing.

From 1883 until 1900, Harper's principal base was the WCTU. Introductions of Harper as a speaker and writer frequently emphasized her title and affiliation with the WCTU, with little mention of her other reform and literary activities. Harper was the second black woman to serve on the WCTU Executive Committee and the Board of Superintendents. By 1888, another black woman, Sarah J. Early, was elected to the Board of Superintendents, ostensibly to superintend the WCTU "colored work" in the South. Harper argued for the integration of unions. However, she defended, without advocating, the right of African American women to maintain separate unions. She felt that in some cases separation was beneficial in that black women could have an opportunity to develop their leadership skills and address specific race issues, free from the scrutiny and intercession of white women. Harper insisted that Frances Willard and the WCTU Executive Committee address the issue of integrated unions, particularly in the South; that the WCTU move beyond rhetorical commitment to the sanction of human and fiscal resources for "colored work"; and that the WCTU take a position against lynching and for African American suffrage. Harper's agenda conflicted with that of Willard and the Executive Committee. Willard was closely allied with Susan B. Anthony and other white feminists, who reached the conclusion by 1890 that the support of southern white women for woman suffrage and other causes was more important than African American aspirations.

In 1887 Frances Willard, in the face of great opposition, made woman suffrage a major priority for the WCTU. Harper and Willard disagreed not over the need for woman suffrage but over the strategies for achieving that goal. It appeared to Harper that for the sake of expediency the WCTU was capitulating to southern racism. By 1890 Harper was in direct conflict with the organization's leadership. After 1890 her role in the WCTU was effectively diminished through a series of reorganizations that removed Harper from the Executive Committee and the Board of Superintendents and eliminated Colored Work as a separate department. Unfortunately, Harper and Early were unable to finance their temperance work on the limited funds of black unions and sparse contributions from the African American community. In order to be an effective superintendent, organizing unions and galvanizing grass-roots support, one needed to travel extensively and to communicate frequently with local and state WCTU leaders.

Harper and Early were caught in a double bind when the WCTU rewrote its constitution to create a division of "Organization." Former departments, such as "Work among Foreigners," "Young Women's Work," "Juvenile Work," "Evangelists World's WCTU," and "American Organizers for World's WCTU" were placed under the direction of one superintendent. The Department of Organization included two categories of organizers, persons assigned to work as local and regional organizers under a particular subdivision and others designated as national organizers, also assigned to work with a subdivision. The WCTU Executive Committee voted salaries to the national organizers. Harper and Early elected to be national organizers for "Colored Work."

But in the reorganization the Department of Colored Work disappeared because Harper and Early chose to be national, instead of regional, organizers and because in the new structure they could not be superintendents. Although Harper's and Early's titles prior to 1890 suggested a more regional work, Harper had always worked in the North, South, East, and West. By placing one superintendent over varied work, listed under "Organization," the WCTU shut black women out of the Executive Committee, which made key policy decisions for the organization. This reflected the growing conservatism of Willard and the WCTU, so evident in their publications and at their conventions during the early 1890s. It was no longer advantageous to the organization to have a distinct department related to African Americans. Harper's and Early's names were listed with the other seventeen national organizers. The WCTU also included a white woman, Mary Marriage Allen, as the third national organizer for the "Colored." When the Department of Colored Work disappeared, the Department for Work among Foreigners continued as a subdivision of Organization and expanded to include not only Europeans but also Chinese and Spanish.

The reorganization effectively made African Americans invisible in the WCTU. Since there was no Department of Colored Work, there were no reports on this subject, which for years had been a feature in the *Union Signal*, the WCTU's major publication. Further, in 1892, the editor of the paper announced that branch news reporting would be replaced by state reports. Since most black unions were auxiliaries, they could not submit articles directly to the paper. They were obliged to report directly to the state presidents who decided what information to include. Thus information on the work of the black unions in the North, South, East, and West declined. This pattern of invisibility continued until 1895.

In 1895 the WCTU reinstated the Department of Colored Work, with Lucy Thurman of Michigan as the new superintendent. This action was taken to squelch the charge of racism and to offset the indictment by Ida Wells-Barnett that Willard was an apologist for lynching. In 1894, while lecturing in the British Isles, Wells-Barnett was asked about Willard's and the WCTU's support for the antilynching cause. She replied that Willard and the organization had never condemned lynching, that the WCTU refused black membership in the South, and that it operated segregated unions in the North. Wells-Barnett's data were not entirely accurate, but the coupling of these two issues drew extensive press comments and polarized the black and white leadership. Josephine St. Pierre Ruffin, editor of *Woman's Era*, in February 1895 indicated her support for Wells-Barnett's efforts. As the organ of the Boston-based New Era Club, *Woman's Era* was widely read by black female reformers, many of whom represented a new and highly vocal young feminist leadership that had come of age in the 1890s. The New Era Club was a key link in the formation of the National Federation of Afro-American Women, one of the first national organizations of black women, which in 1896 united with the District of Columbia–based National League of Colored Women to form the National Association of Colored Women (NACW). In part, the New Era Club and the NACW were formed as a reaction to the escalating lynching controversy, which eventually brought other issues to the fore.

The antilynching controversy, which pitted Wells-Barnett and African Americans against Willard and the WCTU, placed Harper in a difficult position. Harper continued to speak and write on the injustice of lynching. But she neither supported nor refuted the claims of Wells-Barnett that Willard was an "apologist" for lynching. Harper's success in the antislavery movement had convinced her that speeches and writings could be effective weapons in the winning of white allies and supporters to the cause of African Americans and that the same technique could be utilized for mobilizing African Americans. But the new black feminists of the 1890s were impatient with this method. Many of them questioned the efficacy of attending the meetings and working in white women's organizations that exhibited signs of paternalism and racism and would not support human rights for African Americans. In her lifetime effort to influence public opinion, Harper skillfully utilized and relied upon the press and the public platform in her efforts to bring about social reform. Lacking a solid organizational base, particularly among African Americans, Harper's position as a literary leader and feminist reformer was sustained by her unique talents, which for some Americans were larger than life, particularly since she was "black and a woman."

By 1895 Harper's leadership on all fronts was in eclipse. Paul Laurence Dunbar's strident dialectical verse placed him in the forefront of a new literary movement. In 1896 Dunbar was propelled to fame by an exceptionally favorable review of *Majors and Minors* by William Dean Howells, a renowned white literary critic, which appeared in *Harper's Review*. After that date, Frances Harper's poetic accomplishments were overshadowed by Dunbar's works. Harper's leadership as the most prominent African American female reformer was eclipsed by the rise of a new leadership, which was much younger, well educated, articulate, attractive, and extremely impatient with their white counterparts. Unlike Harper, Truth, Smith, and Tubman, the new leadership had a national organization, the NACW, which provided a forum and base of support for their programs and ideas. The NACW became a powerful vehicle for articulating and addressing the concerns of black women in a national context. Harper was selected as a vice-president of the organization, but she does not appear to have played a major role in its deliberations.

The decline in Harper's leadership after 1895 is partially related to the limited visibility she received in the black press after that date. This might be connected to the rise of Booker T. Washington and the Tuskegee Machine, which was actively involved in the suppression of persons whose views and philosophies differed from those of Washington. Harper's philosophy was closely related to the W. E. B. Du Bois tradition of protest. She believed that political action was of the utmost importance. She cautioned African Americans against placing a high priority on "mere money making." She was against accommodation of any kind, and like Ida Wells-Barnett she viewed economic success only as a means to an end, mainly as an element of power that could be used to restructure white attitudes and, most importantly, white behavior. Harper believed that when the Civil War ended African Americans had to have civil and political rights or they would again be forced into a state of subservience akin to that of slavery.

Throughout most of her public career, Harper appealed to the conscience of white Americans. This was a forceful strategy which had served the abolitionist movement well. However, once the slave was free, many white abolitionists felt that their job was done. Harper appealed to all classes of whites but was most often heard and read by the white elite. Her postbellum efforts to advance African Americans through appeals to the white conscience were largely unsuccessful. White men and women had other agendas; black Americans would have to find their own salvation. Though the white leadership did not necessarily agree with Harper, they admired and praised her talents. Like Du Bois and Wells-Barnett, Harper amassed a significant amount of data and tried to educate white Americans about the real plight of African Americans. Her audiences, white and black, were fascinated by her data and her ability to articulate cogent arguments rooted in history and philosophy. However, white racial attitudes regarding African Americans largely remained the same.

When Booker T. Washington ascended to the pinnacle of black leadership, Harper was seventy-one years of age. She appeared to be as active in the civil rights and woman's rights movements as she had been almost thirty years earlier. Throughout her career she had always received extensive press coverage and frequently spoke to black and white groups. After 1895 the black press curtailed its reportage of her activities, and she appears to have received fewer invitations to lecture. Between 1865 and 1885 she frequently had been invited to deliver her lectures in black churches. However, she was unsuccessful in her bid for the support of black ministers, who sometimes gave tacit support but were unwilling to turn their members and money over to any long-term cause they did not control. In addition, in the 1880s as black church women pressed for more equality in the church polity, many ministers were afraid to sanction Harper, who became more and more outspoken on the issue of woman suffrage and equality. And finally, after 1895 the press and the public were beginning to focus more on the new black female leadership. Ida Wells-Barnett, Josephine St. Pierre Ruffin, Margaret Murray Washington, Mary Church Terrell, Fannie Barrier Williams, Josephine Silone Yates, and Alice Moore Dunbar were among the rising stars to whom Harper's mantle was being passed.

Although Harper never became destitute, toward the end of her life her finances were more restricted. Because her philosophy conflicted with that of Booker T. Washington and there were many younger women who were closely allied with his wife, Margaret Murray Washington, a leader in the black woman's club movement, Harper may have been excluded at a time when her experience could have added valuable insights. Harper continued to attend the meetings of the WCTU and the Universal Peace Union; she worked with more recently formed organizations, such as the NACW and the National Association of Colored Educators; and she supported woman suffrage.

At Frances Ellen Watkins Harper's death in 1911, many tributes were written. Since she had outlived most of her contemporaries who had been active in the abolitionist movement and during the Reconstruction era, few of the eulogies were comprehensive in their description of her career and accomplishments. W. E. B. Du Bois, writing in the magazine *Crisis,* noted her literary accomplishments but paid little attention to her extensive reform work. T. Thomas Fortune reminded the readers of the *New York Age* that she had worked with Lucretia Mott, William Lloyd Garrison, and many of the great reformers of the nineteenth century. George Freeman Bragg's editorial in the *Baltimore Afro-American* was one of the few that exhibited a breadth of knowledge about her life and work and captured the essence of her life.

Notes

1   Dr. Marshall W. Taylor, quoted in Monroe A. Majors, *Noted Negro Women, Their Triumphs and Activities* (Chicago: Donahue and Henneberry, 1893).

2   The 1984 republication of *Our Nig,* a novel by Harriet E. Wilson published in 1859, challenged Harper's status as the first black woman novelist. See Henry Louis Gates, *Our Nig: Or Sketches from the Life of a Free Black* (New York: Random House, 1983).

3   The term "woman's reform movement" is frequently referred to by scholars as the woman's rights movement.

Note on Sources

This is the first full-length, analytical essay to examine the life of Frances Ellen Watkins Harper as an abolitionist and feminist reformer. Several essays published since this presentation (1987) provide excellent examinations of Harper as a writer and challenge previous evaluations written after Harper's death. A superb analysis of Harper as a novelist and of her relationship to traditional models of women's fiction in the United States is "Of Lasting Service for the Race," a chapter in Hazel V. Carby, *Reconstructing Womanhood: The Emergence of the African American Woman Novelist* (New York: Oxford University Press, 1987). In addition to providing customary biographical data, this work significantly looks at the impact of Harper's feminism on her writing and of the cultural position of Harper and other black female intellectuals.

In *Discarded Legacy: Politics and Poetics in the Life of Frances E. W. Harper, 1825–1911* (Detroit: Wayne State University Press), Melba Joyce Boyd, a self-described "poet-scholar," uses a biographical framework to explore the themes and structures employed by Harper in her writing. This is a very useful work for examining Harper's poetry and placing it in the context of her work as a feminist reformer. Though the work includes biographical details that demonstrate the relationship between Harper's poetry and politics, it is not an analysis of her work as a feminist reformer.

Although a large body of her poetry has been available for many years in rare original published editions, an excellent collection of Harper's poetry is found in Theodora Daniel Williams, "The Poems of Frances E. W. Harper, Edited with a Biographical and Critical Introduction, and Bibliography" (M.A. thesis, Howard University, 1937). A comprehensive collection of Harper's poetry, which includes an excellent introduction by Maryemma Graham, is *Complete Poems of Frances E. W. Harper* in *The Schomburg Library of Nineteenth-Century Black Women Writers,* ed. Henry Louis Gates (New York: Oxford University Press, 1988). There is one published collection of Harper's poetry, letters, essays, speeches, and fiction: Frances Smith Foster, *A Brighter Coming Day: A Frances Ellen Watkins Harper Reader* (New York: Feminist Press, 1990). This work provides an incomplete but excellent sample of Harper's writings for the period 1853–1911. Two reprints of Harper's novel, *Iola Leroy: Or Shadows Uplifted,* ed. Deborah McDowell (Boston: Beacon Press, 1987) and *Iola Leroy: Or Shadows Uplifted,* in Gates, *Schomburg Library of Nineteenth-Century Black Women Writers,* include excellent introductions by Hazel V. Carby and Frances Smith Foster respectively. In an excellent critical study of black women's literature at the turn of the century, Mary Helen Washington utilizes a novel excerpt from *Iola Leroy* to explore the historical context which propelled Harper and other black women writers to defend "the vicious and prevailing stereotypes" that distinguish American cultural thought. See Mary Helen Washington, *Invented Lives: Narratives of Black Women 1860–1960* (New York: Doubleday, 1988). A recent work that includes three unpublished novels, *Minnie's Sacrifice, Sowing and Reaping, and Trial and Triumph: Undiscovered Novels,* ed. Frances Smith Foster (Boston: Beacon Press, 1994), expands our knowledge of Harper as a black feminist writer. These works, in many ways autobiographical, are an indispensable source for research scholars and teachers.

There is a need for a comprehensive publication of Harper's collective writings. For over sixty years Harper's work appeared in diverse white and black publications, including the *Liberator, National Anti-Slavery Standard,* A.M.E. *Church Review, Frederick Douglass' Paper, New National Era,* A.M.E. *Christian Recorder, English Woman's Review,* and any number of other local and national publications. The best collection of Harper's letters for the period 1854 to 1870 is found in William Still, *The Underground Railroad* (Philadelphia: Porter and Coates, 1872). A number of Harper's letters, speeches, and writings are listed in the index to *The Black Abolitionist Papers,* ed. C. Peter Ripley (Ann Arbor: University Microfilms International, 1986).

Although there are biographical sketches and articles that discuss individual female abolitionists, there are few full-length scholarly biographies of black women abolitionists. A noncritical, but useful, study of Mary Ann Shadd Cary's diverse career as a newspaper editor, abolitionist, and activist is Jim Bearden and Linda Jean Butler, *Shadd: The Life and Times of Mary Shadd Cary* (Toronto: NC Press, 1977). Works in progress include a forthcoming biography of Sojourner Truth by Nell Painter (Norton) and a biography of Frances Ellen Watkins Harper by Bettye Collier-Thomas (University of North Carolina Press). Few works mention or discuss to any extent the role of African American women in the abolitionist movement. This is a subject that needs to be more fully explored. Shirley J. Yee's *Black Women Abolitionists: A Study in Activism, 1828–1860* (Knoxville: University of Tennessee Press, 1992), although derivative of several earlier studies, is an important effort to look at black women abolitionists as a group. One of the best critiques of Harper's role as a poet can be found in Joan R. Sherman, *Invisible Poets: African Americans of the Nineteenth Century* (Urbana: University of Illinois Press, 1974).

There are numerous biographical sketches of Harper's life from 1825 to 1890. With few exceptions, most of the earlier works derive from the description of her life found in Still, *Underground Railroad.* Most of the recent works provide more analysis of her literary work. For a representative sampling of biographical sketches, see Louis Filler, "Frances Ellen Watkins Harper," in *Notable American Women, 1607–1950: A Biographical Dictionary* (Cambridge, Mass.: Harvard University Press, 1971); Margaret Hope Bacon, " 'One Great Bundle of Humanity': Frances Ellen Watkins Harper (1825–1911)," *Pennsylvania Magazine of History and Biography* 113 (January 1989): 21–43; Hallie Quinn Brown, "Frances Ellen Watkins Harper," in *Homespun Heroines and Other Women of Distinction* (Xenia, Ohio: Aldine Publishing, 1926); Maryemma Graham, "Frances Ellen Watkins Harper," in *African American Writers before the Harlem Renaissance,* ed. Trudier Harris and Thadious M. Davis (Detroit: Gale Research, 1986); Ann Allen Shockley, *Afro-American Women Writers, 1746–1933* (Boston: G. K. Hall, 1988); Nagueyalti Warren, "Frances E. W. Harper (1825–1911)," in *Notable Black American Women,* ed. Jessie Carney Smith (Detroit: Gale Research, 1992); and Frances Smith Foster, "Harper, Frances Ellen Watkins (1825–1911)," in *Black Women in America: An Historical Encyclopedia,* ed. Darlene Clark Hine, Elsa Barkley Brown, and Rosalyn Terborg-Penn (Brooklyn, N.Y.: Carlson Publishing, 1993).

Harper's activities in the woman's movement may be traced through the records of the WCTU, AWSA, NAWSA, AAW, ICW, and NACW. The best description of the WCTU collection is Randall C. Jimerson, *Guide to Microfilm Edition of Temperance and Prohibition Papers* (Ann Arbor: University of Michigan, 1978). An excellent reference source for materials on other women's reform organizations, printed conference records, and individual collections is Andrea Hinding, *Women's History Sources: A Guide to Archives and Manuscript Collections in the United States* (New York: R. R. Bowker, 1979). For information regarding Harper's role in the woman suffrage movement, consult Rosalyn Terborg-Penn, "Afro-Americans in the Struggle for Woman Suffrage" (Ph.D. diss., Howard University, 1977), and Elizabeth Cady Stanton et al., eds., *History of Woman Suffrage,* 3 vols. (1881–1887; rpt., New York: Arno Press, 1969). For information regarding Harper's role in the NACW, see *Records of the National Association of Colored Women's Clubs, 1895–1992: Part 1, Minutes of National Conventions, Publications, and President's Office Correspondence* (Lanham, Md.: University Publications of America, 1993).

Harper's other reform activities, including her involvement with the peace movement and efforts for African American education, are recorded in the proceedings of the Universal Peace Union and the American Association of Educators of Colored Youth.

For information regarding women's associations, see Anne Firor Scott, *Natural Allies: Women's Associations in American History* (Urbana: University of Illinois Press, 1991). This work traces the history of women's associations from the late eighteenth century to the recent period. It provides a context for understanding the development and focus of many of the organizations that with which Harper was affiliated. It makes mention of African American women and some of their associations, although it is not a history of those associations. There are scholarly articles that discuss various aspects of black women's associational work, but there is no book-length publication of the history of the black woman's club movement. Existing scholarship on the NACW makes little reference to Harper's role in the organization. For discussion of black women's associational work, see Emma Field, "The Women's Club Movement in the United States" (M.A. thesis, Howard University, 1948); Tullia Hamilton, "The National Association of Colored Women, 1896–1920" (Ph.D. diss., Emory University, 1978); Floris Cash, "Womanhood and Protest: The Club Movement among Black Women, 1892–1922" (Ph.D. diss., SUNY–Stony Brook, 1986); Dorothy Salem, *To Better Our World: Black Women in Organized Reform, 1890–1920,* vol. 14 of *Black Women in the United States,* ed. Darlene Clark Hine (Brooklyn, N.Y.: Carlson Publishing, 1990); Gerda Lerner, *The Majority Finds Its Past: Placing Women in History* (New York: Oxford University Press, 1979); Anne Firor Scott, "Most Invisible of All: Black Women's Voluntary Associations," *Journal of Southern History* 56 (February 1990):3–22; Deborah Gray White, "The Cost of Club Work, the Price of Black Feminism," in *Visible Women: New Essays on American Activism,* ed. Nancy A. Hewitt and Suzanne Lebsock (Urbana: University of Illinois Press, 1993), 247–69; Stephanie J. Shaw, "Black Club Women and the Creation of the National Association of Colored Women," *Journal of Women's History* 3 (Fall 1991):10–25; and Deborah Gray White, *Too Heavy a Load: Race, Class, and Gender in Black Women's Associational Activities, 1896–1980* (forthcoming).

To Catch the Vision of

Freedom: Reconstructing

Southern Black Women's

Political History, 1865–1880

Elsa Barkley Brown

After emancipation, African American women, as part of black communities throughout the South, struggled to define on their own terms the meaning of freedom. Much of the literature on Reconstruction-era African American women's political history has focused on the debates at the national level over the Fifteenth Amendment, which revolved around the question of whether the enfranchisement of African American men or the enfranchisement of women should take precedence.[1] Such discussions, explicitly or not, contribute to a political framework that assumes democratic political struggles in the late-nineteenth-century United States were waged in pursuit of constitutional guarantees of full personhood and citizenship. A careful investigation of the actions of African American women between 1865 and 1880, however, leads one to question that framework. Historians seeking to reconstruct the post–Civil War political history of African American women have first to determine whether the conceptualizations of republican representative government and liberal democracy, which are the parameters of such a discussion, are the most appropriate ones for understanding southern black women's search for freedom—even political freedom—following the Civil War.

The family and the concept of community as family offered the unifying thread that bound African Americans together in the postslavery world. The efforts to reunite family and to establish ways of providing for all community members occupied much of freedpeople's time and attention. In their June 1865 petition to President Andrew Johnson, black men and women in Richmond, Virginia, for example, took note of the considerable efforts many had undergone in the two months since emancipation to reunite "long estranged and affectionate families." It was probably in recognition of the hope inherent in emancipation's possibility of family units existing physically together that the city's African Baptist churches replaced the prewar seating patterns, which had placed men and women separately, with families sitting together.[2]

Family members provided a variety of support—physical, economic, emotional, and psychological. Camilla Jones cared for her husband and two children and for the home and son of her widowed brother who lived in a separate apartment in the same tenement. Rachel and Abraham Johnson, who had no children, shared their home with Mary Jones, Rachel's widowed sister, and her three children. While the thirty-four-year-old widow Catherine Green went to work in a tobacco factory, her thirty-five-year-old single sister, Laura Gaines, cared for Catherine's son and took in washing to add to the family income. Elderly parents moved in with children, like Mariah Morton who lived in the 1870s with her two daughters, one a widow as well and the other single. Parents opened bank accounts for their children, even those who were adult, away from home, married, and employed. And children who left Richmond to search for work elsewhere provided for the money in their savings accounts to be used by other relatives, if needed, during their absence.[3] In all these ways African American women and men testified to the notion of family members as having a mutual and continuing responsibility to help each other and to prepare for hard times.

This sense of shared responsibility extended past blood ties to include in-laws and even fictive kin. Thus Eliza Winston, a sixty-year-old washerwoman, took in a fourteen-year-old girl, saw to it that she was able to attend school rather than seek employment, and made her beneficiary of her savings account. Those who had a place to live made room in their homes for those with whom they had labored as "fellow servants" during slavery. Unmarried or widowed mothers moved in with other single mothers in order to provide mutual support.[4]

Churches and secret societies, based on similar ideas of collective consciousness and collective responsibility, served to extend and reaffirm notions of family throughout the black community. Not only in their houses but also in their meeting halls and places of worship, they were brothers and sisters caring for each other. The institutionalization of this notion of family cemented the community. Community/family members recognized that the understanding of collective responsibility had to be maintained from generation to generation. Such maintenance was in part the function of the juvenile branches of the mutual benefit associations, as articulated by the statement of purpose of the Children's Rosebud Fountains, Grand Fountain United Order of True Reformers:

> Teaching them . . . to assist each other in sickness, sorrow and afflictions and in the struggles of life; teaching them that one's happiness greatly depends upon the others, . . . Teach them to live united. . . . The children of different families will know how to . . . talk, plot and plan for one another's peace and happiness in the journey of life.
>
> Teach them to . . . bear each other's burdens . . . to so bind and tie their love and affections together that one's sorrow may be the other's sorrow, one's distress be the other's distress, one's penny the other's penny.[5]

The institutions that ex-slaves developed give testament to the fact that their vision of freedom was not merely an individual one or, as historian Thomas C. Holt has put it, "that autonomy was not simply personal" but "embraced familial and community relationships as well." While Fanny Jackson, a student at the Lincoln Institute in Richmond in 1867, might declare, "I am highly animated to think that slavery is dead, and I am my own woman," the vision of autonomy which she then articulated embraced her husband, her children, and her community at large.[6] African Americans throughout the South in the post–Civil War period emphatically articulated their understanding that freedom and autonomy could not be independently achieved. In 1865 women in Richmond who attempted to support themselves and their families through domestic work noted the impossibility of paying the "rents asked for houses and rooms," given "the prices paid for our labor." They feared that many would be led "into temptation" out of economic necessity.[7] Mutual benefit societies and churches sought to provide some relief; a number of single black women banded together in homes and in secret societies. Despite these efforts, their worst fears were realized and an unknown number of black women were reduced to prostitution in order to feed, shelter, and clothe themselves and their loved ones. Ann Lipscomb, a single mother who worked, when possible, as a seamstress, was one such woman. Yet in 1872 when she joined with other single mothers to organize the Mutual Benevolent Society, they elected her president and entrusted their bank account to her.[8] Thus they quite emphatically demonstrated the notion of collective autonomy; they understood that none of them would be free until and unless Ann Lipscomb was also free. Their fates were intimately tied together; individual freedom could be achieved only through collective autonomy.

This understanding of autonomy was shared by those who had been slave and those who had been free.[9] In fact, the whole process of emancipation may have, at least momentarily, reaffirmed the common bonds of ex-slave and formerly free, for, despite their individual freedom in law, "freedom" in actuality did not come to free black men and women until the emancipation of slaves. Thus their own personal experiences confirmed for formerly free men and women as well as ex-slaves the limitations of personal autonomy and affirmed the idea of collective autonomy.[10]

The vision of social relations that Ann Lipscomb and her fellow black Richmonders articulated was not the traditional nineteenth-century notion of possessive individualism whereby society is merely an aggregation of individuals, each of whom is ultimately responsible for her/himself.[11] In this individual autonomy, "whether one eats or starves depends solely on one's individual will and capacities." According to liberal ideology, it is the self-regulating impersonality of contractual relations that makes social relations just.[12] Such a notion of freedom and social responsibility was diametrically opposed to the one that undergirded black institutional developments in Richmond and elsewhere in the post–Civil War period, where the community and each individual in the community were ultimately responsible for every other person. Whether one eats or starves in this setting depends on the available resources within the community as a whole. Individuals must each do their part and are free to make decisions about their lives, but ultimately it is the resources of the whole that determine the fate of the individual. This vision of social responsibility was expressed in the Richmond Humane Society's September 1865 proposal that the approximately 18,000 black Baptists and Methodists in the city contribute twenty cents each to a coffer of $3,600 which could be the basis for providing relief for the poor in the community.[13] Black Richmonders were proud of their communal consciousness. In their 1865 petition to President Johnson they asserted that "none of our people are in the alms-house and when we were slaves, the aged and infirm who were turned away from the homes of hard masters, who had been enriched by their toil, our benevolent societies supported while they lived, and buried them when they died." Because of this assumption of communal responsibility, they proudly proclaimed, "comparatively few of us found it necessary to ask for Government rations, which have been so bountifully bestowed upon the unrepentant Rebels of Richmond."[14]

It is a striking example of the different vision held by white Freedmen's Bureau officials throughout the South that they regarded this ethos of mutuality as one of the negative traits that had to be curtailed in the process of preparing freedpeople for life in a liberal democratic society. One South Carolina bureau agent, John De Forest, lamented the tendency among freedpeople to assume obligations to "a horde of lazy relatives and neighbors, thus losing a precious opportunity to get ahead on their own." A case in point was Aunt Judy, who, though supporting herself and her children on her meager income as a laundress, had "benevolently taken in, and was nursing, a sick woman of her own race. . . . The thoughtless charity of this penniless Negress in receiving another poverty-stricken creature under her roof was characteristic of the freedmen. However selfish, and even dishonest, they might be, they were extravagant in giving."[15] As historian Jacqueline Jones has pointed out, De Forest's notion that the willingness to share constituted a "thoughtless" act was a product of assumptions "that a 'rational' economic being would labor only to enhance her own material welfare."[16] The different vision of African American women, and of freedpeople in general, posed a persistent problem for northern white men and women, who consistently sought to reeducate and assimilate freedpeople to the requirements of the free labor ideology by introducing a different cultural world view as a means of imposing a different economic and political world view as well.

Recent historical explorations of the transition from slavery to freedom have provided substantial evidence that the economic vision of many African American women and men differed fundamentally from that imposed even by freedpeople's most supportive white allies. Northern white men and women assumed that ex-slaves would, in the postwar world, form a disciplined working class. Ex-slaves, in large part, shared a different economic vision.[17] They were "always on the move," searching for family, denying their labor to "dishonest or oppressive employers," and asserting their independence through their mobility. Rather than staying in place, working as much as possible for as high a wage as possible, and thus possibly, accumulating greater material goods, a large number of freedpeople sought not to maximize income but to minimize the amount of "time spent at work on other people's behalf." Domestic workers who moved from employer to employer, thus exasperating white women who despaired of ever finding reliable—that is, stable, permanent—servants, showed elements of this pattern.[18] Black men and women throughout the South, whether laboring on small farms or plantations or in homes or factories, generally made economic decisions based on family priorities rather than individual aspirations. For many men and women, higher wages served as an incentive not to greater work but to less, for they allowed one to obtain the basic necessities in shorter periods of time and thus eliminate the need for long-term employment under someone else's control. Such behavior appeared lazy or irrational to those who assumed freedpeople should adopt naturally those habits of thrift, diligence, and acquisitiveness that were a cornerstone of free labor ideology.[19]

In a larger society that assumed economic behavior to be a reflection of innate human characteristics rather than socially defined ones, freedwomen's, like freedmen's, behavior left them subject to a variety of assumptions about their inherent "nature," in light of their obvious nonconformity to what was presented as normal human behavior. Racist ideology was thus fed by ex-slaves' adoption of a different economic world view than that which was increasingly becoming the norm in the late-nineteenth-century United States. So deeply embedded are these assumptions that historians, too, have often assumed the imperative of a free wage labor system to be the equivalent of normal behavior and thus have either berated ex-slaves for not voluntarily adopting these modes of behavior at emancipation or, more sympathetically, have tried to defend ex-slaves against charges of being lazy by arguing that they did follow this norm but racist white people just did not admit it. As the works of historians Barbara Fields and Thomas Holt point out, both of these sets of interpretations stem from a framework much like that adopted by post–Civil War white northerners.[20] Rather than accepting ex-slaves' behavior as evidence of a different and equally valid consciousness which refutes our socially defined assumptions about innate economic behavior, both interpretations assume an absolute norm and then proceed to demonstrate how well ex-slaves either did or did not measure up. While the purpose of one may be proving the inferiority of African Americans, and the other rescuing ex-slaves from such declarations of inferiority, both begin with the same externally imposed parameters and thus miss the ex-slaves' experiences altogether.

The ex-slaves' economic world view developed from different criteria than those of the larger white society. The world view that defined the black community's notions of the function of labor equally defined its image of freedom and the approach to secure it. It is this world view from which all social, political, and economic institutions took shape. If an understanding of the different world views from which African Americans and Euro-Americans operated in the post–Civil War South is necessary to analyze work, family, and community behavior, then a similar understanding is also fundamental to an analysis of the political position of African American women in this same time period. Relatively little has been written about southern black women's participation in Reconstruction-era politics; what has been cited has often been descriptive and anecdotal. The few efforts to analyze have failed to consider the possibility of a radically different political world view in the African American community. For example, Jacqueline Jones notes the fundamental difference in Aunt Judy's "ethos of mutuality" and John De Forest's "possessive individualism" as it pertained to Aunt Judy's economic behavior, but she then fails to adopt a similar logic in her political analysis. Instead, she falls back on notions of republican representative government which stem from the same theory of possessive individualism she has rejected as inappropriate to her economic analysis. Thus Jones "searches in vain for any mention of women delegates in accounts of formal black political conventions . . . —local and state gatherings during which men formulated and articulated their vision of a just postwar society." Jones does note that "freedwomen sometimes spoke up forcefully at meetings devoted to specific community issues." But she concludes that "black men . . . like other groups in nineteenth century America . . . believed that males alone were responsible for—and capable of—the serious business of politicking." Freedwomen, Jones tells us, "remained outside the formal political process" and thus occupied "in this respect . . . a similarly inferior position" as white women.[21] Jones's analysis assumes a universal meaning to the fact that men—black and white—were able to cast a vote and women—black and white—were not. She thus invests the meaning in the act of voting itself rather than in the relations in which that act is embedded. As this essay will demonstrate, just what, in any given case, voting or not voting means has to be investigated and determined, not presumed. Having looked for and not found women delegates, women officeholders, or women otherwise exercising a *legal* franchise—all the important political liberties in a republican representative government—Jones misses what she does see: women participating in democracy in a most fundamental way. Jones's perspective rests on a common contemporary assumption, drawn from nineteenth-century political ideology, that the key political right, and responsibility, is the exercise of a legally granted franchise. The obsession in African American women's political history with questions of legal enfranchisement, thus, stems from this larger preconception.[22]

A thorough effort to uncover evidence of southern black women's political behavior during the latter half of the nineteenth century is vitally needed. In addition, there is a need to develop an interpretative framework consistent with the alternative economic, institutional, and cultural world view of freedpeople. The following analysis is based on my ongoing research on Richmond, Virginia, and on published materials on the postwar years in other areas of the South.[23]

The Reconstruction Act of 1867 required all the former Confederate states, except Tennessee, to hold constitutional conventions. Black men were enfranchised for the delegate selection and ratification ballots. In Virginia, Republican ward clubs elected delegates to the party's state convention, where a platform was to be adopted. On 1 August, the day the Republican state convention opened in Richmond, thousands of African American men, women, and children absented themselves from their employment and joined the delegates at the convention site, First African Baptist Church. Tobacco factories, lacking a major portion of their workers, were forced to close for the day. This pattern persisted whenever a major issue came before the state and city Republican conventions held during the summer and fall of 1867 or the state constitutional convention which convened in Richmond from December 1867 to March 1868. A *New York Times* reporter estimated that "the entire colored population of Richmond" attended the October 1867 local Republican convention where delegates to the state constitutional convention were nominated. Noting that female domestic servants composed a large portion of those in attendance, the correspondent reported: "as is usual on such occasions, families which employ servants were forced to cook their own dinners, or content themselves with a cold lunch. Not only had Sambo gone to the Convention, but Dinah was there also."[24]

It is important to note that these men and women did not absent themselves from work just to be onlookers at the proceedings. Rather, they intended to be active participants. They assumed as equal a right to be present and participate as the delegates themselves, a fact they made abundantly clear at the August 1867 Republican state convention. Having begun to arrive four hours before the opening session, African American women and men had filled the meeting place long before the delegates arrived. Having shown up to speak for themselves, they did not assume delegates had priority—in discussion or in seating. Disgusted at the scene, as well as unable to find seats, the conservative white Republican delegates removed to the Capitol Square to convene an outdoor session. That was quite acceptable to the several thousand additional African American men and women who, unable to squeeze into the church, were now able to participate in the important discussions and to vote down the proposals of the conservative faction.[25]

Black Richmonders were also active participants throughout the state constitutional convention. A *New York Times* reporter commented on the tendency for the galleries to be crowded "with the 'unprivileged,' and altogether black." At issue was not just these men's and women's presence but also their behavior. White women, for example, certainly on occasion sat in the convention's gallery as visitors silently observing the proceedings; these African Americans, however, participated from the gallery, loudly engaging in the debates. At points of heated controversy, black delegates turned to the crowds as they made their addresses on the convention floor, obviously soliciting and relying upon mass participation. Outside the convention hours, mass meetings were held to discuss and vote on the major issues. At these gatherings vote was either by voice or by rising, and men, women, and children voted. These meetings were not mock assemblies; they were important gatherings at which the community made plans for freedom. The most radical black Republican faction argued that the major convention issues should actually be settled at these mass meetings with delegates merely casting the community's vote on the convention floor. Though this did not occur, black delegates were no doubt influenced by the mass meetings in the community and the African American presence in the galleries, both of which included women.[26]

Black Richmonders were, in fact, operating in two political arenas—an internal and an external one. Though these arenas were related, they each proceeded from different assumptions, had different purposes, and therefore operated according to different rules. Within the internal political process women were enfranchised and participated in all public forums—the parades, rallies, mass meetings, and conventions themselves.[27] Richmond is not atypical in this regard.[28]

It was the state constitutional convention, however, that would decide African American women's and men's status in the political process external to the African American community. When the Virginia convention began its deliberations regarding the franchise, Thomas Bayne, a black delegate from Norfolk, argued the inherent link between freedom and suffrage and contended that those who opposed universal suffrage were actually opposing the freedom of African American people:

> If the negro was out of the question, I think it would be admitted that it [suffrage] was a God-given right. . . . the State of Virginia [has] no rights to give to the black man. . . . How can any man assume to give me a right, . . . I want this Convention to understand that the right of suffrage and the right of liberty cannot be separated. . . . When one

ceases, the other ceases. . . . No sooner did separation take place between these rights, than the strong began to oppress and predominate over the weak. . . . I repeat it as the sincere conviction of my heart, that this is an inherent right, this right of suffrage. . . . If you tell a man that this right is a privilege that you have to confer upon him, he will want to know where you got it. . . . If it is a right that men can confer, that power of the right to confer is because of their strength. . . . When we have the right to exercise this right of suffrage . . . the weak can stand up in their manhood and in their knowledge that it is God-given, and bear down all opposition.[29]

In rejoinder, E. L. Gibson, a conservative white delegate, enunciated several principles of republican representative government. Contending that "a man might be free and still not have the right to vote," Gibson explained the fallacy of assuming that this civil right was an inherent corollary to freedom: If the right were inherent then it would belong to both sexes and to all from "the first moment of existence" and to foreigners immediately. This was "an absurdity too egregious to be contemplated."[30] And yet this "absurd" notion of political rights was in practice in the Richmond black community, where males and females voted without regard to age and the thousands of rural migrants who came into Richmond suffered no waiting period but immediately possessed the full rights of the community.[31] What was absurd to Gibson and most white men—Republican or Democrat—was obviously quite rational to many black Richmonders. Two different conceptions of freedom and public participation in the political process were in place.

Gibson's arguments relied on several assumptions which were by then basic to U.S. democracy.[32] First were the ideas that freedom and political liberty were not synonymous and that people could be free without having political liberty. In fact, not all free people were entitled to political liberty because some persons were not capable, that is, not "fit" to exercise political liberty. Thus only those persons who had acquired the manners and morals that enabled them to exercise their freedom responsibly and properly were entitled to political liberty. A certain uniformity was expected; persons who had not yet learned to regulate their lives appropriately—to be thrifty, industrious, and diligent—were not yet capable of responsibly exercising this liberty. Those not capable of political liberty would rely on those capable of it to protect their freedom.[33]

Although Gibson did not specifically articulate this next point, the logic of his assumptions leads to the conclusion that even those with political liberty— as indicated by the right of suffrage—were not equally capable of political decision making. Thus the majority of the people, including the majority of those with suffrage, were expected to leave political decision making to those more qualified. Such political assumptions required that an individual, having once achieved freedom, hand over to others the responsibilities and rights of preserving her/his freedom. In fact, late-nineteenth-century assumptions concerning republican representative government required that the majority of people be passive in their exercise of freedom for the proper operation of democracy. Suffrage granted people not the right to participate in political decision making but the right to participate in choosing political decision-makers. Having become accustomed to this political process by now, we often act as if the two are synonymous. Freedpeople knew they were not.

In a frequently noted observation on women in Reconstruction-era politics, Elizabeth Botume, a northern white teacher in Beaufort, South Carolina, made clear that the political view many white northerners tried to impose was consistent with a particular economic view, too:

> Most of the field-work was done by the women and girls; their lords and masters were much interrupted in agricultural pursuits by their political and religious duties. When the days of *"conventions"* came, the men were rarely at home; but the women kept steadily at work in the fields. As we drove around, we saw them patiently "cleaning up their ground," "listing," "chopping down the old cotton stalks and hoeing them under," gathering "sedge" and "trash" from the riverside, which they carried in baskets on their heads, and spread over the land. And later, hoeing the crops and gathering them in.
>
> We could not help wishing that since so much of the work was done by the colored women,—raising the provisions for their families, besides making and selling their own cotton, they might also hold some of the offices held by the men. I am confident they would despatch business if allowed to go to the polls; instead of listening and hanging around all day, discussing matters of which they knew so little, they would exclaim,—
>
> "Let me vote and go; I've got work to do."[34]

Botume's analysis hinged on several assumptions: that adoption of habits of thrift and diligence were the factors that qualified one for suffrage; that voting equaled political participation; and that "listening and hanging around all day, discussing matters," were not important forms of political participation. Botume, like so many northern allies, thought free black people were to earn the rights of freedom by adopting the proper habits of responsibility and industry. Her lament was that these African American women, who had been "reconstructed" in that sense, were not rewarded by the franchise.[35] Central to her complaint about African American women's disfranchisement is her exasperation at African American men's assumption that political rights included the right to participate in political discussions (and thereby political decision making). She believed these industrious women, having come to exercise their proper economic role, would also adopt their appropriate role in the political system and would properly exercise the suffrage. They would vote and get on back to work rather than hang around engaging in political issues which, she thought, neither they nor the men had capacity to understand. Botume would leave it to others more capable to make the important political decisions. Thus even the slight support southern black women mustered among white northerners for their enfranchisement came in a context that would have preferred to leave them far less active in the political process than they had been in the most immediate post–Civil War days.

The history of African American women's political involvement in South Carolina and elsewhere leaves one dubious about Botume's predictions regarding how black women would exercise the franchise. Nevertheless, Botume's observations do point to the fact that in the end only men obtained the legal franchise. The impact of this decision is neither inconsequential nor fully definitive. African American women were by law excluded from the political arena external to their community. Yet this does not mean that they were not active in that arena—witness Richmond women's participation in the Republican and the constitutional conventions.

Southern black men and women debated the issue of woman suffrage in both the external and internal political arenas, with varying results. Delegates to the South Carolina convention, 56 percent of whom were black, adopted a constitution that included "male" as a qualification for voting, despite a stirring argument for woman suffrage from William J. Whipper, a black delegate from Beaufort. Nevertheless, a significant proportion of South Carolina's Reconstruction-era black elected officials favored woman suffrage or were at least open to a serious discussion of the issue. It was the South Carolina House of Representatives, which was 61 percent black, that allowed Louisa Rollin to speak on the floor of the assembly in support of woman suffrage in March 1869. Several black male representatives argued in favor of the proposal then and again two years later, when Lottie Rollin led a woman suffrage rally at the state capital. In March 1872 Beverly Nash, state senator, and Whipper, then state representative, joined with other delegates to propose a woman suffrage amendment to the state constitution. Alonzo J. Ransier, U.S. congressman from South

Carolina and later the state's first black lieutenant governor, presented his argument on the floor of the U.S. House of Representatives in 1874: "until [women as well as men have the right to vote] the government of the United States cannot be said to rest upon the 'consent of the governed.'" According to historian Rosalyn Terborg-Penn, Ransier, who was president of the South Carolina Woman's Rights Association, was widely supported by his black South Carolinian colleagues. In fact, six of the eight black men who represented South Carolina in the U.S. Congress during the Reconstruction era supported woman suffrage.[36]

The question of woman suffrage was a subject of discussion in other southern legislative chambers as well. It was often raised by white men to demonstrate the absurdity of black delegates' argument for the inherent right of suffrage. Black delegates, even when they rejected woman suffrage, were far more likely to treat it as a matter for serious discussion. If not, as they often did, expressing support, black delegates were far more likely to express at least ambivalence rather than firm conviction of the absurdity of woman electorates. Thomas Bayne, the Virginia delegate who so articulately delineated the argument for suffrage as an inherent right, presents one of the more complex cases. Unsupported by white Republicans in his assertion of inherent right and jeered by Gibson and other white conservative delegates, Bayne retorted,

> In speaking of the right to women to vote, I thought it an inherent right, and that women were wrongfully deprived of it. While I do not say that this is my opinion, yet I would simply say, in answer to that, that woman's right is a right to stay home. It is woman's right to raise and bear children, and to train them for their future duties in life. When she does that she is performing high duties which God himself has imposed upon her, in order that those children may carry out and exercise this very God-given right.[37]

Thus Bayne followed the logic of his "inherent right" argument, rejected his opponents' belief that woman suffrage was an absurdity, and conceded that as an inherent right "women were wrongfully deprived of it." He then, however, proceeded to what on the surface appears a very traditional statement of women's roles as confined to the domestic arena. But, by stating domestic roles as "rights," given the context of Reconstruction labor relations, he perhaps implies that his quarrel was not with those who supported woman suffrage but with those who would deny black women the right to domestic duties by obligating them to labor outside the home. Bayne did not, for example, say that a woman's right to stay home was her only right, nor did he suggest that training children was her highest duty or only duty. Historian Michael Hucles has pointed out that Bayne himself, in a discussion of his own terminology, said he often used the word "men" to stand for "human beings," male and female, thus affirming the possibility that his arguments for suffrage were intended as statements regarding universal suffrage, as in fact they were taken by Gibson and other white conservatives and radicals. Until more detailed research is done, determining Bayne's true meaning is well-nigh impossible. He does, however, clarify the problems with simplistic gender analyses of black male and female behavior in a time period when all economic, political, and social relations were in a state of redefinition. Black women and men had to redefine their rleationships within the context of their own world view and the realities of late-nineteenth-century U.S. society. Bayne may well have found himself confronted with the ambiguities inherent in such a situation, and his own position may be as contradictory as it sounds. Alternatively, he may have been stating quite clearly two distinct and contradictory rights of black women—rights in what historians would call both the public and private spheres—thus making clear the artificiality of the distinctions that historians make.[38] Whatever Bayne's particular position, it is clear that serious discussion of woman suffrage in southern legislative chambers during the Reconstruction era seemed to depend upon a strong African American representation.

The debate over woman's suffrage occurred in the internal arena as well, with varying results. In Nansemond County, Virginia, a mass meeting held that women should get the legal franchise; in Richmond, while a number of participants in a mass meeting held for female suffrage, the majority opinion swung against it.[39] But the meaning of that decision was not as straightforward as it may seem. The debate as to whether women should be given the vote in the external political arena occurred in internal political arena mass meetings where women participated and voted not just before and during *but also after* the negative decision regarding legal enfranchisement. This mass meeting's decision maintained the status quo in the external community; ironically enough, the status quo in the internal community was maintained as well—women continued to have a vote. Both African American men and women clearly operated within two distinct political systems. Eventually the external system would have its effect and the debate over women's enfranchisement would come to be more fully related to the internal political system. When this occurred, it had ramifications far into internal community institutions as well. Thus African American women sitting in Richmond's First African Baptist

Church in the 1880s had to fight for the right to vote in church meetings and were in the 1890s even asked to defend their presence at these meetings.[40]

Focusing on formal disfranchisement, however, obscures the larger story. The economic and political circumstances of African Americans underwent significant change in the years following emancipation. We may imagine that the political frameworks thus significantly changed as well. Black women's vision of freedom and democracy, like that of black people as a whole, may never have been that expansive again. Yet we must be alert to the persistence of old patterns along with the adoption of new. In the changing political frameworks one might expect to find a continuing thread of women's political participation even at the same time as one finds them more and more fundamentally excluded from both the external and the internal political process.

In Richmond and throughout the South exclusion from legal enfranchisement did not prevent African American women from affecting the vote and the political decisions. They organized political societies such as the Rising Daughters of Liberty which actively engaged in the political campaigns by educating the community on the issues, raising funds for the candidates, and getting out the vote. Coal miners' wives living outside Manchester, Virginia, played a similar role through the United Daughters of Liberty. Mississippi freedwomen placed themselves in potentially dangerous positions by wearing Republican campaign buttons during the 1868 election. In some instances the women walked "all the way to town, as many as twenty or thirty miles," to "buy, beg, or borrow one, and thus equipped return and wear it openly in defiance of . . . master, mistress, or overseer" and sometimes of husband as well. Domestic servants also risked job and perhaps personal injury by wearing their buttons to work. "To refuse, neglect, or lack the courage to wear that badge . . . amounted almost to a voluntary return to slavery," according to many freedwomen and freedmen.[41]

Black women initially took an active role in the South Carolina political meetings. Those disfranchised women whom Botume imagined would vote and go home, not involving themselves in political discussion, displayed a particular insistence on continued *public* political activity. The assumptions that underlay these women's activities are instructive. Laura Towne, a northern white teacher, tells us it was the white Republicans who first announced to the freedpeople that "women and children ought to stay at home on such occasions." Yet it does not appear to be merely the presence of females that disturbed these white men, for they quickly made it clear that Towne, of course, was welcome. Their announcement was meant to exclude "outsiders who were making some noise." Probably because of protests or disregard of the exclusion notice, the white Republicans modified their initial ban to state that "the *females* can come or not as they choose, . . . but the meeting is for men voters." It was clearly the women's failure to take the position of passive observers that was being censured.[42] Some black men took their cue, one even using the occasion to prompt women to " 'stay at home and cut grass,' that is, hoe the corn and cotton fields—clear them of grass!" while the men were at the political meetings.[43]

Even though they were excluded from further participation in the Republican meetings by the late 1860s, African American women in South Carolina, Louisiana, and elsewhere were still attending the meetings in the 1870s.[44] Although women were never elected delegates, it does appear that occasionally women were sent to the political meetings on behalf of their community. Lucy McMillan, a South Carolina widow, reported that her attendance at a political meeting was the result of community pressure: "They all kept at me to go. I went home and they quizzed me to hear what was said, and I told them as far as my senses allowed me."[45]

Women's presence at these meetings was often anything but passive. In the violent political atmosphere of the last years of Reconstruction, they had an especially important—and dangerous—role. While the men participated in the meeting, the women guarded the guns—thus serving in part as the protectors of the meeting. This was not a symbolic or a safe role in a time when "men are shot at, hunted down, trapped and held till certain meetings are over, and intimidated in every possible way." During the violent times of late Reconstruction, African American women in South Carolina were reported "in arms, carrying axes or hatchets in their hands hanging down at their sides, their aprons or dresses half-concealing the weapons." One clergyman, contending African Americans could defend themselves if necessary, noted that "80,000 black men in the State . . . can use Winchesters and 200,000 black women . . . can light a torch and use a knife." At times women as well as men actually took up arms. In 1878 Robert Smalls, attacked by redshirts while attempting to address a Republican meeting in Gillisonville, sought refuge and later reported that "every colored man and woman seized whatever was at hand—guns, axes, hoes, etc., and ran to the rescue." Some of these women probably had double incentive as the redshirts had "slap[ped] the faces of the colored women coming to the meeting."[46]

African American women took the political events to heart and took dramatic steps to make their political sentiments known. They also expressed their outrage when the political tide turned against their interests. Alabama women, reportedly, "were converted to Radicalism long before the men and almost invariably used their influence strongly for the purpose of the League." South Carolina Democrats believed African American women to be "the head and fount of the opposition." Thomas Holt has suggested that the South Carolina black woman's "reputation for political partisanship was . . . enhanced by her frequent appearance at the head of angry Charleston mobs, like the one which wreaked havoc on the German merchants after the Republican defeat in the municipal elections of 1871."[47]

African American women in South Carolina and elsewhere understood themselves to have a vital stake in African American men's franchise. The fact that only men had been granted the vote did not mean that only men should exercise that vote. Women reportedly initiated sanctions against men who voted Democratic. One South Carolina witness reported that "no mens were to go to the polls unless their wives were right alongside of them; some had hickory sticks; some had nails—four nails drive in the shape of a cross—and dare their husbands to vote any other than the Republican ticket." In the highly charged political atmosphere of the late 1870s it was no small matter for these women to show up at the election site carrying weapons. Armed Democrats patrolled the polling areas, and Republicans were often "driven from the polls with knives and clubs. Some of them were badly wounded."[48] We might wonder whether the weapons the women carried were for use on their husbands or on the Democratic opponents, but in either case these women very publicly declared their stake in their husband's vote.

Black Republican politicians throughout the South took women's participation seriously and publicly encouraged them to abstain from sexual relations with any man who voted Democratic. Some women left their Democratic husbands. Engaged women were encouraged to postpone the wedding until after the election when they could obtain assurance that their future husband was not a Democrat. In Alabama women banded together in political clubs to enforce these sanctions collectively. Some politicians also endorsed women's use of weapons to influence their husbands' vote.[49] It is likely that, rather than initiating these actions on the part of African American women, Republican legislators merely recognized and endorsed actions initiated by the women themselves. These examples all suggest that African American women and men understood the vote as a collective, not an individual, possession and, furthermore, that African American women, unable to cast a separate vote, viewed African American men's vote as equally theirs. Their belief that the franchise should be cast in the best interest of both was not the nineteenth-century patriarchal notion that men voted on behalf of their wives and children. By the latter assumption, women had no individual wills; rather, men operated in women's best interest because women were assumed to have no right of input. African American women assumed the political rights that came with being a member of the community, even though they were not granted the political rights they thought should come with being citizens of the state.

The whole sense of the ballot as collectively owned is most eloquently presented by Violet Keeling, a tobacco worker who testified in February 1884 before a Senate committee investigating the violence in the previous year's elections in Danville, Virginia. Assenting in her husband's decision not to vote in that election for fear he might be killed, she made it clear that she would not, however, assent in his or anyone else's voting Democratic: "as for my part, if I hear of a colored man voting the Democratic ticket, I stay as far from him as I can; I don't have nothing in the world to do with him. . . . No, sir; I don't 'tallow him to come in my house." Asked why she should "have such a dislike to a colored man that votes the Democratic ticket," she replied:

> I think that if the race of colored people that has got no friends nohow, and if they don't hang together they won't have none while one party is going one way and another the other. I don't wish to see a colored man sell himself when he can do without. Of course we all have to live, and I always like to have a man live even if he works for 25 cents a day, but I don't want to see him sell himself away. . . . I think if a colored man votes the Democratic ticket he has always sold himself. . . . If I knew a colored man that voted the Democratic ticket to come to my house, I would tell him to go somewhere else and visit.

Asked "suppose your husband should go and vote a Democratic ticket," she responded: "I would just picke up my clothes and go to my father's, if I had a father, or would go to work for 25 cents a day."[50]

Violet Keeling clearly articulated the notion that a black man could not exercise his vote only in his own behalf. If he sold his vote, he sold hers. The whole issue of the ostracism of black Democrats reveals very clearly the assumptions regarding suffrage that were operative throughout African American communities. Black Democrats were subject to the severest exclusion: disciplined within or quite often expelled from their churches; kicked out of mutual benefit societies; not allowed to work alongside others in the fields or accepted in leadership positions at work or in the community. Ministers were dismissed from their churches or had their licenses to preach revoked; teachers who voted Democratic found themselves without pupils. Democrats' children were not allowed in schools. And, perhaps the most severe sanction of all, black Democrats found themselves unaided at time of death of a family member. Women participated in all of these actions as well as in the mobs that jeered, jostled, and sometimes beat black Democrats or rescued those who were arrested for such behavior. In fact, women were often reported to be the leaders of such mob involvements.[51] One historian noted that "the average negro . . . believed it was a crime 'to vote against their race.' "[52]

From the perspective of liberal democratic political ideology, these activities might be perceived as "unconscionable" "interference with the [individual voter's] expression of . . . political preference."[53] But African Americans in the post–Civil War South understood quite clearly that the actions of one member of the community affected, and in this instance endangered, all others in that community. Thus they understood there was no such thing as an individual action or a "possessive individual," owing nothing to society. This understanding was most clearly put by Robert Gleed, a Mississippi state senator, in his 1871 testimony before the U.S. Senate:

> it is traitorous in these men to acquiesce with a party who says we have no rights in the community in common with other citizens. . . . They [black Democrats] have the right [to vote Democratic] just like Benedict Arnold had a right to trade off the army just like he did; but that does not make it justice and equity because he did.[54]

The issue, as Gleed and many black men and women understood it, was not autonomy but responsibility. It was that sense of suffrage as a collective, not an individual, possession that was the foundation of much of women's political activities.[55]

Sarah Nash, Nancy Hodges, and the other female hucksters who gathered in Portsmouth, Virginia, in May 1866 "to consult each other and talk our troubles over" made that collective possession clear. Nash and Hodges, along with seven other women "representing many hundreds" of others "who huckster for a living," signed a petition to General O. O. Howard complaining about the unfair taxation policies that were driving them out of business; about their husbands' and children's loss of jobs; and about the general "obbitrary power" controlling them in many matters regarding which they had "never been consulted." These women were speaking, however, not of whether they each individually had voice and representation but of whether their community had a voice. Thus they noted that "their husbands, though called upon to pay a head tax of ($4.00) four dollars, have no voice in making city, State or national government."[56] This is not to suggest that African American women did not desire the vote or that they did not often disagree with the actions taken by some black men. One should, however, be careful about imposing presentist notions of gender equality on these women. Clearly for them the question was not an abstract notion of individual gender equality but rather one of community. That such a vision might over time lead to a patriarchal conception of gender roles is not a reason to dismiss the equity of its inception.

Women's presence at the polls was not just a negative sanction; it was also a positive expression of the degree to which they understood the men's franchise to be a new political opportunity for themselves as well as their children. They reinforced this idea of black men's voting as a new freedom which they had all achieved by turning the occasion into a public festival and celebration, bringing lemonade and gingercakes and spending the day at the polls. Of course, the principal reason for the group presence at the polls was protection. The tendency for "crowds" of freedmen to go to the polls together was seen by their white contemporaries and by some historians as evidence that they were forced to vote the Republican ticket or that they did not take seriously the franchise but instead saw election day as an opportunity for a picnic or other entertainment. Henderson Hamilton Donald, for example, noting that freedmen "always voted in companies," found this behavior "odd and sometimes amusing." Yet his own description suggests the real meaning: "When distances were great, crowds of them under leaders went to the polling places a day in advance and *camped out like soldiers on the march*."[57] Women and children often went along, their presence reflecting their excitement about the franchise but also their understanding of the dangers involved in voting. Women may have gone for additional protection of the voters, like those women in South Carolina who carried weapons, or to avoid potential danger to those left alone in the countryside while the men were gone. But, in any case, the necessity for a group presence at the polls reinforced the sense of collective enfranchisement. What may have been chiefly for protection was turned into festivity as women participated in a symbolic reversal of the meaning of the group presence.

African American women throughout the South in the Reconstruction era assumed *publicly* the right to be active participants in the political process long after they had been formally removed—and they did so, in part, through their husbands. They operated out of an assumption that his vote was theirs. Unlike many northern white middle-class women, southern black women in the immediate post–Civil War era did not base their political participation in justifications of superior female morality or public motherhood. They did not need to; their own cultural, economic, and political traditions provided rationale enough—"autonomy was not simply personal."

One of the ramifications of liberal democratic political theory is that our notion of politics is severely circumscribed. In a context where only certain persons have the rights and abilities to participate fully, the *formal* political process takes on an exclusivity and sanctity all its own. Historians operating from this perspective often ascribe the totality of politics to the formal political arena. With this assumption, Jacqueline Jones asserts that "the vitality of the political process, tainted though it was by virulent racial prejudice and violence, provided black men with a public forum distinct from the private sphere inhabited by their womenfolk."[58] But these women's actions were fundamentally *political.* That African American women did not operate inside the formal political process does not negate the intensely political character of their actions. These actions represented a continuous significant political participation on their part. Black women, therefore, were hardly confined (even without the franchise or elective office) to a private sphere.[59] They were certainly not confined to any less bloody sphere.[60]

African American women understood "that freedom meant above all the right to participate in the process of creating it."[61] Being denied this right in the external political arena and having this right increasingly circumscribed in the internal arena as well, these women created their own political expression, thus inventing the power their freedom required. Their actions were not merely a grievance against their own lack of political rights or lack of rights of the black community but, more importantly, a critique of the absence of freedom and democracy, as they understood it, in the society at large. By their actions and assumptions they challenged the fundamental assumptions of the U.S. political process itself.

Citizenship entails constitutionally granted political rights and privileges which make one a full-fledged and active member of the body politic. Thus one must be granted the right to be active in the political process. But these women operated out of a notion of community, wherein all—men, women, and children; freeborn and formerly slave; native and migrant—had inherent rights and responsibilities requiring no higher authority than their commitment to each other. Their sense of community, related to the collective character of their notion of freedom, had foundation in their understanding that freedom, in reality, would accrue to each of them individually only when it was acquired by all of them collectively. It was this very sense of community rather than citizenship, of peoplehood rather than personhood, that was the basis for their activities. In other words, it was their vision of freedom that granted them the right to assume the political responsibilities which neither the state nor some members of their own community acknowledged to be theirs.

It is clear that to understand southern black women's political history in the post–Civil War era requires that we develop alternative political definitions to those defined by liberal democratic thought. Even the terminology by which we understand African American women's political struggle must be rethought, for we currently have no language in which to express the concepts that these women understood. The significance of this may be difficult to contemplate— both for black women historically and for our notions of how far we have progressed today. For understanding African American women's involvement in the political process in the post–Civil War era, even without the franchise, requires us at least to consider the possibility that when black women, like those in Richmond, obtained the legal franchise in the 1920s they may actually have been far less involved in the political decision-making process than were their unenfranchised foremothers in the immediate post–Civil War period.[62]

Ultimately northern and southern white men may have denied African American women the freedom fully to shape their own lives in the post–Civil War era. But we, trapped in our own mental prisons, have denied them their freedom as well, insisting instead that they accept our very limited and pessimistic vision of human possibilities. There is an enormous amount of work yet to be done on southern black women's political history in the last four decades of the nineteenth century. Just as African American women, as part of black communities throughout the South, struggled in the post–Civil War era to catch, that is, to make real, their vision of freedom, we, as historians, must now struggle to catch, that is, to understand, their vision of freedom. In the process we need not only to refine our base of information but also to reconstruct our frameworks, creating new ones that allow us to interpret these women's lives in ways that do justice to their vision of freedom.

Notes

This essay had its origins in my students' questions and insights as we explored definitions of freedom in African American Studies 100 and History 202 at Emory University, 1986–87. Their excitement about the ideas and their willingness to challenge not only my assumptions but their own deeply held convictions were inspirational as well as informative. Earlier versions of this essay were presented at the "Afro-American Women and the Vote, 1837 to 1965" conference, University of Massachusetts at Amherst, 14 November 1987, where I benefited from the comments of Ena Farley; the Social History Seminar, Newberry Library, Chicago, Illinois, 16 October 1991; and the workshop on "Historical Perspectives on Race and Racial Ideologies," Postemancipation Studies Project, Center for Afroamerican and African Studies, University of Michigan, 22 November 1991. I would like to thank Thea Arnold, Jacquelyn Dowd Hall, Nancy Hewitt, Thomas C. Holt, Lillian Jones, Dee Dee Joyce, Joseph Reidy, Leslie S. Rowland, Rebecca Scott, David Thelen, and Dale Tomich for their careful readings and critiques of this essay.

1   See, for example, Angela Davis, *Women, Race, and Class* (New York: Random House, 1981), 70–86; Paula Giddings, *When and Where I Enter: The Impact of Black Women on Race and Sex in America* (New York: William Morrow, 1984), 64–71; Rosalyn Terborg-Penn, "Afro-Americans in the Struggle for Woman Suffrage" (Ph.D. diss., Howard University, 1977), chap. 2; Bettina Aptheker, "Abolitionism, Woman's Rights, and the Battle over the Fifteenth Amendment," in *Woman's Legacy: Essays on Race, Sex, and Class in American History* (Amherst: University of Massachusetts Press, 1982).

2   *New York Tribune*, 17 June 1865; Peter Randolph, *From Slave Cabin to Pulpit* (Boston: Earle, 1893). For discussions of freedpeople's efforts to reunite families throughout the South, see Robert H. Abzug, "The Black Family during Reconstruction," in *Key Issues in the Afro-American Experience*, ed. Nathan I. Huggins, Martin Kilson, and Daniel M. Fox, vol. 2: *Since 1865* (New York: Harcourt Brace Jovanovich, 1971), 32–34; Ira Berlin, Steven F. Miller, and Leslie S. Rowland, "Afro-American Families in Transition from Slavery to Freedom," *Radical History Review* 42 (1988): 89–121; Eric Foner, *Reconstruction: America's Unfinished Revolution, 1863–1877* (New York: Harper and Row, 1988), 82–85; Leon F. Litwack, *Been in the Storm So Long: The Aftermath of Slavery* (New York: Random House, 1979), 229–47; Peter J. Rachleff, *Black Labor in the South: Richmond, Virginia, 1865–1890* (Philadelphia: Temple University Press, 1984), 15–16.

3   Using the records of the Freedman's Savings and Trust Company and the manuscript census, Peter J. Rachleff has done an extensive job of re-creating this family network (*Black Labor in the South*, 15–23).

4   Rachleff, *Black Labor in the South*, 17, 22, 26; *Freedmen's Record* 2, no. 3 (March 1866): 53.

5   W. P. Burrell and D. E. Johnson, Sr., *Twenty-five Years History of the Grand Fountain of the United Order of True Reformers, 1881–1905* (Richmond: Grand Fountain, United Order of True Reformers, 1909), 76–77.

6   Thomas C. Holt, " 'An Empire over the Mind': Emancipation, Race, and Ideology in the British West Indies and the American South," in *Region, Race, and Reconstruction: Essays in Honor of C. Vann Woodward*, ed. J. Morgan Kousser and James McPherson (New York: Oxford University Press, 1982), 299; Fanny Jackson to Friends of the North, 22 March 1867, in *Freedmen's Record* 3, no. 6 (June 1867): 106. See also David Montgomery, *The American Civil War and the Meanings of Freedom: An Inaugural Lecture Delivered before the University of Oxford on 24 February 1987* (Oxford: Clarendon Press, 1987), 11–13: "the former slaves' own conception of freedom . . . was above all a collective vision, rooted in generations of common experience in the United States. . . . The point is not simply that former slaves lacked experience in bourgeois ways but rather that they did not define

either freedom or property in the same individualistic and market-oriented terms that their northern liberators employed."

7   Rachleff, *Black Labor in the South,* 37–38.

8   Ibid., 26–27.

9   Locating the origins of this collective world view is beyond the scope of this essay, but several works are suggestive of both African origins and the degree to which this democratic ethos was a response to the necessities of life for black people—slave or free—in a slave society. On the African origins of one of the primary institutional expressions of this collective world view, see Betty M. Kuyk, "The African Derivation of Black Fraternal Orders in the United States," *Comparative Studies in Society and History* 25 (October 1983): 559–92. Lawrence Levine offers evidence of a collective world view, African in origin but transformed to meet the needs of life under slavery and freedom; see *Black Culture and Black Consciousness: Afro-American Folk Thought from Slavery to Freedom* (New York: Oxford University Press, 1977). One of the most striking evidences of the democratic ethos under slavery comes to us from a study of children at play. David K. Wiggins tells us that slave children played no games that eliminated players: The rules they devised for their various games of dodge ball and tag prevented the removal of any participants. When one of the main fears of daily life was being removed from the community—sold or hired out—slaves chose not to duplicate that fear in their own social structure. Slave children attempted to provide some security by ensuring that none of them would be excluded from participating and thus through their play reinforced the basic communal values of the slave community. See "The Play of Slave Children in the Plantation Communities of the Old South, 1820–1860," in *Growing Up in America: Childhood in Historical Perspective,* ed. N. Ray Hiner and Joseph M. Hawes (Urbana: University of Illinois Press, 1985), 181–82. See also Thomas L. Webber, *Deep like the Rivers: Education in the Slave Quarter Community, 1831–1865* (New York: W. W. Norton, 1978), esp. 63–70, 144, 224–44; Herbert G. Gutman, *The Black Family in Slavery and Freedom, 1750–1925* (New York: Pantheon Books, 1976), esp. chap. 5; Ira Berlin, *Slaves without Masters: The Free Negro in the Antebellum South* (New York: Pantheon Books, 1974), chap. 9.

10   My effort in this essay is to distinguish the collective vision of these African Americans from the individualistic vision of the government officials, businessmen, missionaries, and teachers who developed and implemented Reconstruction policies. This is not to suggest that there was a monolithic "black" versus a monolithic "white" vision of freedom. Northern white industrial workers and southern white yeoman farmers also often expressed a collectivist vision and understood the individualistic assumptions of free labor ideology in a market economy as detrimental to their collective (and individual) self-interest (Montgomery, *American Civil War*). Contemporary U.S. historians' own socialization often leads them to assume individualism as natural human behavior and thus to assume that collective identity is the "peculiarity" that needs explaining, when in fact collective identity has been the foundation of many people's understandings of self. "Throughout most of human history the antithesis of slavery has not been autonomy but belonging; defining freedom as individual autonomy is a phenomenon of the modern era" (Thomas C. Holt, "Of Human Progress and Intellectual Apostasy," *Reviews in American History* 15 [March 1987]: 58).

11 C. B. Macpherson, *The Political Theory of Possessive Individualism: Hobbes and Locke* (Oxford: Oxford University Press, 1962).

12 Holt, " 'An Empire over the Mind,' " 287.

13 John Thomas O'Brien, Jr., "From Bondage to Citizenship: The Richmond Black Community, 1865–1867" (Ph.D. diss., University of Rochester, 1974), 78, 174–75, 277–78. For a discussion of institutional developments in Richmond's black community as an outgrowth of this collective consciousness and its attendant understandings of social responsibility, see Rachleff, *Black Labor in the South*. For similar discussions regarding other southern black communities in the post–Civil War era, see Edward Magdol, *A Right to the Land: Essays on the Freedmen's Community* (Westport, Conn.: Greenwood Press, 1977); Herbert G. Gutman, "Schools for Freedom: The Post-Emancipation Origins of Afro-American Education," in Herbert G. Gutman, *Power & Culture: Essays on the American Working Class*, ed. Ira Berlin (New York: Pantheon Books, 1987), 260–97.

14 *New York Tribune*, 17 June 1865.

15 John William De Forest, *A Union Officer in the Reconstruction* (1948; rpt., Hamden, Conn.: Archon Books, 1968), 97–99. For an extended discussion of the ways in which this ethos of mutuality shaped a variety of freedpeople's communities, see Magdol, *Right to the Land*. Habits of mutuality are not exclusive to persons of African descent. For similar discussions of European and Euro-American working-class and rural communities, see, for example, E. P. Thompson, *The Making of the English Working Class* (London: Victor Gollancz, 1963); Jacquelyn Dowd Hall, James Leloudis, Robert Korstad, Mary Murphy, LuAnn Jones, and Christopher B. Daly, *Like A Family: The Making of a Southern Cotton Mill World* (Chapel Hill: University of North Carolina Press, 1987); Steven Hahn, *The Roots of Southern Populism: Yeoman Farmers and the Transformation of the Georgia Upcountry, 1850–1890* (New York: Oxford University Press, 1983).

16 Jacqueline Jones, *Labor of Love, Labor of Sorrow: Black Women, Work, and the Family from Slavery to the Present* (New York: Basic Books, 1985), 65–66. Assumptions of individual autonomy permeate the conceptual frameworks that shape much contemporary discussion of African American women's economic conditions as well. Consider, for example, analyses of women's wages that treat the closing gap between the earnings of full-time black and white female employees as evidence of increasing economic parity among women. Such analyses extract women from their families and communities, assume they are "possessive individuals" whose well-being and status are determined solely by their individual resources. Yet in reality the economic base and status of black and white full-time wage earning women are markedly different, since the majority of these white women live in households in which there are two full-time wage earners and the majority of these black women live in households in which they are the only full-time wage earners. A critique of such analyses was presented by Linda Burnham, "Struggling to Make the Turn: Black Women and the Transition to a Post-Industrial Society," at the Schomburg Center for Research in Black Culture "Survival and Resistance: Black Women in the Americas" symposium, 9 June 1989.

17 Gerald David Jaynes, *Branches without Roots: Genesis of the Black Working Class in the American South, 1862–1882* (New York: Oxford University Press, 1986); Barbara Jeanne Fields, *Slavery and Freedom on the Middle Ground: Maryland during the Nineteenth Century* (New Haven: Yale University Press, 1985); Holt, " 'An Empire over the Mind,' " 283–

314; Julie Saville, "A Measure of Freedom: From Slave to Wage Laborer in South Carolina, 1860–1868" (Ph.D. diss., Yale University, 1986); Ira Berlin, Steven Hahn, Steven F.
Miller, Joseph P. Reidy, and Leslie S. Rowland, "The Terrain of Freedom: The Struggle
over the Meaning of Free Labor in the U.S. South," *History Workshop Journal*, no. 22
(Autumn 1986) 108–30; Armstead L. Robinson, " 'Worser dan Jeff Davis': The Coming of
Free Labor during the Civil War, 1861–1865," in *Essays on the Postbellum Southern Econ-
omy*, ed. Thavolia Glymph and John J. Kushma (Arlington: University of Texas, 1985), 11–
47; Harold D. Woodman, "The Reconstruction of the Cotton Plantation in the New
South," in Glymph and Kushma, *Postbellum Southern Economy*, 95–119; Lawrence N.
Powell, *New Masters: Northern Planters during the Civil War and Reconstruction* (New
Haven: Yale University Press, 1980), esp. chap. 6.

18   Fields, *Slavery and Freedom*, 157–65.

19   Ibid., 157–66; Saville, "Measure of Freedom"; Holt, " 'An Empire over the Mind.' "

20   Fields, *Slavery and Freedom*, 165–66; Holt, " 'An Empire over the Mind.' "

21   Jones, *Labor of Love*, 66–67.

22   For studies of black women's struggle for legal enfranchisement, see n. 1 above; see also
Beverly Lynn Guy-Sheftall, "Books, Brooms, Bibles and Ballots: Black Women and the
Public Sphere," in *"Daughters of Sorrow": Attitudes toward Black Women, 1880–1920*
(Brooklyn, N.Y.: Carlson Publishing, 1990).

23   This analysis is necessarily generalized. Further research will no doubt reveal important
distinctions in black women's political activism across regions within the South, within
states, between rural and urban areas.

24   *Richmond Dispatch*, 1, 2 August, 30 September, 9 October 1867; *New York Times*, 1, 2,
6 August, 15, 18 October 1867. My discussion of these events follows closely Rachleff,
Black Labor in the South, 45–46. See also Richard L. Morton, *The Negro in Virginia
Politics, 1865–1902*, Publications of the University of Virginia Phelps–Stokes Fellowship
Papers, no. 4 (Charlottesville: University of Virginia Press, 1919), 40–43. Similar reports
issued from other areas throughout the South, causing one chronicler to report that "the
Southern ballot-box" was as much "the vexation of housekeepers" as it was of farmers,
businessmen, statesmen, or others. "Elections were preceded by political meetings, often
incendiary in character, which all one's servants must attend." Election day itself could
also be a problem. As one Tennessean reported in 1867, "Negro women went [to the
polls], too; my wife was her own cook and chambermaid" (Myrta Lockett Avary, *Dixie
after the War: An Exposition of Social Conditions Existing in the South, during the Twelve
Years Succeeding the Fall of Richmond* [1906; rpt., New York: Negro Universities Press,
1969], 282–84). For similar occurrences in Florida, see Susan Bradford Eppes, *Through
Some Eventful Years* (1926; rpt., Gainesville: University of Florida Press, 1968), 282–86.

25   *Richmond Dispatch*, 1, 2 August 1867; *New York Times*, 2, 6 August 1867; see also Rachleff,
Black Labor in the South, 45; Morton, *Negro in Virginia Politics*, 40–43.

26   The October 1867 city Republican ward meetings and nominating convention adopted
the practice common in the black community's mass meetings: a voice or standing vote
that enfranchised men, women, and children. See, for example, the 8 October Second
Ward meeting for delegate selection: "All who favored Mr. Washburne were first requested to rise, and forty were found on the floor, including women." *Richmond Dispatch*, 30 September, 9 October 1867, 2, 4, 14, 23, 24 January, 15, 25 February, 3, 8, 25 April

1868; *New York Times,* 6 August, 15, 18 October 1867, 11 January 1868; Rachleff, *Black Labor in the South,* 45–49; Avary, *Dixie after the War,* 229–31, 254.

Throughout the state of Virginia, the internal community political gatherings adopted measures by a voice or standing vote that could often enfranchise not only women but children as well. See, for example, the minutes of the mass meeting of colored citizens of Elizabeth City County, Virginia, 5 December 1865: "When upon this motion the entire audience rose to their feet and remained standing some time." Brig. Gen. S. Brown to Brig. Gen. B. C. Card, Washington, D.C., 19 December 1865, "Negroes, Employment of," Consolidated Correspondence File, ser. 225, Central Records, Records of the Office of the Quartermaster General, Record Group 92, National Archives, Washington, D.C. [Y-719]. Bracketed numbers refer to file numbers of documents in the Freedmen and Southern Society Project, University of Maryland. I thank Leslie S. Rowland, project director, for facilitating my access to these files.

The issue of children's participation is an interesting one, suggestive of the means by which personal experience rather than societal norms shaped ex-slaves' vision of politics. A similarly telling example was in the initial proposal of the African National Congress that the new South African constitution set the voting age at fourteen, a testament to those young people, like those in Soweto, who experienced the ravages of apartheid and whose fight against it helped bring about the political negotiations to secure African political rights and self-determination.

27   Compare southern black women's active participation in formal politics—internal and external—in the first decades after the Civil War to Michael McGerr's assessment that nineteenth-century "women were allowed in to the male political realm only to play typical feminine roles—to cook, sew, and cheer for men and to symbolize virtue and beauty. Men denied women the central experiences of the popular style: not only the ballot but also the experience of mass mobilization." McGerr's analysis fails to acknowledge the racial basis of his study, i.e., that it is an assessment of white women's political participation. Michael McGerr, "Political Style and Women's Power, 1830–1930," *Journal of American History* 77 (December 1990): 864–85, esp. 867. My analysis also differs substantially from Mary P. Ryan, *Women in Public: Between Banners and Ballots, 1825–1880* (Baltimore: Johns Hopkins University Press, 1990). Ryan gives only cursory attention to African Americans but finds black women's political expression in the Civil War and Reconstruction eras restricted "with particular severity" and "buried beneath the surface of the public sphere"; see 146–47, 156, passim.

28   For women's participation in political parades in Louisville, Kentucky, Mobile, Alabama, and Charleston, South Carolina, see Gutman, *Black Family in Slavery and Freedom,* 380; *Liberator,* 21 July 1865, and *New York Daily Tribune,* 4 April 1865, both reprinted in *The Trouble They Seen: Black People Tell the Story of Reconstruction,* ed. Dorothy Sterling (Garden City, N.Y.: Doubleday, 1976), 2–4. In other areas of Virginia besides Richmond, and in South Carolina, Louisiana, and Arkansas, men and women participated in the political meetings. See, for example, Vincent Harding, *There Is a River: The Black Struggle for Freedom in America* (New York: Harcourt Brace Jovanovich, 1981), 294–97; Rupert Sargent Holland, ed., *Letters and Diary of Laura M. Towne Written from the Sea Islands of South Carolina, 1862–1884* (1912; rpt., New York: Negro Universities Press, 1969), 183; testimony of John H. Burch given before a Senate committee appointed to investigate the

exodus of black men and women from Louisiana, 46th Cong., 2d Sess., S. Rept. 693, pt. 2, 232–33, reprinted in *A Documentary History of the Negro People in the United States,* ed. Herbert Aptheker (New York: Citadel Press, 1951), 2:721–22; Thomas Holt, *Black Over White: Negro Political Leadership in South Carolina during Reconstruction* (Urbana: University of Illinois Press, 1977), 34–35; Randy Finley, "Freedperson's Identities and the Freedmen's Bureau in Arkansas, 1865–1869," paper presented at Southern Historical Association annual meeting, Orlando, Florida, 11 November 1993 (cited with permission of Finley). Graphic artists recognized the participation of women as a regular feature of parades, mass meetings, and conventions as evidenced by their illustrations; see "The Celebration of Emancipation Day in Charleston" from *Leslie's Illustrated Newspaper,* reprinted in Francis Butler Simkins and Robert Hilliard Woody, *South Carolina During Reconstruction* (1932; rpt., Gloucester, Mass.: Peter Smith, 1966), facing 364; "Electioneering at the South," *Harper's Weekly,* 25 July 1868, reprinted in Foner, *Reconstruction,* fol. 386; "Colored People's Convention in Session," reprinted in Sterling, *The Trouble They Seen,* 65.

29 *New York Times,* 11 January 1868; *The Debates and Proceedings of the Constitutional Convention of the State of Virginia, Assembled at the City of Richmond* (Richmond, 1868), 524–27.

30 *New York Times,* 11, 22 January 1868; *Debates and Proceedings, Virginia,* 505–7.

31 Estimates of the number of black people who migrated into Richmond in the immediate postemancipation period run as high as 15,000. Rachleff, *Black Labor in the South,* 14; Virginius Dabney, *Richmond: The Story of a City* (Garden City, N.Y.: Doubleday, 1976), 208; Randolph, *From Slave Cabin to Pulpit,* 59.

32 My discussion of liberal democratic political ideology draws on Macpherson, *Political Theory of Possessive Individualism;* C. B. Macpherson, *Democratic Theory: Essays in Retrieval* (Oxford: Oxford University Press, 1973) and *The Life and Times of Liberal Democracy* (Oxford: Oxford University Press, 1977).

33 For a similar and extended discussion focused on Jamaica and Britain, see Thomas C. Holt, *The Problem of Freedom: Race, Labor, and Politics in Jamaica and Britain, 1832–1938* (Baltimore: Johns Hopkins University Press, 1992); also Thomas C. Holt, " 'The essence of the contract': The Articulation of Race, Gender, and Political Economy in British Emancipation Policy, 1838–1866," paper presented at "Seminar on Racism and Race Relations in the Countries of the African Diaspora," Rio de Janeiro, Brazil, 6 April 1992 (in Barkley Brown's possession; cited with permission of Holt).

34 Elizabeth Hyde Botume, *First Days amongst the Contrabands* (1893; rpt., New York: Arno Press and New York Times, 1968), 273. See Jones, *Labor of Love,* 66–67; Margaret Washington Creel, "Female Slaves in South Carolina," *TRUTH: Newsletter of the Association of Black Women Historians,* Summer 1985.

35 For a discussion of the idea of emancipated slaves earning freedom and political liberties through proper orientation to a market economy, see Holt, " 'An Empire over the Mind.' " An explicit statement of that assumption was given by white Republicans during the Virginia constitutional convention debates. Disagreeing with Bayne's argument regarding the inherent right of suffrage, Judge John Underwood contended, "I hold that the colored men . . . ought to have the right of suffrage. . . . they have shown themselves competent . . . they have shown their industry and their effort and desire to elevate

themselves. . . . I do not think that the Indians, wandering upon the plains, . . . having no fixed homes, no habits of industry—I do not think that such a class of people should be entitled to vote. . . . Just so soon as they become settled and industrious in their habits like the colored men of this State, then I will go for giving the Indians the right to vote." Bayne, on the other hand, supported suffrage for Indians. *Debates and Proceedings, Virginia,* 527.

36   Percentages computed from figures given by Holt, *Black over White,* 35, 97. *Proceedings of the Constitutional Convention of South Carolina, held at Charleston, South Carolina, beginning January 14 and ending March 17, 1868* (Charleston: Denny and Perry, 1868), 836–38; *New York Times,* 3 April 1869; Terborg-Penn, "Afro-Americans in the Struggle for Woman Suffrage," 52–54; Rosalyn Terborg-Penn, "The Rollin Sisters," in *Black Women in America: An Historical Encyclopedia,* ed. Darlene Clark Hine, Elsa Barkley Brown, and Rosalyn Terborg-Penn (Brooklyn, N.Y.: Carlson Publishing, 1993), 990–91. There are some reports that black women actually voted in Reconstruction-era South Carolina. Benjamin Quarles states that in some "districts in the South Carolina elections of 1870 colored women under the encouragement of Negro election officials, exercised the privilege of voting. By this act the Negro became the first practical vindicator of woman's right to the ballot" ("Frederick Douglass and the Woman's Rights Movement," *Journal of Negro History* 25 [January 1940]: 35). Others have suggested that, whenever black men were ill and unable to come to the polls to cast their ballot, their wives or other female relatives were allowed to vote in their place.

37   *Debates and Proceedings, Virginia,* 254.

38   Eric Foner sees Bayne as a primary example of the "distinction between the public sphere of men and the private world of women" that developed with freedom. Quoting only Bayne's "It is woman's right to raise and bear children, and to train them for their future duties in life," Foner sees this "militant Virginia political leader" as having a "severely restricted definition of women's rights" (*Reconstruction,* 87). This may be true, but such a conclusion is not necessarily the meaning of Bayne's statement when taken in its full context; only further research on Bayne and his colleagues will clarify these issues. But Bayne's self-conscious explication of his own terminology further reinforces my reading of his discussion of domestic roles of women as in addition to not instead of political roles. (Hucles, having pointed out Bayne's terminology, still accepts Foner's reading of Bayne's domestic roles statement and thus accepts Foner's conclusions regarding Bayne's sexism and exclusion of women from political rights; Michael Hucles, "Many Voices, Similar Concerns: Traditional Methods of African-American Political Activity in Norfolk, Virginia, 1865–1875," *Virginia Magazine of History and Biography* 100 [October 1992]: 543–66.)

I am not ignoring the importance of language but emphasizing the importance of historicizing and investigating language. Bayne, like other Afro-Virginians, used a conventional political language, just as they used conventional political forms, but gave each larger meaning than conventionally intended. A recent literary study that takes these questions of language, gender, citizenship, and freedom as its core is Claudia Tate, *Domestic Allegories of Political Desire: The Black Heroine's Text at the Turn of the Century* (New York: Oxford University Press, 1992). Like most studies, however, its concentration on northern middle-class black women and its reading of postemancipation through late-nineteenth-century eyes and texts ignore the different language and meanings of the immediate emancipation era among ex-slaves in the South. Tate thus assumes that "discourses of citizenship . . . were *inherently* gendered until the ratification of the Twenty-second [*sic*] Amendment in 1920" (21, 243 n.; emphasis mine). My effort is to understand how an explicitly gendered discourse on citizenship and rights *developed* within late-nineteenth-century black communities, rather than assuming it was either inherently there at emancipation or immediately and uncontestedly assumed thereupon. For a fuller explication of this, see Elsa Barkley Brown, "Negotiating and Transforming the Public Sphere: African American Political Life in the Transition from Slavery to Freedom," *Public Culture* 7 (Fall 1994): 107–46.

39   *Richmond Dispatch*, 18 June 1867; Rachleff, *Black Labor in the South*, 48.

40   First African Baptist Church, Richmond, Virginia, Minutes, Books II and III, Virginia State Library Archives, Richmond. These developments are explored in Barkley Brown, "Negotiating and Transforming the Public Sphere." The whole question of the operating procedures of internal community institutions such as churches and mutual benefit and fraternal societies needs investigation; surviving church minute books and denominational minutes offer a promising source for future analyses. In any case, the question of women's participation in the external political arena should be analyzed in the context of developments within internal community institutions. These debates over gender roles within black churches occurred on congregational and denominational levels. For studies that examine these debates at the state and/or national level in the late nineteenth–early twentieth century, see Evelyn Brooks Higginbotham, *Righteous Discontent: The Women's Movement in the Black Baptist Church* (Cambridge, Mass.: Harvard University Press, 1993); Glenda Gilmore, "Gender and Jim Crow: Women and the Politics of White Supremacy in North Carolina, 1896–1920" (Ph.D. diss., University of North Carolina, Chapel Hill, 1992); Cheryl Townsend Gilkes, " 'Together and in Harness': Women's Traditions in the Sanctified Church," *Signs: Journal of Women in Culture and Society* 10 (Summer 1985), 678–99.

41   Rachleff, *Black Labor in the South*, 31–32; A. T. Morgan, *Yazoo; or, On the Picket Line of Freedom in the South: A Personal Narrative* (New York: Russell and Russell, 1884), 231–33; W. L. Fleming, *The Civil War and Reconstruction in Alabama* (New York: Peter Smith, 1905), 777.

42   This censuring of women's political participation was part of a larger pattern whereby northern white men attempted to teach southern black men and women "proper" relations. Towne noted that "several speakers have been here who have advised the people to get the women into their proper place" (Holland, *Letters and Diary of Laura M. Towne*, 183–84). It was the participation, not merely the presence, of black women at political meetings that was the issue elsewhere as well. In Richmond, for example, white women certainly on occasion sat in the convention's gallery as visitors, merely watching the proceedings. The problem with the black women and men, as many white observers saw it, was that they participated from the gallery. Avary, *Dixie after the War*, 254–57.

43   Holland, *Letters and Diary of Laura M. Towne*, 183. Despite this example, the various continued activities of women, often with the approval of men, makes clear that ex-slaves' compliance with these norms of "proper" relations was not immediately forthcoming. However, more detailed investigations of the ways in which freedmen and

freedwomen came to work out family and community relationships—political, economic, and social—in various areas of the South are needed. Until then, the various formulations that lay out a well-developed public/private dichotomy and patriarchal construction of black family and community life as a fairly immediate occurrence after emancipation amount to nothing more than a presentist reading of an as yet not fully explored past.

44   Holt, *Black over White*, 34–35. A witness before the Senate investigating committee testified in 1872 that the women "have been very active since 1868 in all the political movements; they form a large number in all the political assemblages" in Louisiana. Testimony of John H. Burch in Aptheker, *Documentary History*, 2:721.

45   Lucy McMillan testimony taken at Spartanburg, South Carolina, 10 July 1871, in U.S. Congress, *Testimony Taken by the Joint Select Committee to Inquire into the Condition of Affairs in the Late Insurrectionary States*, 42d Cong., 2d sess., S. Rept. v. 2, n. 41, pt. 4: *South Carolina*, vol. 2 (Washington, D.C.: Government Printing Office, 1872), 605 (hereafter cited as *Ku Klux Klan Testimony*).

46   Holt, *Black over White*, 35; Avary, *Dixie after the War*, 362; Holland, *Letters and Diary of Laura M. Towne*, 284–91.

47   Fleming, *Civil War and Reconstruction in Alabama*; Joel Williamson, *After Slavery: The Negro in South Carolina during Reconstruction, 1861–1877* (Chapel Hill: University of North Carolina Press, 1965), 344; Holt, *Black over White*, 35.

48   U.S. Congress, *Smalls v Tillman*, 45th Cong., 1st sess., H. Misc. Doc. no. 11 (1877), quoted in Dorothy Sterling, ed., *We Are Your Sisters: Black Women in the Nineteenth Century* (New York: W. W. Norton, 1984), 370; Holland, *Letters and Diary of Laura M. Towne*, 284.

49   *Smalls v Tillman*, in Sterling, *We Are Your Sisters*, 370; Fleming, *Civil War and Reconstruction in Alabama*, 564–65, 776.

50   Violet Keeling's testimony before the Senate investigating committee, 18 February 1884, 48th Cong., 1st sess., S. Rept. no. 579, reprinted in Aptheker, *Documentary History*, 2:739–41.

51   Avary, *Dixie after the War*, 285–86, 347; Fleming, *Civil War and Reconstruction in Alabama*, 564–65, 776–78; *Ku Klux Klan Testimony: North Carolina*, 9, 289, *Georgia*, 236, 248, 290, 1184, *Alabama*, 684, 878, 1072–73, 1078–80, *Mississippi*, 725, *Florida and Miscellaneous*, 50; Thomas J. Evans, Alexander H. Sands, N. A. Sturdivant, et al., Richmond, to Major General Schofield, 31 October 1867, reprinted in *Documents of the Constitutional Convention of the State of Virginia* (Richmond: Office of The New Nation, 1867), 22–23; John H. Gilmer to Schofield, reprinted in the *New York Times*, 30 October 1867; Joe M. Richardson, *The Negro in the Reconstruction of Florida, 1865–1877* (Tallahassee: Florida State University, 1965), 237–38; Lerome Bennett, Jr., *Black Power U.S.A.: The Human Side of Reconstruction, 1867–1877* (Chicago: Johnson Publishing, 1967), 359; Frenise A. Logan, *The Negro in North Carolina, 1876–1894* (Chapel Hill: University of North Carolina Press, 1964), 22–23; Henderson Hamilton Donald, *The Negro Freedman: Life Conditions of the American Negro in the Early Years after Emancipation* (1952; rpt., New York: Cooper Square Publishers, 1971), 203–5; Charles Nordhoff, *The Cotton States in the Spring and Summer of 1875* (New York: Burt Franklin, 1876), 11, 22; Simkins and Woody, *South Carolina during Reconstruction*, 512; Sir George Campbell, *White and Black: The Outcome of a Visit to the United States* (1879; rpt., New York: Negro Universities Press, 1969), 181, 317; *New York Times*, 3 November 1867; Proceedings before Military Commissioner, City

of Richmond, 26 October 1867, in the case of Winston Jackson, filed as G-423 1867, Letters Received, ser. 5068, 1st Reconstruction Military District, Records of the U.S. Army Continental Commands, Record Group 393, pt. 1, National Archives [SS-1049].

52 Fleming, *Civil War and Reconstruction in Alabama*, 776.

53 Quote is from James E. Sefton, "A Note on the Political Intimidation of Black Men by Other Black Men," *Georgia Historical Quarterly* 52 (December 1968): 448. My analysis here leans heavily on an unpublished essay by Joseph Reidy on Reconstruction-era politics.

54 Robert Gleed testimony before Mississippi Subcommittee, 10 November 1871, *Ku Klux Klan Testimony: Mississippi*, 725. Gleed's statement also challenges that feminist theory that attempts to dichotomize men and women's ideas of justice by arguing that men accept a more abstract equal application of the law as justice, whereas women insist upon a notion of justice more closely tied to issues of morality and outcome. See Carol Gilligan, *In a Different Voice* (Cambridge, Mass.: Harvard University Press, 1982). This is, of course, a problematic argument as it assumes gender to be an analytical category removable from the context of race and class. For a critique of Gilligan that emphasizes the degree to which that which she sees as female might also be seen as African American, common to both males and females in black communities, see Carol Stack, "The Culture of Gender: Women and Men of Color," *Signs: Journal of Women in Culture and Society* 11 (Winter 1986): 321–24. See also Carol B. Stack, "Different Voices, Different Visions: Gender, Culture, and Moral Reasoning," in Maxine Baca Zinn and Bonnie Thornton Dill, eds., *Women of Color in U.S. Society* (Philadelphia: Temple University Press, 1994), 291–301.

55 The larger society reinforced this sense of collective ownership of the vote. Black women (and children) were included in the retribution black men faced when they cast a Republican vote. Harriet Hernandes, a South Carolina woman, testified that her entire community lay out at night to avoid whippings or murder. "Mighty near" everyone in her neighborhood had been whipped "because [when] men . . . voted radical tickets they [the Ku Klux Klan] took the spite out on the women when they could get at them. . . . Ben Phillips and his wife and daughter; Sam Foster; and Moses Eaves, they killed him—I could not begin to tell all—Ann Bonner and her daughter, Manza Surratt and his wife and whole family, even the least child in the family, they took it out of bed and whipped it. They told them if they did that they would remember it." Violet Keeling reported that on election day she carried a knife with her as she walked to and from work for fear that if the Republicans were victorious black women as well as black men would be held responsible. Harriet Hernandes' testimony taken at Spartanburg, South Carolina, 10 July 1871, in *Ku Klux Klan Testimony: South Carolina*, 586; Keeling testimony in Aptheker, *Documentary History*, 2:739.

56 Petition from Nancy Hodges and other hucksters filed as Geo. Teamoh to Gen. O. O. Howard, 21 May 1866, T-173 1866, Letters Received, ser. 15, Washington Headquarters, Records of the Bureau of Refugees, Freedmen, and Abandoned Lands, Record Group 105, National Archives [A-7619].

57 Avary, *Dixie after the War*, 282–83; Donald, *Negro Freedman*, 207 (emphasis mine).

58 Jones, *Labor of Love*, 66. Jones is not alone in her assessment. In his generally rigorous analysis, Eric Foner, apparently adopting Jones's analysis, also suggests the public/private dichotomy between black men and women based in part on men's participation in

the formal political process; Nell Irvin Painter assumes that, since black women were unenfranchised in the Reconstruction era, "they could not act politically as men could." Foner, *Reconstruction,* 87; Nell Irvin Painter, "Comment," in *The State of Afro-American History: Past, Present, and Future,* ed. Darlene Clark Hine (Baton Rouge: Louisiana State University Press, 1986), 82.

59   My work here and elsewhere questions the usefulness of the public/private dichotomy for understanding African American women's history. Others have also raised questions in relation to the larger fields of women's history and women's studies. Linda Kerber, acknowledging the degree to which conceptualizing this dichotomy opened up many avenues of women's lives to historical investigation, also suggests that such a dichotomy has probably outlived its usefulness. Elsa Barkley Brown, "Womanist Consciousness: Maggie Lena Walker and the Independent Order of Saint Luke," *Signs: Journal of Women in Culture and Society* 14 (Spring 1989): 610–33; Linda K. Kerber, "Separate Spheres, Female Worlds, Woman's Place: The Rhetoric of Women's History," *Journal of American History* 75 (June 1989): 9–39. See also Alice Kessler-Harris, "Gender Ideology in Historical Reconstruction: A Case Study from the 1930s," *Gender and History* 1 (Spring 1989): 31–49. Kerber echoes Michele Rosaldo's critique of oppositional modes of thought in general and transhistoric conceptions of home versus public life in particular. Linda Nicholson provides a basis for understanding the reification of these categories as a product of Western liberalism. She argues that liberalism as a political theory rests on the assumption that the family, as the sphere of the private, and the political, as the sphere of the public, are "inherently demarcatable." M. Z. Rosaldo, "The Use and Abuse of Anthropology: Reflections on Feminism and Cross-Cultural Understanding," *Signs: Journal of Women in Culture and Society* 5 (Spring 1980): 389–417; Linda Nicholson, *Gender and History: The Limits of Social Theory in the Age of the Family* (New York: Columbia University Press, 1986). For an example of the ways in which those challenging public/private dichotomies often reinvent the same dichotomy, see Elsa Barkley Brown, "Imaging Lynching: African American Women, Communities of Struggle, and Collective Memory," in *African American Women Speak Out: Responses to Anita Hill–Clarence Thomas,* ed. Geneva Smitherman (Detroit: Wayne State University Press, 1995).

60   Even a cursory reading of Reconstruction-era documents makes this clear. The thirteen volumes of *Ku Klux Klan Testimony,* for example, are filled with reports of whipping and/or raping of black women—for their refusal to work in the fields or in white men's and women's homes; for their husbands' political activities; or for their families' efforts to acquire land. One North Carolina man, Essic Harris, reported that the rape of black women by the Ku Klux Klan was so common in his community that "It has got to be an old saying." Some women, such as Lucy McMillan, reported violent attacks as a direct result of their own political activities. McMillan's house was burned after she attended a political meeting and reported back to her community. She was accused of being a "d——d radical," "making laws," and "bragging and boasting that I wanted the land." Essic Harris testimony, 1 July 1871, *Ku Klux Klan Testimony: North Carolina,* 100; McMillan testimony, ibid., 604–11.

61   Harding, *There Is a River,* 296.

62   The point, of course, is that the meaning cannot be presumed merely from the act. The implications of this are far-reaching, for it recalls to our attention the fact, as stated by

Michele Rosaldo, "That woman's place in human social life is not in any direct sense a product of the things she does . . . but of the meaning her activities acquire through concrete social interactions. And the significances women assign to the activities of their lives are things that we can only grasp through an analysis of the relationships that women forge, the social contexts they (along with men) create—and within which they are defined. Gender in all human groups must . . . be understood in political and social terms, with reference . . . to local and specific forms of social relationship" (Rosaldo, "Use and Abuse of Anthropology," 400). Ignoring this is analytically problematic. See, for example, Susan Mann's explication of black women's status under the sharecropping system. Mann, by design, lifts her exploration of economic roles out of the context of political and cultural roles and ideology and thus explores the meaning of labor removed from its social context. More importantly, her exploration of economic roles assumes that the distinctions between women laboring in the home and men laboring in the field have inherent universal implications rather than ones embedded in a particular historical context. See Susan A. Mann, "Slavery, Sharecropping, and Sexual Inequality," *Signs: Journal of Women in Culture and Society* 14 (Summer 1989): 774–98. One point of my essay is to demonstrate that variables such as enfranchisement/disfranchisement (or work in the fields/work in the homes) mean different things in different social and historical contexts. Our tendency to attribute inherent meaning to certain activities obscures rather than explains historically specific developments of social relations between black men and black women.

The Quest for Justice:

African American Women

Litigants, 1867–1890

Janice Sumler-Edmond

During the latter part of the nineteenth century, African American women used the judicial system to redress racial discrimination and to define the parameters of their newfound citizenship. Such resorts to legal solutions were timely. To paraphrase novelist Charles Dickens's immortal words, the promise of the best of times and the reality of the worst of times existed for African Americans—both women and men—in the decades following the Civil War. Promise of the best of times could be discerned from the ratification of three post–Civil War constitutional amendments. By virtue of the Thirteenth, Fourteenth, and Fifteenth amendments, African Americans gained emancipation, citizenship, and the franchise for black men. However, Congress did not stop with these vitally important amendments. It also passed a host of progressive civil rights laws and created the Freedmen's Bureau. Such actions were intended to assist blacks in the transition from slavery to freedom with all the rights and privileges of citizenship.[1]

Unfortunately, the harsh reality of the worst of times frequently overshadowed the promise of the best of times. At least one historian has labeled the era from the end of the nineteenth century to the beginning of the twentieth century as the nadir of the black experience in America. Promises of equality under the law, due process, and other constitutional rights remained unfulfilled because of widespread racial segregation, prejudice, economic exploitation, political disfranchisement, and even lynching. Indeed, those decades were difficult times for black women and men.[2]

To their credit, however, the African American women examined in this study refused to relinquish their dreams of first-class citizenship, and they remained determined to participate in the mainstream of American life. In the decades following the Civil War, these black women used the legal system to secure for themselves and for their race the rights and privileges many other Americans took for granted. As litigants, black women undoubtedly faced substantial obstacles including the expense of litigation, the time commitment, the confusing legal jargon, and the risk of failure. Nevertheless, court records show that African American women demonstrated great tenacity in their legal pursuits. They hired lawyers, presented evidence, called witnesses, and subpoenaed documents. Their actions did much to challenge a social and political system that frequently and unjustly permitted discrimination against a woman because of her race or skin color.

Though it is less well known than the substantial amount of civil rights litigation initiated by groups and individuals over the past half-century, African Americans have a rich judicial tradition dating back to the eighteenth and nineteenth centuries. In fact, so frequent were the court proceedings with black litigants—both women and men—after the Civil War that the *New York Times* reported how judges of the era described the "rush" to the courts and the "excited conditions" of blacks suing in courts.[3] To document that judicial tradition, this essay examines a selection of lawsuits initiated by African American women. The study explores the issues and experiences faced by black women litigants and revisits the historical interpretations and applications of the Fourteenth Amendment, related civil rights statutes, and common law precedents. The study focuses on litigation in the areas of public transportation, miscegenation, and the inheritance of property. Court opinions provide unique glimpses of nineteenth-century life, portraits of the black women litigants, as well as the numerous problems they encountered.

Two such problems encountered by black women who traveled by rail and steamboat were racial discrimination in seating arrangements—Jim Crow accommodations—and poor treatment aboard trains and boats. Too often the color of the traveler's skin determined the seat or the kind of treatment she received. Take, for example, the facts surrounding the 1867 lawsuit of *West Chester & Philadelphia Railway Company* v. *Miles*. In that case, Judge Pierce of the Philadelphia Court of Common Pleas decided whether the railroad's discriminatory seating arrangement was permissible under Pennsylvania law. The judge concluded that "a regulation which prohibits a well-behaved colored woman from taking a vacant seat in a car simply because she is colored, is not a regulation the law allows."[4] The well-behaved colored person to whom Judge Pierce referred was Mary E. Miles of Philadelphia. With his decision, the judge upheld Miles's rights both as a citizen and as a railroad passenger. He also awarded her the sum of five dollars for personal injuries incurred.

Several months earlier, Miles had boarded a train in Philadelphia on her way to Oxford, Pennsylvania. Observing many vacant seats, Miles chose one toward the middle of the car. What had begun as a pleasant journey turned into an ugly altercation. A conductor approached and assigned Miles a seat in a section set aside for black passengers at the end of the car. When Miles refused to change seats, the conductor sternly admonished that she had no choice in the matter. Angry words were exchanged, after which the conductor forced Miles from her seat and then from the train. In response she filed suit charging that the railroad company violated her rights.

At the trial before Judge Pierce, the railroad flatly denied any wrongdoing on two grounds. First, the railroad argued that the conductor had acted well within the scope of his authority and in accordance with the company's seating regulation. Second, the railroad contended that Mary Miles's assigned seat was comfortable and in all respects equal to the one she had been asked to vacate. Unconvinced by the railroad's arguments, Judge Pierce challenged the legality of the seating regulation. He concluded that a rule based on color prejudice was offensive to the state's judicial system and must be struck down.

This judicial victory for Mary Miles proved to be short-lived, however. Later that same year, on 4 November 1867, in an appeal to the Pennsylvania Supreme Court, the railroad company won a reversal of the previous judgment in Miles's favor. The state's highest court defined the issues in terms of a public carrier's private property rights and the reasonableness of the seating arrangement. In its ruling for the railroad the court determined that the separation of passengers based on mere prejudice was unlawful. Nevertheless, the court reasoned that segregated seating would be permitted due to "the natural and well-known repugnances, which are liable to breed disturbances by promiscuous sitting."[5] The court concluded that, so long as passengers were carried in safety and comfort, such seating regulations constituted a sound policy in the best interest of the carrier and the public at large.

Though the court flatly denied that the *Miles* case involved any assertion of racial inferiority, the judicial opinion ultimately bowed to the prejudices of the day under the guise of maintaining peace between the races. An excerpt from the opinion reads as follows:

> The danger to the peace engendered by the feeling of aversion between individuals of the different races cannot be denied. It is a fact with which the company must deal. If a negro takes his seat beside a white man or his wife or daughter, the law cannot repress the anger, or conquer the aversion which some will feel. However unwise it may be to indulge the feeling, human infirmity is not always proof against it. It is much wiser to avert the consequences of this repulsion of race by separation, than to punish afterward the breach of peace it may have caused.[6]

In spite of the Pennsylvania Supreme Court's endorsement of the railroad's regulation, the Pennsylvania legislature had rejected such discriminatory policies. On 22 March 1867, eight months before the state supreme court issued the *Miles* opinion, the legislature prohibited railroad companies from making distinctions between passengers because of race or color. Although the court made a reference to this new law in its opinion, it refrained from applying the law retroactively to the *Miles* case. Future black passengers in Pennsylvania would receive some protection from discrimination, but Mary Miles had become a casualty of racial prejudice.

Numerous questions remain concerning the personal dynamics as well as motivations behind the *Miles* litigation and the other lawsuits examined. We do not know, for example, whether indignation arising from her treatment by the railroad employee or race-conscious motives prompted Mary Miles to file her lawsuit. Additonal questions concern the funding resources available to Miles and other black women litigants. Likewise, there is little information on the degree to which these women could rely on their communities or community institutions for assistance in their legal pursuits. Interestingly enough, a majority of the black women in the study—even those identified as married women—filed lawsuits as individuals in their own behalf. Questions persist about the level of independence from male dominance experienced by black women who ventured into the legal arena alone. While court opinions provide valuable information about the legal issues of a particular case, they offer few details on the personal, social, or even political forces behind those issues.

We do know, however, that the *Miles* case was not an isolated incident. Nineteenth-century court records reveal that numerous black women encountered similar humiliating experiences; many such victims chose to litigate their grievances. Several common themes linked the public transportation cases examined in this study. Trial courts, especially state trial courts, were more likely to rule in favor of black women litigants than were appellate courts. One possible explanation for such a pattern of decisions is that trial judges and juries could view the appearance and demeanor of the women and their supporting witnesses. These litigants garnered compelling facts that frequently proved persuasive. It was not uncommon for the judges to criticize and reprimand the conductors and brakemen who used force and abusive language to eject black women passengers.

Nineteenth-century judges grappling with the issue of discrimination in public transportation decided cases one by one, the facts and circumstances of each being determinative. To the judges' credit the records reveal that they labored over their opinions, paying scrupulous attention to the particular set of facts surrounding each case. Although justice did not always prevail, the majority of black women litigants discussed in this study did have their day in court.

Unlike Mary Miles's litigation for open seating on a Pennsylvania railroad, other black women asserted their right to sit in the ladies' car, a first-class accommodation for women passengers and their male escorts. Most often, trains providing intercity transportation included two or more cars. The forward car, located directly behind the engine, typically had a smoking section. In addition to poor air quality caused by engine smoke and passengers using tobacco products, the forward car was occupied by passengers prone to loud talking, profanity, and drinking. In sharp contrast, the ladies' car, located at the rear of the train, offered first-class passengers more pleasant surroundings and kept them at a distance from the rowdy, less refined travelers. It is not surprising that black women who could afford the higher fare paid for and then demanded seats in the ladies' car.

Such was the case with Anna Williams, a black resident of Illinois. In 1870 Williams journeyed from Rockford, Illinois, to Belvidere aboard the Chicago and Northwestern Railroad. As she proceeded to enter the ladies' car, a brakeman blocked her way and prevented her from taking a seat. Subsequently, the brakeman permitted several white women to enter the ladies' car without incident. Sometime later, asserting her right to sit in the ladies' car, Williams brought suit in an Illinois circuit court. The facts in the case of the *Chicago & Northwestern Railway Company* v. *Anna Williams* were compelling. Williams presented evidence that the brakeman had used force and verbally abused her. At the trial, testimony given on Williams's behalf by several white women passengers probably brought additional credibility to her argument in the eyes of the court. In the final analysis, the court was persuaded by Williams's evidence and awarded her $200 in damages.

In an opinion affirming the circuit court's ruling in favor of Anna Williams, the Illinois Supreme Court framed the issue in terms of the racial exclusion of a first-class ticket holder from a car set aside for ladies and their gentlemen escorts. Justice Scott's opinion expressed his annoyance with the railroad employee's treatment of Williams, whom he described as "a well-behaved, mannerly colored woman of good character."[7] In the court's view, evidence that the company had no seating regulations for black passengers, as well as evidence that black women had used the ladies' car previously, demonstrated that the brakeman's actions had been arbitrary. While acknowledging the company's right to promulgate rules, the court urged that "such regulations must always be reasonable and uniform in respect to persons."[8] By referencing the *Miles* case in Pennsylvania, the Illinois Supreme Court cautioned against discrimination on prejudicial grounds alone. The court declared itself the final arbiter of such regulations and concluded that reasonableness was to be determined under all circumstances on a case-by-case basis.

Although Anna Williams won a favorable ruling in the Illinois Supreme Court, Ida B. Wells was less successful with a similar effort in Tennessee. Many students of American history are familiar with the litigation initiated by Wells beginning in 1884 and extending for three years against the Chesapeake, Ohio and Southwestern Railroad.[9] As a passenger on the Memphis-to-Woodstock line one afternoon, Wells tried to enter the ladies' car. When the conductor assigned her a seat in the forward smoking car, Wells refused to surrender her ticket unless allowed to choose her own seat. Following a brief scuffle between Wells and the conductor, a black porter escorted her from the train. Within several hours Wells returned to Memphis where she retained a lawyer.

Initially, Wells prevailed before both the magistrate and the circuit courts of Tennessee by convincing those courts that the railroad had violated her rights as a passenger. However, when the railroad company appealed to the Tennessee Supreme Court in 1887, Wells did not prevail. By placing his emphasis on Wells's refusal to relinquish her ticket and not on the conductor's actions, Chief Justice Turney ruled that the railroad was not liable to her. Crucial factors underlying the court's ruling against Wells were evidence of the similarities between the forward car and the ladies' cars as well as conflicting testimony on the amount of smoke present in the forward car. The court further stated that it knew of no rule requiring a railroad to provide passengers with the exact seat of their choice. In the court's estimation, the railroad company had complied with the law by furnishing equal accommodations for Wells. Implying that Wells's motive was litigation, not comfortable and safe passage, the court queried why she had refused to ride in the forward car for the short ten-mile trip.

Undoubtedly, Ida Wells must have been surprised to learn that her case was used as a precedent to deprive a white man of a seat in a ladies' car. According to the facts in *Memphis & Charleston Railroad Company v. Benson*, also argued before the Tennessee Supreme Court in 1887, Benson, a white male passenger, had been unable to secure a seat in the ladies' car. Claiming a physical aversion to the "foul air" in the forward smoking car, Benson, like Wells, refused to surrender his ticket until he had obtained his desired seating. When no seat became available, the conductor ejected Benson from the train. His suit for wrongful ejectment soon followed. Citing the *Wells* case, the Tennessee Supreme Court, in an opinion written by Justice Lurton, ruled in favor of the railroad. According to the court, both plaintiffs—Wells and Benson—in their respective lawsuits had no grounds for complaints since each had been furnished accommodations equal in all respects to those available for other passengers.[10]

Mandated to hear controversies arising under the United States Constitution or laws of the United States and generally perceived as more neutral than their state counterparts, nineteenth-century federal courts attracted black women litigants. An examination of case law, however, contradicts the notion of widespread impartiality from the federal bench. For example, in 1882, Belle M. Smoot, a black woman, and her husband, Edward J. Smoot, filed a lawsuit in the Circuit Court for the District of Kentucky, alleging the violation of Belle Smoot's rights under the Fourteenth Amendment and the Civil Rights Act of 1875. Belle Smoot had purchased a first-class ticket on the Kentucky Central Railroad for the trip from Paris to Lexington. Although the Smoots repeatedly insisted that they should be allowed to sit in the ladies' car, the conductor refused their requests. Apparently irritated by the Smoots' persistence, the conductor put them off the train between stations. Sometime later, in court, the Smoots argued that the railroad's discriminatory seating arrangement had unconstitutionally denied Belle Smoot equal protection under the law.[11] To support this argument, the Smoots proffered evidence demonstrating the inferiority of the forward smoking car.

Instead of determining the reasonableness of the railroad's action as was done in the *Miles* and *Williams* cases, Judge Barr queried whether his circuit court or any other federal court had jurisdiction to decide the case. According to Judge Barr's interpretation, the due process and equal protection clauses of the Fourteenth Amendment prohibited state-sponsored discrimination but did not reach discriminatory acts by private corporations or individuals. Belle Smoot had alleged no state action in her complaint, nor could she attribute the railroad's racially biased actions to the state. Possibly anticipating the *Civil Rights Cases* of 1883, in which the Supreme Court of the United States held that the Fourteenth Amendment did not authorize Congress to prohibit private discrimination, Judge Barr granted the railroad's motion to dismiss the Smoots' lawsuit.[12] In an afterthought, the court advised Belle Smoot that she was not devoid of any judicial recourse. Judge Barr suggested that she might resolve her lawsuit in a state court that employed the common law doctrine governing common carriers. Further, the court advised that if a Kentucky law or a Kentucky state court were to uphold the discriminatory treatment she had suffered Belle Smoot could seek relief in the Supreme Court of the United States.

In contrast to the adverse ruling against Smoot, other federal courts upheld black women's rights to sit in the ladies' cars. In 1882 and in 1888 respectively, two women, Gray of Lexington, Kentucky, and Lola Houck of Victoria, Texas, received favorable court rulings and substantial damage awards. On a Saturday evening in August of 1881, Gray, her husband, and their sick child were returning home to Kentucky from a visit in Cincinnati, Ohio. Although they held first-class tickets on the Cincinnati Southern Railroad, the Grays were denied entrance to the ladies' car. Instead, the brakeman directed them to the forward smoking car. When Gray's husband, a Baptist minister, demanded an explanation for the brakeman's actions, the employee admitted that the couple's race was determinative. The husband did return to Lexington aboard the smoking car, but his wife and child elected to take another route several days later.

When the case of *Gray* v. *Cincinnati Southern Railroad Company* came before the Circuit Court of the Southern District of Ohio in 1882, Judge Swing reprimanded the company about its legal duty to provide first-class passengers, irrespective of race, with first-class accommodations. The judge also allowed the $1,000 verdict for Gray to stand. Concerning the issue of racial equality, Judge Swing stated:

> In the eyes of the law, we all stand now upon the same footing. We stand before the law equal. Whatever the social relations of life may be, before the law we all stand upon the broad plane of equality. And this company was bound to provide for this colored woman precisely such accommodations, in every respect, as were provided upon their train for white women.[13]

The court in the *Gray* case mentioned, but did not decide, the issue of whether the facts in the lawsuit arose under the civil rights bill or under natural laws.

Instead, the court decided the case pursuant to common law precedents governing public carriers.

Compelling facts also aided Lola Houck in her litigation against the Southern Pacific Railway Company in 1888. Houck sued, alleging she had sustained serious personal injuries while a passenger on one of the company's trains. From the court's opinion, we know that Houck was an African American woman, living with her husband and child in Victoria, Texas. The Houcks were both graduates of a Texas colored high school, which specialized in teacher training. At the time of the incident that was the subject of her lawsuit, Houck, who was several months pregnant, was en route from Victoria to Galveston, Texas, some ninety miles away. She had received a telegram that her infant child had become ill while visiting his grandmother in Galveston.[14]

The train she boarded had two passenger cars. The rear car with padded seats and other first-class features was set aside for white passengers by the company's rules. The forward car, known as the Jim Crow car, contained inferior seating and was designated for black passengers. Houck purchased a first-class ticket at the Victoria station, but she was not permitted to enter the first-class car. This was an unusual turn of events for Houck. The record reflects that she could pass for white and that she had traveled with the railroad before, each time sitting in the first-class car without incident. However, on this particular occasion, the bootblack at the station had informed the brakeman that Houck was a black woman. Armed with this information, the railroad's brakeman and conductor spent the afternoon making Houck's life miserable aboard their train. They began by locking her out of the first-class car while, at the same time, permitting whites to enter by the rear door. The brakeman also taunted her with rude remarks, shut the door in her face, and made fun of her. At one point, the brakeman pushed her, causing her to fall against the wheel of the brake where she tore her dress. He also threw her pots of flowers off the train.

Entering the forward Jim Crow car, which was filled with loud and boisterous passengers of both races, some of whom were drinking and smoking, was simply not an option that Houck was willing to entertain that afternoon. To make matters even worse, the brakeman had repeatedly ridiculed and pointed to Houck; as a result, the other passengers knew she was riding on the platform. Apprehensive and humiliated, Houck remained on the train's platform during the entire trip where she got soaking wet from a rainstorm. Several white witnesses corroborated every grisly detail of Houck's story. Upon reaching her destination, she was confined to her bed for several weeks and suffered a miscarriage.

The jury in the *Houck* case decided two issues. The first query concerned whether the railway had satisfied its duty under the law of public carriers to provide substantially equal accommodations to the black and the white passengers it elected to separate. Houck prevailed on this issue. Undoubtedly crucial to her case was the fact that the company sold her a first-class ticket but then failed to provide her with first-class accommodations. The jury also determined whether the injuries Houck sustained were caused by the rude and wrongful actions of the brakeman. Instructions to the jury indicated that she could not prevail on this issue if the injuries resulted from her own contributory negligence in staying on the platform. The jury found in favor of Houck on this second issue as well.

Lola Houck claimed damages in the amount of $7,500. The jury awarded her a total of $5,000, consisting of $2,000 in punitive damages to punish the railroad company and $3,000 to compensate her for injuries. The railroad appealed and requested a new trial, which Judge Boarman of the court of appeals denied. The judge agreed with the jury's overall findings except for the amount of the compensatory damage award, which he reduced from $3,000 to $500. Judge Boarman permitted the punitive damages award to stand, noting, with obvious annoyance, that instead of receiving a dismissal for his actions toward Houck the brakeman had been promoted.[15]

Cases involving interstate travelers over the nation's waterways also provide a yardstick to measure the extent of black women's rights in the post–Civil War era. The evidence reveals that an African American woman's formula for legal success rested more with compelling facts than with a reliance on liberal judicial interpretations of the law. The *Sue* litigation, argued before Chief Judge Morris of the Federal District Court of Maryland in 1885, illustrates this point. The *Sue*, a steam-operated passenger boat, made interstate journeys overnight on the Potomac River. In August of 1884, a black woman, described in the judge's opinion as a person of "unobjectionable character and conduct," purchased a first-class ticket for the trip from Baltimore, Maryland, to Virginia. At bedtime the woman was turned away from the ladies' sleeping cabin. Instead of retiring to the second-class cabin, she sat up all night with occasional walks on deck. Upon arriving at her destination in Virginia, she sued the steamboat company.[16] At trial this black woman, whose name is not mentioned in the court's opinion, called several other black women to testify about the dirty conditions found in the second-class sleeping cabin. Their statements revealed that in sharp contrast the ladies' sleeping cabin had fresh linen, washing facilities, and even a maid in attendance.

In his opinion Judge Morris queried whether the Fourteenth Amendment had eliminated all racial discrimination. Nevertheless, by his application of the reasonableness standard, the judge concluded that an interstate carrier did possess the legal authority to separate the races. He cautioned, however, that this authority touched the limit of the carrier's power and could be invalidated if the separate accommodations were discriminatory in comfort, attention, or appearance. According to the court, first-class passengers of both races must be afforded first-class accommodations. If the steamboat company could not provide separate and equivalent accommodations, they must allow both races to use the same facilities. The steamboat's potential liability to passengers remained the only alternative. Judge Morris ruled in favor of the black woman litigant and awarded her $100 in damages.

Six years earlier, a Georgia court reached a different result in *Green v. City of Bridgeton,* decided in 1879.[17] Green, a black woman traveling from Darien, Georgia, to Savannah, filed a legal action for damages against the owners of a steamboat called *City of Bridgeton.* Green, accompanied by her three-year-old nephew, had boarded the steamboat at Darien and proceeded to the upper deck of the vessel, a section set aside for white passengers in accordance with company regulations. When Green offered the ship's purser five dollars, the price for her ticket, he refused to take the money. He insisted that she would have to take a seat on the lower deck, which had accommodations for black passengers. Instead of complying with the purser's wishes, she appealed to the captain but was rebuffed. The purser then offered Green a ticket entitling her to use a stateroom on the lower deck. Once again, Green rejected his suggestion, relating that she and her nephew would still be obliged to use the lower deck adjacent to the staterooms.

By this time, the vessel was nearing the wharf at Doboy. The purser admonished Green that she must either move to the lower deck or he would remove her from the vessel. Worried that she might be thrown overboard, Green reluctantly left the boat. To add insult to injury, Green waited some six hours for another steamboat to continue her journey to Savannah. Claiming that the steamboat company, through its employees, had unlawfully denied her safe passage and in the process had also caused her great emotional suffering and humiliation, Green asked the court to award her a total of $3,000 in damages. Judge Erskine of the District Court for the Southern District of Georgia heard all the evidence and then promptly dismissed the suit, ordering Green to pay the litigation costs.

The different outcomes in the *Sue* and *City of Bridgeton* cases turn largely on the nature of the accommodations provided for blacks by the respective steam-boats. In the *Green* case, the judge concluded that the *City of Bridgeton*'s upper deck for whites and its lower deck for blacks were substantially equal. Thus Green had no legal basis for her lawsuit. With respect to Green's claims of humiliation and insult, the judge determined that the weight of the evidence simply did not support her story. Conversely, in the *Sue* litigation the court ruled that a steamboat company was liable if it could not provide suitable accommodations for blacks who purchased first-class tickets.

Despite the courageous efforts of black women litigants, their victories in public transportation cases were individual and narrow in scope. Though their motives may have been to achieve a ruling that would benefit the black race, the judicial outcomes proved less far-reaching. Instead of setting down a broad rule that could then govern future cases, the judges applied a reasonableness standard to the facts before them. Complicating this task, judges were obliged to decide cases in a manner that brought the Fourteenth Amendment and civil rights statutes into harmony with the law of common carriers and inns. Pursuant to the Civil Rights Act of 1875, for example, those persons who operated public accommodations had the duty to serve orderly, paying customers. Carriers and innkeepers could promulgate "reasonable" regulations for safety and comfort so long as customers paying the same amount received equal accommodations. The opinions make it evident that many judges accepted racially segregated seating on public transportation as both reasonable and constitutional so long as equal facilities were available.[18] Because the reasonableness standard, applied to the facts of a particular case, provided a workable, albeit time-consuming, method of deciding cases, a definitive ruling on separate accommodations was not forthcoming until *Plessy* v. *Ferguson* in 1896. In its opinion in the *Plessy* case, the Supreme Court of the United States gave federal approval to the "separate but equal doctrine."[19]

The fact that miscegenation remained a punishable taboo in the late nine-teenth century created another arena of legal conflict for black women. Many women, who believed the post–Civil War amendments and civil rights statutes assured them equality under the law and due process, received rude shocks upon encountering the coercive power of state criminal justice systems enforc-ing laws against miscegenation. Judicial rulings in miscegenation cases of that era were consistent. Using a racially biased logic, state and federal judges helped to maintain a rigid social code for the races. While grudgingly giving lip service to the propriety of legal equality for blacks, many judges rejected the notion that blacks should be afforded social equality with whites. Privacy rights, equal protection under the laws, and the obligations of the marriage contract were all swept away by an adherence to the social status quo.

The case of *Scott* v. *State of Georgia* illustrates this point. In 1869 Charlotte Scott, an African American woman, appeared before Judge Clark of the Dougherty County Superior Court in Georgia to answer an indictment charging her with cohabitation and fornication with one Leopold Daniels, a Caucasian.[20] The indictment described Scott as an unmarried woman and Daniels as a single man. Scott's attorney disputed this characterization and presented testimony by Scott's daughter that the couple was married. On the witness stand, Daniels corroborated his stepdaughter's testimony. Daniels informed the court that he was a Frenchman, born in León; he also testified that a black preacher in Macon, Georgia, had performed the marriage ceremony.

Claiming the couple had misplaced their marriage license, Scott's attorney requested that Judge Clark perform a second marriage ceremony on the spot. The judge refused to marry them and denied Charlotte an opportunity to testify on her own behalf. The judge also refused to instruct the jury that if the testimony showed Scott and Daniels were married they must acquit her. Instead, Judge Clark advised the jury that if Scott had married Daniels their marriage was null and void. After reviewing the evidence presented, the jury found Scott guilty as charged.

The Georgia Supreme Court affirmed Scott's conviction. The central issue for consideration by the high court was whether Georgia's state constitution and code of laws permitted marriage between blacks and whites. This issue was quickly resolved by reference to Georgia Code Section 1707, which expressly prohibited marriage between the races and declared all such unions null and void. The justices of the Georgia Supreme Court ruled that Code Section 1707 was a valid provision under the state constitution as well as "an enlightened enactment of wise statesmanship."[21] The court also concluded that though the recent Civil War had guaranteed blacks certain legal rights there had been no accompanying grant of social equality with whites. In the court's view social equality was not desired by "the thoughtful and reflecting portion of either race."[22]

By utilizing a shrewd kind of logic, the Georgia Supreme Court countered Charlotte's argument that Code Section 1707 had been repealed by its inconsistency with another section of the state constitution. Charlotte's attorney pointed to the provision rendering impotent any legislation regarding the social status of Georgia residents. The court rejected that argument by reasoning that the latter provision applied to future laws that sought to change social status.

According to the court, Section 1707, on the other hand, remained valid and enforceable as a pronouncement of an existing social classification.

Writing a separate, concurring opinion in the *Scott* case, Justice McCay rejected the argument that the Georgia Code of Laws impaired Scott's obligations to contract as guaranteed by the United States Constitution. Quite to the contrary, the justice explained that, similar to the state's power to set the minimum marriageable age and the acceptable blood relationship between the marriage partners, the state also had the power to dictate the race of marriage partners.

Circumstances similar to those faced by Charlotte Scott brought Rose Ward Tutty, a former slave, and Charles Tutty, a white man, face to face with a criminal indictment of fornication in 1890.[23] In April of the previous year, a federal grand jury convened in Liberty County, Georgia, and announced the indictment. Two weeks later the couple traveled to Washington, D.C., to be married. Following their wedding ceremony, the Tuttys returned to Georgia.

At the trial to answer the charges, James Atkins, the couple's attorney, attempted to have the charges dismissed, citing the Tuttys' marriage ceremony. As an alternative strategy, Atkins also argued that the Georgia marriage code denied the Tuttys their constitutional right to fulfill all obligations of the marriage contract. In a lengthy opinion Judge Speer of the federal Circuit Court for the Southern District of Georgia upheld the constitutionality of the Georgia statute. According to the court, the Tutty marriage contract was not protected by the United States Constitution but was instead within the rightful domain of the state's police power. Referring to the 1819 U.S. Supreme Court case of *Dartmouth College* v. *Woodward*, Judge Speer noted that the federal Constitution covered contracts respecting property or objects of value. Conversely, marriage contracts involved a fundamental social institution and as such could be regulated by public authority.

Asserting that a marriage which is valid where solemnized is valid everywhere, Attorney Atkins sought judicial recognition of the couple's marriage ceremony performed in the District of Columbia. The court summarily rejected this argument by citing a Georgia Code section that prohibited Georgia residents from evading state law by marrying outside the state with the intention of residing in Georgia. As a final defense, the Tuttys' attorney asked the court to rule that an interracial marriage was neither an evil nor an injury to the state, but the court declined to address this issue.

Outside the bonds of marriage, interracial couples discovered that the criminal justice system forced them to pay a higher penalty than required of couples of the same race. In the 1881 case of *Pace & Cox* v. *State of Alabama,* Tony Pace, a black man, and Mary Ann Cox, his white paramour, unsuccessfully argued that their Fourteenth Amendment rights had been violated.[24] Their conviction of the crime of adultery, with a sentence of two years in prison, was a more severe punishment than was given to similarly convicted white couples or black couples.

In affirming what amounted to a discriminatory sentencing scheme, the Alabama Supreme Court found no equal protection violation. Writing for the court, Justice Somerville stated that "[t]he discrimination is not directed against the person of any particular color or race, but against the *offense,* the nature of which is *determined by the opposite color of the cohabiting parties*"[25] (emphasis in original). Through the prism of the court's reasoning, the punishment of each offending party—black and white—was exactly the same; there was no difference or discrimination in the punishment. Moreover, the justice agreed with the sentence handed down in the *Cox* case. In his opinion, the greater evil tendencies resulting from fornication by an interracial couple, "producing" what he termed "a mongrel population and a degraded civilization," mandated a different punishment in the interest of sound public policy.[26]

In addition to harsh laws that either restricted or prohibited interracial relationships, the post–Civil War remnants of antebellum state property laws frequently thwarted the enterprising efforts of black women to own land and to pass on estates to their descendants. Then, as now, the acquisition and ownership of land constituted economic wealth. During the late nineteenth century, both state and federal judges felt obliged to decide property disputes in accordance with the relevant state law in force at the time of the particular land transaction. As a result, racially biased laws worked to the disadvantage of African American women. Problems arose from statutes like an 1818 Georgia law prohibiting free blacks from holding real estate in three Georgia cities, Savannah, Augusta, and Darien. Black women who defied such discriminatory laws did so at their financial peril.

Take, for example, the plight of Aspasia Mirault, a black woman who attempted to circumvent the 1818 Georgia law.[27] In 1842 she gave George Cally, a white resident, the purchase money for lot number 22, Pulaski Ward, in Savannah. Cally took title to the property, but he did so with the understanding that he held the land as a trustee for Mirault and her heirs. Mirault assumed immediate possession of the property, made improvements, and also paid the taxes and ground rent. The court record reflects that on numerous occasions Cally acknowledged Mirault as the true owner. Unfortunately, this trust arrangement between Mirault and Cally dissolved at Mirault's death. Asserting his ownership by way of the title and deed, Cally initiated action to keep the property for himself. However, having fallen on hard times, Cally failed to pay the annual ground rent tax of $41.43. Soon thereafter, the city of Savannah gave public notice of its intention to sell the property. Swoll, a bona fide purchaser, then became the new owner.

Mirault's heirs, Mary Jackson, Louisa Burton, and Robert Oliver, filed a lawsuit in 1878, seeking title to the property. The jury decided that Mirault had been the rightful owner and awarded the property to her heirs. The jury also concluded that the city's resale to Swoll had been illegal. During its August 1878 term, the Georgia Supreme Court reversed the jury's verdict in favor of the heirs. Crucial to the court's decision was its application of the 1818 Georgia law prohibiting free blacks from owning real property in Savannah. The court reasoned that as a black woman Mirault could not own the lot; therefore, the trust she had created with Cally in 1842 was invalid and unenforceable. If Georgia law had rendered Mirault incapable of enforcing the trust, her heirs were likewise powerless to do so. Although Cally had successfully cheated Mirault's heirs out of their inheritance, as fate would have it neither he nor his descendants kept the property. The Georgia Supreme Court also ruled that since the city had given Cally adequate notice of the delinquent tax bill the sale to Swoll was valid and enforceable by law.

In the case of *Woods* v. *Pearce* argued before the Georgia Supreme Court in 1881, John Woods, a former slave, filed a lawsuit to eject the purchaser and current owner from his deceased mother's land.[28] In the alternative, Woods requested the court to award him $5,000, the estimated value of the land located in Muscogee County on the Chattahoochee River. In 1840 Celia Woods, John's mother, had received her freedom in Florida and migrated to Columbus, Georgia. In compliance with then existing state law, Celia secured a guardian and trustee, a white man named Lee. Celia gave Lee $1,000. Lee then purchased a piece of real estate, taking title to the land as guardian for Celia. When she died in 1856, Lee took control of the property and subsequently sold it to Tillman Pearce. Both men were aware of Celia's ownership. Sometime thereafter, Pearce sold the property to an innocent purchaser for value.

In deciding the case against John Woods, the court acknowledged that he was the son and only surviving heir of Celia Woods. The court proceeded to explain that, while Georgia law allowed free blacks to bequeath real estate as well as personal property to their descendants, the law required that the descendants would be free men and women. When Celia Woods died in 1856, slaves were considered chattel and could not inherit an estate of any kind. John Woods did not receive his freedom until 1865. Nine years earlier, when the title to the property would have passed to him, John was incapable of holding property under Georgia law. Unlike the circumstances confronted by Mirault's heirs in Savannah, Celia Woods's purchase of real estate in Columbus had been a legitimate transaction. Nevertheless, the court's interpretation of Georgia's property laws denied John Woods the benefits of his inheritance.

John Woods lost his appeal to the Georgia Supreme Court, but three black women were more fortunate in their litigation. In 1879, after a protracted trial and an appeal, the Georgia Supreme Court upheld the inheritance of the daughters of Henry Lowe and his slave Sophy Lowe.[29] The three sisters, Victoria Monroe, Maria Gray, and Missouri Overton, filed suit in Muscogee County, Georgia, to recover over $4,000 from the estate of their deceased guardian, Pleasant J. Phillips. Phillips had died without a will, and his administratrix refused to give the sisters an accounting of their assets. The administratrix justified her actions by arguing that the three women had been slaves in 1854—the alleged date Phillips became their guardian—and as slaves they had no rights to real or personal property.

During the trial of *Monroe* v. *Phillips* the sisters proffered the following facts and arguments. They showed that their father, Henry Lowe, a white planter, had arranged for Phillips, who was also white, to serve as guardian for them and their mother beginning in 1854. The sisters claimed that Phillips had been given a sum of money to be used for their sole benefit and support. As evidence of their claims, the women introduced a certificate establishing the free status of their mother, Sophy Lowe, a black woman. The women also introduced several account returns which Phillips had made in previous years. The women further asserted that Phillips's conversion of their trust money into Confederate bonds and treasury notes constituted an illegal and unwise investment, for which his estate should be held liable. Apparently unconvinced by the sisters' arguments, the jury decided the case in favor of Phillips's administratrix.

The women then appealed to the state's highest court. In his opinion, Justice Bleckley of the Georgia Supreme Court made reference to the various movements and activities of the women since their father's death. He noted that all three sisters had married, and two had emigrated to Liberia becoming permanent residents of that West African nation. Bleckley's opinion quickly dismissed the notion that the three women had been slaves in 1854 and thereby incapable of holding property. According to the court, in the era before the Civil War, Georgia law required free blacks to have guardians. Thus Phillips's appointment as their guardian was clear and convincing evidence of the sisters' free status. Justice Bleckley's opinion proceeded to explain how, following the recent war, guardians holding money in trust for free blacks assumed the new status of general trustees. The justice determined that Phillips and, after his death, his estate were accountable for all such funds entrusted to Phillips.

A similar ruling was the end result of *Smith* v. *Du Bose*. In that case, decided in 1887, the Georgia Supreme Court also upheld the inheritance rights of Amanda Dickson, an African American woman.[30] The court ruled that the Fourteenth Amendment of the United States Constitution as well as the Georgia constitution guaranteed legal rights for blacks. The court went so far as to declare that all distinctions restricting black citizenship had been abolished. According to the court, African Americans stood on an equal footing with whites and could assert their civil rights under the law. In a liberal pronouncement the court ruled as follows: "whatever rights and privileges belong to a white concubine, or to a bastard white woman and her children, under the laws of Georgia, belong to a colored woman and her children, under like circumstances, and the rights of each race are controlled and governed by the same enactments or principles of law."

At issue in the *Smith* case was a valuable bequest in the will of David Dickson, a wealthy white man who had died in Hancock County, Georgia. The parties contesting the will argued that Amanda Dickson and her mother, Julia Dickson, had obtained the will by perpetrating fraud and undue influence on David Dickson. The attorney for the will contestants also argued that the will provided for future illegal cohabitation and, thereby, was void as contrary to public policy.

In a lengthy opinion, the court sifted through the complicated facts of the case. Substantial evidence surfaced proving Amanda Dickson was the natural daughter of David Dickson and Julia Dickson, a black woman. Dickson's will left the lion's share of his estate to Amanda Dickson for her own use and as a trustee for her minor children, Julian and Charles. The court's examination of the public policy issue uncovered no Georgia law prohibiting blacks from receiving an inheritance under a will. Without evidence that the bequest was compensation for future cohabitation, the gifts to Amanda Dickson and her sons remained valid. Important evidence in the court's determination revealed that Julia Dickson, who had been David Dickson's mistress, received nothing under the will. In addition, the court deemed the bequests valid in the absence of a state law prohibiting a father from leaving his estate to his illegitimate child, whether the child be white or black.

An examination of postbellum case law suggests that the quest for justice, including legal justice, required that every avenue to achieve victory be tested and every method be explored. In those decades following the Civil War, many African American women used judicial redress to secure for themselves and for their race the rights and privileges many other Americans took for granted. Litigating cases took considerable courage and tenacity. The stakes for bringing such legal actions remained high; as a result, black women litigants took substantial risks. Personal dignity, money, property, and, ultimately, the dismantling of the racial status quo all hung in the balance. Advanced in their thinking, it is likely that these nineteenth-century black women—against overwhelming odds—held fast to a vision of America to be realized many decades in the future. Indeed, racism proved to be a formidable adversary but one that nonetheless could sometimes be overcome.

Of the cases examined in this essay, the success rate for the black women litigants was low. Far too frequently, state and federal appellate courts reversed lower court decisions that favored black women. Perhaps, however, the number of actual courtroom victories is less important than the legacy these women left behind. The litigation records reveal that the women were aware of their entitlement to both citizenship and participation in the mainstream of American life. As a result, their individual quests for justice have left us a rich legacy of legal activism and a blueprint for equality and justice in American life.

Notes

1 Morroe Berger, *Equality by Statute: The Revolution in Civil Rights* (Garden City, N.Y.: Doubleday, 1967), 4–8.

2 Derrick A. Bell, Jr., *Race, Racism, and American Law,* 2d ed. (Boston: Little, Brown, 1980), 34–38; Charles A. Lofgren, *The Plessy Case: A Legal-Historical Interpretation* (New York: Oxford University Press, 1987), 23; John Hope Franklin, *From Slavery to Freedom: A History of Negro Americans,* 6th ed. (New York: Alfred A. Knopf, 1988), 206–7, 226–27, 231–32; Donald G. Nieman, *Promises to Keep: African-Americans and the Constitutional Order* (New York: Oxford University Press, 1991), 56–57, 59–61, 106–8.

3 Quoted in Stephen J. Riegel, "The Persistent Career of Jim Crow: Lower Federal Courts and the 'Separate but Equal' Doctrine, 1865–1896," *American Journal of Legal History* 28 (1984): 22. See also Nieman, *Promises to Keep,* 67–68, 86–87.

4 *West Chester & Philadelphia Railway Company* v. *Miles,* 55 Pennsylvania 209, 210 (1867).

5 Ibid., 211.

6 Ibid., 212; see also Lofgren, *Plessy Case,* 118–21.

7 *Chicago & Northwestern Railway Company* v. *Anna Williams,* 55 Illinois 185, 187 (1870).

8 Ibid., 188; see also Lofgren, *Plessy Case,* 122.

9   *Chesapeake, Ohio & Southwestern Railroad Company* v. *Wells*, 85 Tennessee 613 (1 Pickle 613) (1887); Ida B. Wells, *Crusade for Justice: The Autobiography of Ida B. Wells*, ed. Alfreda M. Duster (Chicago: University of Chicago Press, 1970), 18–20. Following her 1895 marriage to Ferdinand L. Barnett, Ida B. Wells was known as Ida Wells-Barnett.

10 *Memphis & Charleston Railroad Company* v. *Benson*, 85 Tennessee 627 (1887).

11 *Smoot* v. *Kentucky Central Railroad Company*, 13 Fed. 337 (1882). See also *Logwood* v. *Memphis & Charleston Railroad Company*, 23 Fed. 318 (1885).

12 Franklin, *From Slavery to Freedom*, 238. For a discussion of the Supreme Court's opinion in the *Civil Rights Cases*, 109 U.S. 3 (1883), see Nieman, *Promises to Keep*, 96–97; and Bell, *Race, Racism, and American Law*, 86–93.

13 *Gray* v. *Cincinnati Southern Railroad Company*, 11 Fed. 686 (1882); see also Lofgren, *Plessy Case*, 136.

14 *Houck* v. *Southern Pacific Railway Company*, 38 Fed. 226 (1888).

15 Ibid., 227. See also Lofgren, *Plessy Case*, 139–40.

16 *Sue Case*, 22 Fed. 843 (1885). See also *Hall* v. *De Cuir*, 95 U.S. Sup. Ct. 485 (1877), and *Coger* v. *North West Union Packet Co.*, 37 Iowa 145 (1873).

17 *Green* v. *City of Bridgeton*, 10 Fed. 1090 (1879). See also Lofgren, *Plessy Case*, 135–36.

18 Riegel, "Persistent Career of Jim Crow," 24–25.

19 Lofgren, *Plessy Case*, 116–18; Franklin, *From Slavery to Freedom*. 238. See *Plessy* v. *Ferguson*, 163 U.S. 537 (1896).

20 *Scott et al.* v. *State of Georgia*, 39 Georgia 321 (1867).

21 Ibid., 324. For a discussion of interracial marriage during the post–Civil War era, see Mary Frances Berry, "Judging Morality: Sexual Behavior and Legal Consequences in the Late Nineteenth-Century South," *Journal of American History* 78 (December 1991): 839–40.

22 *Scott et al.* v. *State of Georgia*, 39 Georgia 326.

23 *State of Georgia* v. *Tutty et al.*, 41 Fed. 753 (1890).

24 *Pace & Cox* v. *State of Alabama*, 69 Alabama Reports 231 (1881).

25 Ibid., 232.

26 Ibid. See also Richard Bardolph, ed., *The Civil Rights Record: Black Americans and the Law, 1849–1970* (New York: Crowell, 1970), 94–96.

27 *Swoll et al.* v. *Oliver et al.*, 61 Georgia 248 (1878). See also *Beal* v. *Drane*, 25 Georgia 430 (1858).

28 *Woods* v. *Pearce*, 68 Georgia 160 (1881).

29 *Monroe* v. *Phillips, administratrix*, 64 Georgia 32 (1879).

30 *Smith et al.* v. *Du Bose et al., executors*, 78 Georgia 413 (1887). For a discussion of Amanda Dickson's inheritance from David Dickson and the Dickson will controversy, see Adele Logan Alexander, *Ambiguous Lives: Free Women of Color in Rural Georg'a, 1789–1879* (Fayetteville: University of Arkansas Press, 1991). Amanda Dickson is also the subject of a recent work; see Kent Anderson Leslie, *Woman of Color, Daughter of Privilege, 1849–1893* (Athens: University of Georgia Press, 1995). See also Berry, "Judging Morality," 854.

Advancement of the Race

through African American

Women's Organizations

in the South, 1895–1925

Cynthia Neverdon-Morton

During the period from 1895 to 1925, black women addressed issues and concerns facing them as women and systematically responded to specific needs of the black community through the development and strengthening of local, national, and international social service and self-help organizations. This essay examines the efforts of black women, individually and in groups, to effect social and political change which would result in advancement of the race. Often, their activities were responses to progressivism, imperialism, self-determinism, and racism on both national and international levels. At the same time, more often than not, their activism was coupled with the desire to achieve full equality in American society. In examining the activism of black women, attention is given to two southern locales, Baltimore, Maryland, because of its urban character, and Tuskegee, Alabama, because it served as a model for programs in other rural communities.[1]

Southern women focused on many needs of African Americans: the plight of working women, limited economic opportunities, inferior housing, severe health problems, the political and social straitjacket of Jim Crowism, care for the aged, and programs for the very young. Educational initiatives are highlighted in this essay because the key to solving all of these problems, black women leaders were convinced, was education of the masses of black citizens. Education was seen as the first step toward racial equality, and racial equality was the essential precondition for development of the individual African American's full potential. Thus individual growth and group improvement were viewed as inextricably intertwined, with education as one of the key melding forces.

Even though black women living in different communities realized that there were some needs unique to their areas, they also understood that certain needs were common to all communities where African Americans lived. As a result, black women throughout the South developed programs and organizations to respond to local, state, and regional concerns; the final goal was the advancement of African Americans as a group. Generally, the programs were designed to serve self and others directly and to teach new ways to modify unfavorable conditions. Although the women were unable to provide solutions for all problems, they were able to change some people's behavior, provide services for many, and strengthen ties among separate southern communities. The social service and self-help programs described in this essay demonstrate the many achievements of black women as they were "Defining for Themselves: Consolidating the Struggle."

Defining Self: The Double Burden of Gender and Race

Who were these women who accepted the responsibility to effect social, economic, and political changes for the race? Black women during the period 1895–1925 mirrored the society in many ways and at the same time possessed unique qualities and objectives that provoked reactions from the larger society. To be sure, black women were not monolithic in their thoughts and actions. Margaret Murray Washington, organizer of the Tuskegee Woman's Club and one who articulated a conservative political ideology not unlike that of her husband, Booker T. Washington, stated, "We cannot find the average colored woman any more than we can find the average woman in other races."[2] Regional as well as individual differences influenced the way black women viewed themselves. Some had advantages—urban versus rural location, family structure, education, and personal income were four such variables—which shaped their social status and self-perceptions.

Differences between urban and rural women were obvious. At times the differences, due largely to demographic, political, and economic factors, were even more apparent for those living in northern urban areas. In urban areas women often could interact more readily with each other and with whites, were exposed to more diverse economic opportunities, had greater access to educational facilities—although often substandard in comparison to those for whites—and could agitate more effectively for inclusion in the political process. Nevertheless, Adella Hunt Logan of Tuskegee Institute believed that "the needs of country folk are about the same as those of town and city residents. Means of social uplift do not differ greatly."[3] As a result, it was believed that when a community of women began to think, class differences aside, action would follow. As the black woman assumed new responsibilities, she would have to become knowledgeable about her surroundings, about national and international events, and about the image she projected.

At the same time, it was clear to the women that, unlike their white counterparts, they had an extra burden to bear. Mary Church Terrell, in an article entitled "Being a Colored Woman in the United States," expressed it best when she wrote:

> But the white women of England and the United States have only one burden to bear, after all, the burden of sex. What would they do I wonder if they were double-crossed, so to speak, as the colored women of this country are: if they had two heavy loads to carry through an unfriendly world, the burden of race as well as that of sex?[4]

The tensions and interactions between gender and race, the two sources of discrimination, and black women's varied responses to them must be examined and analyzed in order to better understand the black female experience during the period under consideration. The dual burden of race and sex was quite apparent during the debate over suffrage. Many arguments used by men to justify their opinion as to the role of women resurfaced as women began to agitate for the right to vote. After the Reconstruction era, most black males of the South were systematically denied the right to participate actively in the political process. In American society, the right to vote has never been just an aspect of the political process. Access to the polls also represented an acknowledgment of social equality and the potential for economic actualization. Therefore, it is clear why white males sought to exclude African Americans and to categorize voting as a gender-specific right only for them. The denial of black women's right to vote reinforced the belief held by many whites that the women were not and did not deserve the status of citizens with full participatory rights. Throughout the long struggle for the right to vote, black women realized that they could not rely only upon the vote to bring about positive change for all African Americans in the South; as a result, one response was the implementation of self-help and social service programs.

Programs in Rural Alabama

Programs in Alabama were in some ways representative of self-help and social service programs in other parts of the rural South. Margaret Murray Washington (1865–1925) was the prime force behind social service programs in Alabama. It was largely through her efforts that women, first in Tuskegee and then throughout the state, began to create their own social service programs. Rural communities were generally isolated. Large expanses of land were needed for agricultural pursuits, and in rural areas the majority of the black residents worked in agriculture. Therefore, such residents' needs often were peculiar to the rural South. Women in rural communities such as Tuskegee and Mount Meigs actually helped to create new communities and establish services considered commonplace in cities such as Baltimore and Atlanta.

Rural social programs emphasized industrial education and education for adults. Education for both young and old stressed ways of adjusting to rural agricultural life. Acutely aware of the increasing urbanization in the nation and the migratory patterns of African Africans, educators tried to discourage migration from the farms and the South. Those people who were sent to schools in urban areas were expected to return to assist in the reconstruction of the South and the development of rural African Americans.

It was also in the rural communities that class differences were often more pronounced. Groups such as the Tuskegee Woman's Club retained an elitist composition and sponsored some activities only for the formally educated. There were distinct differences in the type of programs held on Tuskegee's campus and the social uplift programs carried out in the surrounding communities. Those who were not members of the Tuskegee's Woman Club were not actively involved in determining uplift imperatives and programs. Personal attainments and social customs precluded the complete bonding of women from all classes. Rural women were not as motivated to effect changes in the social structure, because in rural areas the separation between African Americans and whites was clearly defined and rigidly enforced. To challenge such customs might have endangered black lives, programs, services, institutions, and communities.

Rural women such as those in Tuskegee relied to a greater extent than urban women on federal and state funds and programs to implement their goals. As the populations in rural communities were not as large or affluent as those in urban ones, local fund-raising activities were less successful, but limited funds did not automatically dictate inferior programs. Since greater resourcefulness was required to obtain funds, people depended on and utilized more fully the natural resources available in the area.

Programs in Baltimore, Maryland

Baltimore, Maryland, was one of the more cosmopolitan southern cities. As a result of its geographic location, its urban character, and the infusion of northern ideals, Baltimore's self-help and social service programs for African Americans exhibited unique qualities. Major fund-raising activities succeeded in involving a cross-section of the citizens; the economic strength of the city and the support of the black press stimulated increased giving to worthy causes. Such giving enabled the Baltimore Colored Empty Stocking and Fresh Air Circle, under the leadership of Ida Rebecca Cummings (1867–1958), to purchase a 10.5-acre farm for economically deprived and handicapped children. The circle remained active for more than forty years with Cummings as the president for most of that time.

Because of the number of black residents in the city, there were many active groups and diverse programs. Baltimore had a history of self-help groups dating from the antebellum period. In the early years and through 1925, the efforts of religious groups, including the Oblate Sisters of Providence, a black order of nuns, resulted in the development of child care facilities and educational institutions.

Interracial efforts also began earlier in Baltimore's urban setting than in many of the rural southern areas. The Women's Cooperative Civic League, an all-black female group, was formed in 1913 at the request of a group of white citizens to address housing, health, sanitation, and educational problems resulting from the rapid urban growth. Under the leadership of Sara Fernandis, the city was organized into wards headed by community activists. By 1914 the membership had grown to 130.[5] At the same time, there were hundreds of persons in the various neighborhoods working closely together in order to actualize the objectives that their ward representatives had helped to determine. With the assistance of whites, the local government was made fully aware of problems in the black communities. Municipal laws and services were monitored to ensure more and better public services for the black communities. The

Cooperative League's activities are notable because the leadership relied upon "grass-roots persons" to implement the goals.

The varied programs initiated by black women made it possible for many African Americans to share the benefits of Baltimore's growth. This was possible in part because of the passage of laws more favorable to the black residents, laws which were enacted because black residents became involved in the political process. Working independently, in groups of black women only, and with black men, residents circulated petitions, wrote letters to the editors of the local newspapers, held protest rallies, and formed protest groups in support of issues black citizens deemed worthy. One combined effort resulted in an educational reform group. Headed by Laura Frances Dickerson Wheatley, the Civic Aid Association lobbied for additional schools, salary increases, and black teachers for black schools. In 1923 Wheatley was unanimously elected the first president of the Baltimore Federation of Colored Parent-Teachers Clubs. With a membership of over 10,000 and branches at twenty-seven schools, the club became a definitive voice in the educational circles of the city.

National Programs and Organizations

Once local efforts were underway, women from different states and regions met to structure a national body to respond not only to local and regional issues but also to national issues and concerns. In 1896 the National Association of Colored Women (NACW) was formed as a result of the merger of the National League of Colored Women and the National Federation of Afro-American Women. The NACW reported a membership of fifty clubs and 500 persons representing many states. During the tenure of Mary Church Terrell, its first president, the NACW defined realistic, purposeful, and lasting objectives. The association not only operated national programs but also constituted the first cohesive national network of black women.[6] The structure of the organization facilitated communication: local clubs at the base, then state federations, regional federations, and at the top the national body. Information and influence flowed, in many cases, as freely from bottom to top as in the reverse direction.

By 1913 the NACW was affiliated with organizations in Canada, Liberia, and Madagascar, as well as thirty states in the United States. Although most members were formally educated, middle-class women, reform for the masses was seen as the essential goal. Mothers' clubs, day nurseries, kindergartens, and schools of domestic science were among the many programs implemented to effect reform. So that all members could keep abreast of local and national programs, Terrell called for biennial conventions to be held in cities where there were many active members.

The small group of national leaders of black women spoke for the masses at national and international conferences. Generally, these educated black women were also regional leaders who served as presidents of state federations of black women's clubs. In many cases the same women concurrently held key local, regional, and national offices and so made public policy decisions for black women. Because the decisions generally flowed from a genuine desire to "lift the race," and in many cases after 1897 emerged from the general and executive sessions of the National Association of Colored Women's national conventions, they reflected the needs of black people. As a direct result of the implementation of national, regional, and local objectives, racial uplift did occur. Dedicated cadres of workers, usually volunteer, always existed at the level of greatest importance for racial advancement—the local community. Capable leadership, adequate funds, community support, and the potential to fulfill a defined need were essential if programs were to succeed.

State Federations: Focus on Alabama

Margaret Murray Washington, in a speech in 1917 at a Nashville Women's Club meeting, indicated that the original NACW concept was still valid when she identified the three key elements of club work: individual or city work, state work, and national programs. Washington also stated that the city federation, as represented by those at the meeting, should be composed of clubs of women at work in various sections of the city, but with one ideal. The state federations were to work on projects for the betterment of the state.[7]

Such was the case in Alabama. The activities of Washington and the Tuskegee Woman's Club gained statewide attention. To preserve the accomplishments of their programs and to draw attention to problems in other areas of the state of Alabama, a convention of black clubwomen was held in Alabama. Washington was the principal organizer and first president of the Alabama State Federation of Colored Women's Clubs organized in 1898. The federation sponsored projects similar to those of the Tuskegee Woman's Club, but because of its larger membership and financial resources it was able to elicit support from whites, influence the allocation of state funds, and, most important, reach greater numbers of African Americans who benefited from the federation's activism.

The federation developed two projects that served as examples for other state groups. More often than not in southern states, young black offenders, male and female, were sent to penal institutions for adults. In some cases, youngsters who were homeless were committed to the institutions because foster homes were not available. Washington credited the NACW as the primary stimulus for the Alabama federation's creation of the Mount Meigs Reformatory for Juvenile Negro Law-Breakers, which housed boys. For the girls, the Mount Meigs Rescue Home was established and supported by the federation.

By the Twenty-seventh Annual Session of the federation in Selma in 1925, it was apparent that the projects were successful and that the goal of networking was broadening the base of the group. Additional clubs had joined, bringing the number of local organizations to fifty-three. The federation president indicated that $3,633.24 had been raised during the year to support the home for girls and other programs.[8] The women had proven that they were responsive and responsible on local and state levels. It was also evident that local and statewide concerns were similar in scope; in later years, this would also be true of regional concerns. Part of the success at the state and regional levels is attributable to the successful models implemented at the local level. The conceptual framework for the majority of state and regional programs had its origin in local communities.

Interracial Cooperation

Because of the urgent need to improve the conditions under which the majority of African Americans lived, black women not only independently structured programs and institutions but consistently demonstrated a willingness to work with whites to achieve specific goals. This willingness was in spite of earlier failures to cooperate across racial lines. One notable effort of interracial cooperation was the Commission on Interracial Cooperation (CIC), organized in 1918 partly in response to the problems facing African Americans as World War I drew to a close. Originally, all of the members were white professional men who had worked in some area of race relations.

In order to involve women in the initiatives of the CIC, two white clubwomen, Estelle Haskin and Mary de Bardelehen, established a framework through which they could organize. Carrie Parks Johnson was appointed the chair of the planning committee. To elicit support from black women, Johnson and Haskin attended the 1920 annual meeting of the NACW at Tuskegee. Lugenia Burns Hope, founder of the Atlanta Neighborhood Union, obtained permission for Johnson to speak to the women on the last day of the conference. At a later conference, Johnson described her impression of the women: "I saw these colored women, graduates of great institutions of learning. I saw lawyers, doctors, poets, sculptors and painters. I saw women of education, culture and refinement. I had lived in the South all my life, but didn't know such as these lived in the land."[9] If the southern social system had permitted greater and varied interaction among the races, Johnson's impressions probably would have been shared by many other middle-class white women. Johnson's words constituted a clear and terrible indictment of the southern social system, which not only did not utilize the talents of many of its citizens but was even unaware of their existence.

The day after the NACW meeting ten premier leaders among black clubwomen met with Johnson and Haskin. The meeting represented a major breakthrough in the South and a significant accomplishment for the ICC because it was generally accepted that among white women the direction fostered by the ICC was not "popular with the rank and file of club women in the South in 1920. Many women were indifferent while others were openly antagonistic."[10] As an outgrowth of the Tuskegee meeting, a hundred white women and four black women assembled in Memphis in October 1920 to commit themselves to interracial cooperation. The four were Elizabeth Ross Haynes from Fisk in Tennessee, Margaret Murray Washington from Tuskegee, Charlotte Hawkins Brown of Sedalia, North Carolina, and Jennie Moton of Hampton, Virginia. The delegates decided to aid African Americans through the establishment of day nurseries, kindergartens, clinics, and playgrounds; the improvement of housing and sanitary conditions; the provision of educational opportunities; the improvement of traveling conditions; the seeking of justice in the courts and suppression of lynching.[11]

During and after the conference, the greatest debate centered around the suppression of lynching. Lugenia Burns Hope represented those who argued against a slow, middle-of-the-road course as the best way to eliminate lynching. She supported the passage of a national law to prohibit lynching and wanted white women to accept responsibility for controlling the behavior of their male family members.[12] Because of her conservative approach and her desire not to alienate those whites with whom she could work, Washington supported the majority opinion. Finally, points from drafts were combined with what was called the "Hope Amendment on Lynching."[13] The debate on the best approach to use in resolving problems was not a new one among black women. Differing opinions led at times to internal conflicts which necessitated skillful mediation by the leaders. At no time, however, did the women permit their differences to become more important than the causes for which they were working. After the meeting, Johnson was appointed chairperson of the Department of Women's Work. Officially, as of 17 November 1920, the department was a unit of the CIC.

Because the concept of broadly based interracial cooperation was alien to many southern white women, the Memphis conference did not bring about immediate, significant changes. Therefore, in 1921, the Southeastern Federation of Negro Women's Clubs published a pamphlet entitled *Southern Negro Women and Race Cooperation*,[14] which was designed to accomplish what meetings with white women, the last of which, during this period, was held in Georgia on 28–30 June 1921, had not been able to achieve. The pamphlet encouraged white women to assist black women in those matters affecting both groups. Lugenia Hope, Lucy Laney, Janie Porter Barrett, Margaret Murray Washington, and Mary McLeod Bethune, all active members of the NACW, were five of the contributors.

Beginning with the statement that all black women, regardless of economic or social status, suffered from racial bias at one time or another, the pamphlet listed areas where black women came into contact with whites and troubling aspects of such contacts. In the area of child welfare, black women had already begun to address the problems of children who did not have adult supervision while their parents worked. The recommendations requested the support of white women in establishing additional day nurseries, playgrounds, and recreational centers; in providing for home and school visitations; and in securing more juvenile probation officers and reform schools. In another area related to children, the pamphlet provided suggestions to improve the educational process. While all of the recommendations had received the attention of African Americans since 1895, the authors of the pamphlet knew that more needed to be done and could be done if white women also agitated for improved facilities, extended terms, vocational training, adequate salaries, and additional training schools for teachers. The task was to convince the whites that improvements for African Americans would bring about benefits for them as well.

In each state where there was a branch of the CIC, much was accomplished in many communities by 1925. Successes attributed to the state commissions and the Women's Department included the building of playgrounds, the establishing of day nurseries, street repairs, fire protection, the observation of Negro Health Week, and the investigation of housing conditions. Through their involvement in the interracial organization, black women proved that they were willing to affiliate with any group that sought the advancement of the race. Even when confronted with inequities in treatment and a reluctance to move at a pace they deemed acceptable, the women remained active members. The interracial cooperation did necessitate, at times, the development of new strategies by the women. In order to gain the support of whites, they modified to some extent their public declarations against social evils; they relinquished the possibility of holding key, visible leadership positions within the group, and they acquiesced at points to priorities determined by black or white males. It was probably easy for many of the women to modify their position because they saw their actions resulting in increased attention to and financial support for programs and goals that they had championed since 1895. In many cases, the interracial thrust simply encouraged and won earlier program sanction from governmental officials, greater exposure for the programs, and greater financial assistance from whites.

International Council of Women of the Darker Races

Not all interracial efforts proved as successful as CIC. While struggling to change conditions at home, black women throughout the United States sought ways to broaden their understanding of international affairs and the conditions under which other peoples of color lived. They were particularly interested in the plight of black people in Africa and in the Caribbean. To fulfill their desire to become more aware, to assist in influencing international affairs, and to help improve life for peoples of color, members of the NACW joined the International Council of Women, an interracial group. By 1920 it was obvious that a separate organization would better enable the women to accomplish specific objectives which more clearly narrowed their areas of interest to those of the African diaspora; thus the International Council of Women of the Darker Races was formed as an adjunct to the NACW.

The stated purpose of the new council was to assist in disseminating information regarding peoples of color and to help instill racial pride. The original members were fifty American women of color and fifty foreign women of color. Mary Church Terrell and Addie Hunton were vice-presidents, and Maggie Walker, Mary McLeod Bethune, and Nannie Burroughs were members of the Executive Council.[15]

In 1922 the council began to hold conventions separate from the general sessions of the NACW. The council's meeting in Washington, D.C., attracted representatives from African nations, Haiti, Ceylon, and the West Indies. A definitive statement of purpose was developed at the 1922 meeting: "The Council has as its object the economic, social, and political welfare of the women of all the darker races."[16] The principal activity for the remainder of 1922 was an investigation of the status of the women and children of Haiti. Emily Williams was sent to Haiti to conduct an on-site study of women there. Williams's trip was partially financed by the council, and her report was submitted to the general body of the NACW at the 1923 convention.

In August 1923 the council met at the National Training School in Washington, D.C. In order to implement the primary goal of the organization, three sections were organized: International Relations, Social and Economic Conditions, and Education. For the 1923–24 convention year, three resolutions were passed and disseminated to the press. The women resolved (1) to commend Adelaide Casely-Hayford for her efforts to found a school for girls in Sierra Leone, (2) to study the condition of women and girls in Africa, and (3) to condemn the French government for its posture in regards to racial discrimination in African nations.[17] The second resolution was crucial; no longer would the council be merely a fact-finding body. After studying conditions in Africa, the next step would be to change conditions. Unfortunately, the International Council of Women of the Darker Races never moved, during this period, far beyond gathering data and proposing solutions. The international political arena was not receptive to black women who attempted to become involved in the internal affairs of colonized nations. By this time, the entire continent of Africa and the West Indies were affected directly or indirectly by the colonization activities of European nations and the United States. Nevertheless, the women were able to expand their knowledge of peoples of color and to aid specific individuals or groups in foreign nations. The women also pressured school superintendents in the United States to order books about people of the diaspora. The council was especially concerned that black youngsters, as well as council members, be exposed to and understand the history and literature of their people. To ensure that all of its own members were as well informed as possible, the council encouraged the development of study groups.

As an adjunct to the council, under its Education Section, the Committees of Seven were formed in 1924 to "study conditions of the darker races of the world." Each community was to form a committee to study problems of African peoples and those of African Americans. Educational, social, religious, and industrial concerns were suggested as broad areas from which specific topics could be selected. It was also recommended that the women read books about Africa and schedule visits from native Africans and missionaries.[18] The local committees, as indicated in articles, letters, and minutes of club meetings, did take suggestions quite seriously and worked to implement them.

While the women labored to make the International Council of Women of the Darker Races a channel for their concerns about African peoples abroad and in the United States, they maintained their affiliation with the International

Council of Women. The year 1925 did not usher in any marked difference in attitudes and behaviors among white Americans. Nor did the majority of those struggling for women's rights embrace black women as a vital component of the movement. There were still many domestic issues that required constant, concerted involvement. In spite of the advances made by women in general, black women still toiled under the heavy yoke of race and sex. Membership in traditionally white organizations did not guarantee greater inclusion, respect, or success. Organizations started by black women in response to their specific needs and interests were still the most important conduits for change and progress.

However, whether in groups of black women only or in biracial groups, the black woman demonstrated her competence, industry, and intelligence. Thus we find the African American woman struggling to come into her own and bringing her race with her. There is no greater evidence of her value to the progress of the race than the lives she influenced, the lasting institutions she founded, the enduring programs she initiated, and the positive course for racial betterment that she set for future generations.

Notes

1 For a fuller discussion of the activism of black women in the South, see Cynthia Neverdon-Morton, *Afro-American Women of the South and the Advancement of the Race, 1895–1925* (Knoxville: University of Tennessee Press, 1989).

2 Margaret Murray Washington, "Are We Making Good?" *Spelman Messenger*, November 1915, 8.

3 Mrs. Warren Logan, "Colored Women of the Country Districts," *Tuskegee Messenger* 29 (April 1913): 3.

4 Mary Church Terrell, "Being a Colored Woman in the United States," Mary Church Terrell Papers, Collection 102, box 3, folder 53, p. 1, Manuscript Division, Moorland-Springarn Research Center, Howard University, Washington, D.C.; hereafter MSRC.

5 S. C. Fernandis, "Report of the Women's Cooperative Civil League," in *Civic Courier, 1912–1914* (Baltimore: Lord Baltimore Press, April 1914), 4.

6 Patricia Hills Collins provides an analysis of the factors and thought undergirding the development of the black women's club movement in "Feminism in the Twentieth Century," in *Black Women in America: An Historical Encyclopedia*, ed. Darlene Clark Hine, Elsa Barkley Brown, and Rosalyn Terborg-Penn (Brooklyn, N.Y.: Carlson Publishing, 1993), 418–25.

7 "Mrs. Booker T. Washington Honored Guest of Nashville's Women's Club," *National Globe*, 11 May 1916, Women's Work file, Monroe Work Collection, Hollis Burke Frissell Library, Tuskegee University's Archival Collection, Tuskegee, Ala.; hereafter TUAC.

8 "Negro Women and Successful Meet," *Montgomery Advertiser*, 10 June 1925, Women's Work file, Monroe Work Collection, TUAC.

9   "Background of the Women's Department," 12, Commission on Interracial Cooperation
    Collection, file 17 B-1, Archives Department, Trevor Arnett Library, Atlanta University,
    Atlanta, Ga.; now titled the Atlanta University Center Woodruff Library; hereafter
    ADAU. Reproduced by permission.

10 Ibid., 4.

11 "Conscience Answers the Call," 5, Commission on Interracial Cooperation Collection,
    file 17 A-Z, ADAU.

12 "Background," 17.

13 Jacqueline A. Rouse provides the most comprehensive analysis of the life and work of
    Lugenia Burns Hope in *Lugenia Burns Hope: Black Southern Reformer* (Athens: Univer-
    sity of Georgia Press, 1989).

14 *Southern Negro Women and Race Cooperation* (Southeastern Federation of Negro Wom-
    en's Clubs, 1921), 2–6, R. R. Moton Collection, Interracial Conference, box 52-file 344,
    TUAC. Due in part to the efforts of black women such as Lugenia Burns Hope, the
    prevention of lynchings remained one of the concerns of the CIC. In 1930 the CIC
    established the Southern Commission on the Study of Lynching. Jessie Daniel Ames,
    director of the CIC Women's Department, further expanded the role of women in the
    cause with the establishment of the Association of Southern Women for the Prevention
    of Lynching (ASWPL) in 1932.

15 International Council of Women of the Darker Races, printed sheet, 10 November 1924,
    Terrell Papers, box 102–12, Manuscript Division, MSRC.

16 "Booker T.'s Wife Heads World Order," *Chicago Defender,* 26 August 1922, in Women's
    Work file, Monroe Work Collection, TUAC.

17 "World International Council—Darker Races," *New York Age,* 18 August 1923, in Wom-
    en's Work file, Monroe Work Collection, TUAC.

18 M. M. Washington, International Council of Women of the Darker Races, prepared
    statement, in Terrell Papers, box 102–12, Manuscript Division, MSRC; and "The Com-
    mittee of Seven," *Tuskegee Alumni Bulletin* 6, nos. 8–9 (Aug–Sept. 1924), 192.

Clubwomen and Electoral

Politics in the 1920s

Evelyn Brooks Higginbotham

Between 1900 and 1930 more than 1.5 million black men and women migrated from the South to the urban North. The massive trek, actually begun in the last decade of the nineteenth century, shifted into high gear during World War I when wartime demands from northern industry promised employment and, most of all, escape from the southern way of life—from its boll-weevil-ravaged sharecrop farming and from its segregation, disfranchisement, and lynching. In the decade between 1910 and 1920 the black population soared upward in such cities as Chicago (from 44,103 to 109,458), Detroit (from 5,741 to 40,878), Cleveland (from 8,448 to 34,451), New York (from 91,709 to 152,467), and Philadelphia (from 84,459 to 134,229).[1] Concentrated in the ghettos of urban centers, the migrants soon transformed their restricted residential opportunities into political opportunity.

With migration stepped up to even higher levels between 1920 and 1930, the growing significance of the black vote did not escape the attention of machine politicians. Blacks played an especially influential role in Chicago's machine politics. For instance, in the city's closely contested mayoral race in 1915, the black vote was critical to the victory of Republican William Hale Thompson. Moreover, growing black populations in the northern cities and border states precipitated the rise of black officeholders. In the first three decades of the twentieth century blacks increasingly sent their own to state legislatures, city councils, judgeships, and clerkships. In 1928 the political clout of Illinois blacks carried Oscar DePriest, the first northern black congressman, to the House of Representatives.[2]

Invisible Politics

Black women played an active and valuable role in the electoral politics of the 1920s, but their role is, too often, overlooked as if it was an unimportant, even impotent factor in the profound political changes underway. Black political behavior during the early decades of the twentieth century has been analyzed in a number of excellent studies. Unfortunately, the overwhelming majority treat black women as invisible participants, silent members of the black electorate. The literature, much of which was written between the 1930s and the 1970s, fails to investigate, to any meaningful extent, either the black female vote or the role of black women leaders in getting out the vote.[3]

While the significance of the female vote has not received serious attention from the traditional literature on black politics, it also has been too easily dismissed by the recent scholarship in women's history. And though a growing body of research has appeared on the suffragist activities among black women leaders, very little is known about their political participation in the decade after the ratification of the Nineteenth Amendment.[4] Feminist scholarship has placed black women's club work firmly within the context of the organizational history of suffragism and has identified such individual leaders as Mary Church Terrell, Ida B. Wells-Barnett, and Nannie Helen Burroughs as outspoken champions of women's suffrage in the first two decades of the twentieth century, but this scholarship fails to recognize their continuing political activism after 1920. The passage of the Nineteenth Amendment, according to this research, appears to portend the end rather than the starting point of black women's involvement in electoral politics for the next decade. This assumption is based on the following realities.

On the eve of ratification, the handwriting on the wall boldly read, "The full meaning of the Nineteenth Amendment would be denied to black women." Historians of the woman's suffrage movement have exposed the racist and class biases of white women suffragists.[5] In a deliberate effort to win southern white support, they disassociated their cause from black voting rights issues. The white women's movement abandoned its earlier nineteenth-century ties with the black freedom struggle in favor of an alliance with white supremacy. The reversal reflected a fundamental shift not only in strategy but also in the rationale upon which suffragism had rested. By the late nineteenth and early twentieth centuries, white suffragists argued from the position of expediency rather than justice. The National American Woman Suffrage Association, having adopted a states' rights policy toward its member organizations in 1903, paved the way for its southern wing to argue the expediency of woman's suffrage in nullifying the intent of the Fifteenth Amendment and buttressing the cause of white supremacy in general. An assent, if not a direct contributor, to the disfranchisement and segregation of southern blacks of both sexes, the strategy assured the denial of black women's ballots. Carrie Chapman Catt, Alice Paul, Ida Husted Harper, and other luminaries of the women's movement added insult to injury by expressing their racist sensibilities in correspondence, segregated marches, and various public statements. The press reported the hard facts once ratification became reality. In state after state in the South, large numbers of black women turned out to register only to be turned back.[6]

Historian Rosalyn Terborg-Penn draws attention to the suffrage clubs of black women in the states that ratified the woman's vote prior to 1920, but she concludes that the postscript to the passage of the Nineteenth Amendment was one of frustration and disillusionment. By the mid 1920s discontented black feminists, Terborg-Penn posits, turned their eyes away from mainstream electoral politics to the renewed antilynching crusade, social service efforts, and separatist or Third World causes such as the International Council of Women of the Darker Races, Pan-Africanism, and the Marcus Garvey movement.[7] Although her assessment correctly emphasizes the hostile, racially charged environment that black women faced, it underestimates the continuing interest of black women leaders in the electoral process.

The work of Ida Wells-Barnett, the great black feminist and antilynching crusader, illustrates the potential of black women leaders in mobilizing voters. Her autobiography tells of her activities with the Alpha Suffrage Club for black women soon after Illinois adopted woman's suffrage in 1913. She credited her club with DePriest's election in 1915 as Chicago's first black alderman, and the large black turnout also played the decisive role in the victory of William Hale Thompson.[8]

Migration and Woman Suffrage

When America returned to normalcy after World War I, the combined realities of Jim Crow and southern disfranchisement, of northern discrimination in housing and jobs, and of pervasive racism both customary and institutionalized created a set of social conditions as inimical to black progress as had existed in previous generations. Although their grievances were just as pronounced, black women, like their men, did not greet these objective conditions with the same degree of resignation and accommodation that had characterized the era of Booker T. Washington. Rather, their response was one of optimism, reflecting a reevaluation of their circumstances and a transformed subjective perception of their own power to bring about change. This subjective transformation was conditioned by new forces at work—namely, migration and the woman's vote. Both appeared to signal a break with the past.

Thousands upon thousands of migrants of voting age annually left states in the Deep South where voting restrictions had been most repressive. That these states simultaneously imposed the greatest economic and social restrictions upon blacks accounts for the eagerness of so many to uproot and search for greater economic and political freedom. Unskilled and semiskilled jobs in the northern cities offered wage rates considerably higher than the southern agricultural work in which most of the migrants previously had been engaged. Florette Henri's study of the Great Migration observes that "to farm workers in the South who made perhaps $.75 a day, to urban female domestics who might earn from $1.50 to $3.00 a week, the North during the war years beckoned with factory wages as high as $3.00 to $4.00 a day, and domestic pay of $2.50 a day." Despite the higher cost of living and the drastic reduction of factory employment for blacks after the war ended, the urban North's higher wages and greater economic opportunity relative to the South continued to lure hundreds of thousands of black migrants throughout the 1920s. For black southern migrants, the ballot box, no less than heightened employment opportunity and greater social mobility, served as a badge of freedom from the Jim Crow world they fled.[9]

When viewed as an indicator of voting behavior, employment suggests its positive role within the critical mix of urban opportunities that encouraged black women's political integration. Women constituted a sizable proportion of the northern black labor force. In 1920 the black married women's employment rate stood at five times that of white married women. In the largest northern cities in 1930 between 34 and 44 percent of black households had two or more members employed. Moreover, successive waves of migrants contributed to the growth of economic and social differentiation within the black urban community. The appearance of a black male and female elite composed of lawyers, educators, physicians, ministers, and entrepreneurs reflected a leadership ever mindful of black political interests and the importance of voter mobilization for the realization of those interests.[10]

Harold Gosnell indicates the political consciousness of black women in his classic *Negro Politicians* (1935), the earliest systematic study of urban black political behavior. More attentive to women than subsequent works by social scientists, Gosnell's several studies of Chicago politics were written in the 1920s and 1930s when the implications of woman's recently acquired right to vote were more consciously observed. Gosnell notes that black women "shared with their men folks an intense interest in politics." He reveals that in the 1923 local election relatively fewer black women than white used the antisuffragist argument as an excuse for not voting. While Gosnell does not dwell on the political mobilization of black women, he clearly acknowledges their importance in augmenting the black vote: "The huge increment in the absolute number of the estimated eligible colored voters between 1910 and 1920 was due largely to the adoption of woman suffrage in 1913 and to the flood of newcomers after 1914."[11] The conflation of woman's suffrage and black urban migration made possible greater political opportunity and leverage for blacks as a group. It also served to broaden black women's perceptions of their own influence and activism. Throughout the 1920s black women leaders, far from abandoning the electoral process, envisioned themselves in politics to stay.

The Black Press and Women's Political Consciousness

The black press served as an important vehicle for promoting the political concerns of black women. Varying in form from lengthy informative articles to mere blurbs, its news announced and promoted organizational activities and noteworthy persons and events rarely covered by the white press. Its pages featured the election or appointment of blacks to prominent and, just as often, quite obscure positions from across the nation. Papers such as the *Chicago Defender, New York Age, Pittsburgh Courier, Norfolk Journal and Guide,* and *Baltimore Afro-American* served not only their local markets but a national one hungry for "race news." The *Chicago Defender,* which had the largest readership of all, is often cited for its influential role in the Great Migration out of the South during World War I. The importance of the black press did not go unrecognized by campaigning politicians. Robert L. Vann, editor of the *Pittsburgh Courier,* was appointed chairman of the publicity committee of the Colored Voters' Division of the Republican National Committee during the 1928 presidential race. Claude A. Barnett, of the Associated Negro Press, was secretary. In fact, the Hoover forces enlisted practically every black news editor on this committee.[12]

Black newspapers frequently reprinted or cited each others' stories along with those from such national magazines as the National Association for the Advancement of Colored People's *Crisis,* the National Urban League's *Opportunity,* and the National Association of Colored Women's *National Notes.* Through the Associated Negro Press important news releases were syndicated in the different papers. Hanes Walton draws attention to the historical role of the black press as a transmitter of political culture—as an agent of political socialization. Its role combated the negative black images presented in the white newspapers. The black press provided the counter orientation to forces affirming black inferiority. In its coverage of women's political activities during the 1920s, it also reinforced the idea of a prominent place for women within black political culture.[13]

The *Baltimore Afro-American,* a weekly during the twenties, concisely illustrates the way black women's political activities were portrayed. In the four issues appearing between 17 September and 16 October 1920, twenty-two articles covered one or another aspect of women's newly acquired right to vote. Three articles presented congratulatory responses by various black and white notables to the ratification of the Nineteenth Amendment. One noted the appointment of Lethia Fleming as head of the black woman's advisory committee to the Republican party during the 1920 presidential campaign, and another covered Daneva Donnell's appointment as the only black on the first all-woman jury in an Indianapolis court. Five articles exposed the thwarted attempts of black women to register in the southern states. Nine reported political activities among women in Baltimore. Most of these activities took the form of meetings and rallies. One of the local stories featured the results of the first two days of registration in the city's predominantly black wards and concluded that "where the colored women are organized as in the 14th and 17th wards their registration nearly equals that of the men."[14]

The final three articles on black women and politics were represented in the column "A Primer for Women Voters," written by Augusta T. Chissell. Chissell, a member of the Colored Women's Suffrage Club of Maryland, designed the weekly column as a tool for political education. Readers were invited to write in questions, which she in turn answered.

> Question—There are some men who will be up for election in this state in November who have bitterly opposed woman suffrage. What do you think of supporting them?

> Answer—Women should weigh this question very carefully, not from the standpoint of resentment but from the standpoint of justice.[15]

Question—What is meant by party platform? And where may I go to be taught how to vote?

Answer—Party platform simply means what either candidate promises to do after he is elected. The Just Government League is conducting a polling booth at its headquarters. . . . You may go there and become acquainted with the whole order of things. You will also do well to attend the Thursday night meetings of the YWCA under the auspices of the Colored Women's Suffrage Club.[16]

Black women leaders used the press to voice their political concerns and programs throughout the 1920s.

Clubwomen and Politics

Even more important to the political activism of black women leaders was the organizational network already in place on the eve of the ratification of the Nineteenth Amendment. The National Association of Colored Women (NACW) had stood at the forefront of the suffragist cause among black women and became the logical springboard for future political work. By the 1920s the NACW came to represent the organizational hub of the women's club movement. It was the linchpin that united hundreds of women's clubs throughout the nation in shared goals and strategies of social service and racial uplift. Divided into districts, under which fell regional and state federations, the elaborate infrastructure established linkages and opened channels of communication between women's organizations in every black community in America. Through its national leaders and committees, plans were centralized and tasks divided. Through its biennial meetings and national magazine, *National Notes*, the NACW functioned as a clearinghouse, providing a communications network for the dissemination of information and the promotion of collective action.[17]

NACW members, largely of middle-class status, received wide coverage in the black press, and the leaders at the state and national levels were, more often than not, prominent in other progressive groups with respect to racial advancement, such as the National Association for the Advancement of Colored People (NAACP), the National Urban League, and the Commission on Interracial Cooperation. Some of these same leaders also occupied places of influence within major religious organizations.[18] Tullia Hamilton's study of the first generation of NACW leaders reveals their privileged status vis-à-vis the great majority of black women. Most of the 108 leaders identified by Hamilton had been born in the South between 1860 and 1885 but had settled in the North a decade or two prior to the onslaught of migrants during the World War I period. Unlike the masses of uneducated and unskilled black women who were restricted to domestic service and other menial employment, NACW leaders enjoyed the benefits of education and greater employment opportunities. Approximately three-quarters of them were married. Most of the clubwomen were career-oriented; about two-thirds were teachers, and a small proportion were clerical workers and entrepreneurs.[19]

In 1926 the NACW boasted affiliated clubs in forty-one states. Its vast scope and influence prompted Mary McLeod Bethune, national president between 1924 and 1928, to remark: "Every organization is looking to the National Association of Colored Women for assistance in some line of advancement."[20] One organization that looked to the NACW for assistance was the Republican National Committee, which had enlisted outgoing president Hallie Q. Brown to direct its voters' drive among black women in 1924.[21] During the presidential race, the NACW's usual social service activities took a back seat to intense partisan politics. Its magazine, *National Notes,* encouraged political consciousness, shared ideas and strategies, and followed the progress of the campaign in the various states. The selection of Brown, NACW president between 1920 and 1924, reflected the Coolidge forces' recognition of her command over hundreds of thousands of black women.

As director of the Colored Women's Department of the Republican National Committee, Brown built her campaign network on the foundation of the existing regional, state, and local structures of her organization. She recruited her army of workers from the NACW's leadership—from women who had already proved their organizing abilities. Brown appointed Maria C. Lawton of Brooklyn to head the eastern division of the Republican campaign and Myrtle Foster Cook of Kansas to head the western division. At the time, Lawton held the presidency of the Empire State Federation, the association of clubwomen at the New York state level. Her mobilizing ability had been responsible for the tremendous growth in affiliated clubs since 1912. As organizer of the Empire State Federation in 1912 and president from 1916 to 1926, Lawton had expanded the number of clubs from a small concentration mostly in New York City and Buffalo to 103 in all parts of the state. Cook afforded the Republican party another strong mobilizing resource. As editor-manager of *National Notes,* she transformed the nationally read magazine into a political organ for the Republican party.[22]

Black women's Republican clubs sprang up everywhere, led by clubwomen already in the vanguard of the civic and political affairs of their communities. The overall operation included precinct captains; ward chairmen; city, county, and district chairmen; together with state chairmen and national organizers and speakers. Each state chairman developed circulars and bulletins for her own territory and sent reports to the black press "with accurate and encouraging accounts of women's campaign activities." Their reports highlighted their cooperation in a cause that "has added to our lives a rich chapter of wider friendships with the mutual confidence born of close acquaintances and hard work." The campaign had a tremendous psychological effect on these workers, who described it as rewarding and personally enriching. Lawton referred to the campaign's emotionally fulfilling impact on black women workers. It became an "outlet for their pent up aspirations and ambitions to be counted as integral parts of the body politic."[23]

Reports from state chairmen and organizers revealed optimism in politics and a belief that their efforts were decisive to the electoral outcome. Although the Republican party had utilized black women leaders in the past, the election in 1924 involved their participation in more extensive, visible, and official ways. The state organizer from Rhode Island typified this attitude in her reflections on Coolidge's victory: "I am sure the work our colored women did during the last campaign helped materially to give the National ticket the large plurality it had in the Nation." Campaign reports indicate that there were hundreds of Coolidge–Dawes clubs and meetings in halls, churches, fraternal lodges, schools, homes, and on the streets. House-to-house canvassing appeared to be their most effective strategy, but bringing in speakers of national reputation also received a good response. Other interesting techniques were employed. The organizer for upstate New York outlined the following activities based on her tour of Elmira, Rochester, Auburn, Buffalo, and Niagara Falls:

> We found the forming of Coolidge–Dawes Clubs using pledge cards an excellent method for tabulating new voters and bringing in old voters who were in the class of stay-at-homes. Another method found very effective was Block Captains in every district. These, with their assistants, kept a list of new voters and registrants of old, in turn. These were given to the chairman of our Get-Out-The-Vote Committee. This committee of twenty women did Yeoman work on election day; no voter of their district was omitted.[24]

Organizers in West Virginia noted the role of special circular letters—one with an appeal to the ministry and another to women directly. West Virginia women also found the question box helpful in identifying issues of concern to voters. The report from Minnesota relied heavily on mass distributions—pamphlets entitled "Important Information for All Legal Voters," "Register Today" cards, and sample ballots. Iowa was the only state to cite telephone canvassing among its techniques. Kentucky reported its least successful technique—getting women to answer mail questionnaires.[25]

Florie Pugh of Oklahoma City held instructional meetings in the evenings and lectured on how to organize a precinct and district, the duty of a precinct committeewoman, how to poll, how to get the voters registered, new voters, the necessity of voting by 10:00 A.M. on election day, and why black people should be Republicans. Lillian Browder, a precinct captain in Chicago, stressed the need to discuss gender politics in house-to-house canvassing. She found that women exhibited greater responsiveness and interest when told of legislation and political affairs vital to home life. Thus Browder talked to women about laws that touched upon their lives—for example, the Child Labor Law, the Pure Food Act, and the law regulating working hours for women—and she associated passage of this legislation with the Republican party.[26]

The presidential race of 1924 and Coolidge's ultimate victory reinforced a growing sense of political efficacy among black clubwomen. They interpreted their role as crucial to Republican victory, and they expected a continued relationship with the party and with political organizations among white women. Estele R. Davis, who served on the Speakers' Bureau during the Coolidge campaign, captured the perceived interconnection between the club movement and political participation:

> How little have we realized in our club work for the last twenty-five years that it was God's way of preparing us to assume this greater task of citizenship. I often wonder what would have happened without our organized club work which has not only trained us for service, but has created a nation-wide sisterhood through which we know the outstanding women of each state who are able to serve our race in the time of need.[27]

The National League of Republican Colored Women

Throughout the summer of 1924 women came to value the need for permanent organization at the state and national levels. In some states political clubs had operated since the adoption of women's suffrage, but in most the presidential campaign had spurred the desire for continued political work. Mamie Williams (Mrs. George S. Williams) and Mary Booze, both NACW women and also the Republican national committeewomen from Georgia and Mississippi, respectively, urged the practicality of uniting black women's Republican clubs in a national organization.[28] On 7 August 1924, hours after the adjournment of the biennial meeting of the NACW, Williams and Booze reconvened a number of the clubwomen for the purpose of forming the National League of Republican Colored Women (NLRCW). Booze and Williams were named honorary presidents, and the official roster also included Nannie Burroughs of the District of Columbia, president; Sue M. Brown (Mrs. S. Joe Brown) of Iowa, vice-president; Daisy Lampkin of Pennsylvania, treasurer and chairman of the Executive Committee; Mary Church Terrell of the District of Columbia, treasurer; and Elizabeth Ross Haynes, parliamentarian. These women were well known for their visibility in political affairs and for their work with the NAACP and the Urban League.[29]

The NLRCW sought to become a permanent political force among black women, adopting the slogan, "We are in politics to stay and we shall be a stay in politics." It distinguished its goals from those of the NACW and other groups that adopted partisan political activities on a temporary basis and specifically at election time.[30] While endorsing the Republican National Committee's appointment of Hallie Q. Brown as director its Colored Women's Department during the presidential campaign, the members of the NLRCW criticized the NACW for abandoning its nonpartisan image and expressed disapproval of its heavy coverage of the Republican campaign through the pages of *National Notes*.

There are several explanations for this reaction on the part of women whose roles as leaders overlapped both organizations. First, the NLRCW ensured continuation of a partisan political emphasis by taking it out of the hands of an organization whose intentions and objectives had historically been to unite black women of all affiliations and persuasions in the work of social service. The NACW's Citizenship and Legislative departments constituted integral parts of the organization's "lifting as we climb" philosophy, but they were designed to inspire civic duty and legislative study for race and sex advancement, not to advance specific political parties.[31] Second, rivalries existed between women. Some of the NLRCW women claimed that certain NACW leaders had used their positions during the presidential campaign to further their own selfish personal ambitions.[32] On the other hand, individuals in the NLRCW might have perceived the new organization as a stepping-stone to a political appointment that had bypassed them in the last campaign.

The crossover of membership in the two organizations invariably blurred distinctions. Reports of campaign activities during the 1924 election were sent to Nannie Burroughs as well as to the NACW officials working with the Republican National Committee.[33] Members of the NLRCW often quoted the slogan of the NACW when confirming their attendance at an event sponsored by the former. In 1928 Daisy Lampkin wrote to Burroughs of Lethia Fleming, an outstanding Republican organizer in Ohio and leader in both the NLRCW and the NACW: "She seemed to confuse the two National organizations, but I made it clear to her that they are in no way connected." By 1926 the NACW, while continuing to urge women's political participation, had relinquished overt partisanship to the NLRCW.[34]

In 1924 Burroughs sent out a questionnaire to black women leaders throughout the country. The exact number mailed is unknown, and only twenty-three responses appear to exist—representing respondents from eleven states. Though this number is too small to be representative of black women in general, the questions themselves reveal the major concerns of the NLRCW in the building of its program. Some of the questions read as follows:

—Did you hear of any vote selling among the women?
—What is being done to educate women as to the value of the ballot?
—Are Negro women taking an active part in local politics?
—Is it true that a number of women failed to register and vote because their husbands are opposed to woman suffrage?
—Did you hear that Whites who hire servants tried to influence their votes?
—What is the general attitude of the White women of your city toward Negro women since they have suffrage?
—Give the names of Congressmen from your State who have poor records on the Negro question.
—What should the Negro demand of the incoming administration?
—Who are the women in your city and State best qualified to organize political clubs to assist in the work?[35]

Meeting in Oakland in August 1926, the Executive Committee of the NLRCW presented its goals and intentions in the form of a resolution, copies of which were sent to Sallie Hert, a vice-chairman of the Republican National Committee and head of its Women's Division, and to the Associated Negro Press for distribution in all the black newspapers. The resolution requested formal and active affiliation with the Women's Division of the Republican National Committee and offered the services and counsel of its state leaders in the upcoming congressional election.[36]

The response by the Women's Division of the Republican National Committee could not have been more promising. Sallie Hert invited Burroughs to represent the NLRCW at its first national conference of women leaders. Eighty-five women from thirty-three states met in Washington between 12 and 14 January 1927 to discuss their role in the Grand Old Party. The group included national committeewomen (Booze of Mississippi and Williams of Georgia being the only other blacks present), state vice-chairmen, and Republican women's clubs. The women discussed a variety of issues of direct interest to Burroughs: maintaining on ongoing functioning organization throughout the year, women's representation in the party organization, problems of organizing and fund raising, party integrity and loyalty, and overcoming differences among Republican women.[37]

Burroughs was among the seventy-five women to visit the White House and receive greetings from President and Mrs. Coolidge. She also heard talks by Secretary of War Dwight Davis and Secretary of Commerce Herbert Hoover. The high point for Burroughs was the opportunity to address the gathering. She began her remarks by stating: "I'm glad to be able to give a touch of color to this meeting. No political party in America is 100 percent American without this touch of color." She proceeded to inform her seemingly quite receptive audience of the work of her own organization.[38]

In May 1927 the NLRCW called its own three-day conference in Washington, D.C. Leaders from twenty-three states came together to discuss their concerns and to hear high-ranking officials in the GOP discuss issues and policies. Included among the array of speakers were Sallie Hert of the Women's Division, Virginia White Speel of the Republican Central Committee for the District of Columbia, Secretary of Labor James Davis, and Secretary of the Interior Hubert Work. Feelings of efficacy continued to run high among black women.[39]

The presidential election in 1928 witnessed NLRCW leaders in prominent campaign positions. Lampkin, chairman of its Executive Committee, was appointed by the Republican high command to direct the mobilization of black women voters in the East. Burroughs had wanted the position, but her nonvoting status as a District of Columbia resident operated to her disadvantage. An eloquent orator, Burroughs was appointed to the National Speakers' Bureau and became one of the most highly sought-after speakers on the campaign trail.[40] Many NLRCW members journeyed to Washington for the inauguration of President Hoover. They rejoiced in his victory. It seemed just as much their own.

By 1932 the honeymoon had ended between the black women and the Republican party. The Depression focused the attention of black leaders, male and female, on questions of economic survival. The Hoover administration had little to say to most Americans, least of all to blacks, on economic relief. Burroughs, like most blacks, continued to support Hoover in that year, but with increasing criticism of his policies toward the black poor. Nor had the party of Lincoln fared well in its civil rights record during Hoover's term. In the throes of unprecedented economic suffering, blacks came to challenge their traditional loyalty to the party responsible for their emancipation from slavery.[41]

Black leaders denounced the various racist actions of the Hoover administration. Hoover's efforts to "lily-white" the Republican party in the South, his segregation of the Gold Star Mothers, and his nomination of an avowed advocate of black disfranchisement to the Supreme Court incurred the wrath of black leaders throughout the nation.[42] However, for members of the NLRCW, the unhappy alliance between blacks and the administration was foreshadowed as early as Hoover's inauguration. In March 1929 the chairman of the Inaugural Charity Ball requested that Burroughs retrieve tickets "accidentally" sent to black women workers in the Hoover campaign. Burroughs acquiesced to Republican wishes for a segregated ball, but not without registering the protest of her coworkers: "It is not easy for me to get the others reconciled to embarrassments for which they are not responsible. One has said already, 'They use us in the crisis and humiliate us at will.'" In 1932 Sallie Hert's replacement by Lena Yost as head of the Republican Women's Division further alienated the black women. Yost lacked the sincerity and interest that had characterized Hert's relationship with the NLRCW. Burrough's correspondence discloses increasing frustration with the party's solicitation of her support at election time, while at all other times treating her suggestions with "silent contempt."[43]

The League of Women Voters

Another organization that captured the interest of black clubwomen during the 1920s was the League of Women Voters (LWV). Lines of communication remained open between the NACW and black units of the LWV. Although individual blacks held membership in some of the predominantly white state leagues, separate black leagues operated in Oakland, San Francisco, Los Angeles, Chicago, and St. Louis. Delegates from the Oakland, Chicago, and St. Louis groups were represented at the league's national conferences in the 1920s. They were also represented on the state boards of the California and Illinois leagues. Leaders of the black leagues were, at the same time, leaders of their state federated clubs—the constituent members of the NACW.

Hettie Tilghman, leader among black California women in the LWV, referred to the overlap in membership for the NACW and her state's two black leagues, the Alameda County League of Colored Women Voters and the San Francisco Colored League. She cited their political activities from the dual role of federated women and League of Women Voters. Delilah Beasley, active member of the NACW and the Alameda County League of Colored Women Voters, devoted press coverage to both in her column "Activities among Negroes," which ran in the white daily, the *Oakland Tribune.* On 25 November 1925, she announced the interest of the Alameda County League of Colored Women Voters in the observance of World Court Day, scheduled for 17 December. Her column also cited an article written by the president of the Alameda County league for the magazine of the NACW. The article, which had appeared a few weeks earlier in *National Notes,* praised the California state league and the national League of Women Voters for their efforts in securing the passage of specific legislation affecting women and children.[44]

On 6 October 1920, the St. Louis LWV organized a "Colored Committee" to bring before the larger body racial concerns related to education, health, child welfare, and citizenship. Nine years later, B. F. Bowles headed the committee, which functioned as an important liaison between the league and the large black female population in St. Louis. Under Bowles's leadership, the committee assumed a number of projects: gathering data on southern election laws and policies, offering lectures on pending legislation, holding citizenship schools, providing scholarships to black students, entertaining national league officers at gatherings in the black community, forming junior leagues among black girls, and contributing financially to the budget of the St. Louis league. In an editorial in the *St. Louis American,* Carrie Bowles, another black league member and member of the NACW, praised the St. Louis league for being "one of the very few leagues in the U.S. in which the colored members enjoy every privilege of the organization on terms of absolute equality." Writing in the national magazine of the NACW in 1928, Bowles again praised her city league for sending a black delegate to the eighth annual conference.[45]

Illinois black clubwomen also contributed to the work of the league. In 1926 the Illinois state League of Women Voters elected a black woman, Margaret Gainer, to membership on its Board of Directors. Gainer, also a member of the Illinois State Federation of Colored Women's Clubs, directed the latter's citizenship department, which included the program of the Illinois LWV. The Illinois State Federation constituted an extensive network of black clubwomen. It organized in 1899 and by 1926 comprised 92 clubs with 2,074 members divided into three districts: the Chicago and Northern, the Central, and the Southern.[46]

Several clubwomen in the Chicago area were league members. The Douglass League of Women Voters, the black unit of the league in the city, was headed by Irene Goins, a leader of the Illinois State Federation as well. On 18 June 1924, Florence Harrison of the national league met with the black members to discuss their plans for the development of citizenship schools. Attached to Harrison's report were the black women's plans for the national "Get-Out-the-Vote Campaign." In addition to incorporating the campaign into the citizenship program of the Illinois State Federation of Colored Women's Clubs, the Douglass league proposed:

1. Frequent meetings open and advertised, to be held in the Community Center . . . to which the League hopes to rally colored women from a large surrounding territory. At its meetings there will be from time to time (a) Ballot demonstrations (repeated); (b) Importance of registration (repeated); (c) Issues of the Campaign; (d) Candidates' meetings.
2. A system of home teaching for the colored women who cannot come to the Community Center . . . will be carried into the homes by members of the Douglass League.
3. "Excursion tickets" indicating a trip to the polls and asking "have you voted?" will be hung on tags on the doors in the neighborhood.[47]

News of league activities encouraged politically minded black women to seek membership in either separate or integrated units. However, they were usually discouraged. Delilah Beasley of Oakland expressed her frustration in establishing a black league in Los Angeles. Her efforts encountered prejudice throughout the state and especially in Los Angeles itself. Urging the formation of "full Colored Leagues" and auxiliaries to the white leagues, she stressed the need for black women to develop their own leadership, separate from whites so that "they do not antagonize the members of the White league by their presence." Yet Beasley did not demur from strongly recommending black representation on the general state board.[48]

On the other hand, Ohio black women opposed racial separatism in league work. Members of the Ohio Federation of Colored Women's Clubs had hoped to integrate various local leagues, after Sybil Burton, president of the state league, addressed their meeting and solicited their cooperation in mobilizing the vote. Ohio black women were ripe for participation. Burton admitted that the Ohio league found it unnecessary to execute educational classes for black women in the state because J. Estelle Barnett, a league member and black woman editor of the newspaper *In the Queen's Garden,* had used her paper to disseminate information on ballot marking and the necessity for voting.[49]

With no uniform guidelines, Burton preferred to leave the decision of accepting blacks to the individual leagues, whose racial policies varied by community. Oberlin accepted blacks freely and equally. Zanesville received black members but made them unwelcome at their luncheons and other social gatherings. The Toledo league sought advice from the national league when black women desired membership. The general consensus of the Toledo league was against integration, but it encouraged black women to form their own separate units. The Cincinnati league likewise contemplated the formation of an all-black unit. The reply from the national league tended to be discouraging in every way. While acknowledging that a few of the states had black leagues and a few others actually integrated individual black women into their ranks, Anne Williams Wheaton, press secretary, asserted: "Those who have expertise in this matter think it is far better not to encourage organizations of colored Leagues."[50] Rather than formal organization, the national league sought to address black issues through its Committee on Negro Problems—the name later being changed, at the request of black members, to the Committee on Interracial Problems.

In 1921 the committee was formed in response to a petition by southern black women whose suffrage rights were denied. Interracial in composition, the committee included representatives from states where "the colored vote is a material and accepted fact." Its purpose was to implement educational and citizenship training programs, not to augment black league membership. Although plans were devised by its three successive chairwomen, Julia Lathrop (1921), Minnie Fisher Cunningham (1921–25), and Adele Clark (after 1925), the small committee left little in the way of accomplishment. A questionnaire was sent out to the states in 1927, but most did not reply, nor did the states that responded always do so thoughtfully and accurately. The ineffectiveness of the committee was evidenced in the infrequency of its meetings, all of which occurred informally at the national conventions and did not carry over into the interim period.[51] By the end of the decade the League of Women Voters had lost, largely by its own choice, the potential for being an important mobilizing force among black women.[52]

Conclusion

At the dawning of the 1930s, blacks found themselves on the brink of a political transition that would greatly accelerate in the next five years. The more dramatic collective action of blacks during the Depression and their strategic placement in the New Deal hierarchy have overshadowed the contribution of the previous decade to their political mobilization and increased political leverage. The ratification of the Nineteenth Amendment in 1920 lent significant impetus to black women's interest in the American political process, although the continuing legacy of racism conditioned the nature and extent of their participation. The racist policies of the National American Woman Suffrage Association continued in the 1920s with its successor organization, the League of Women Voters, to discourage black participation. Black women leaders, while organizing their own separate organizations, encountered racism from the very elected officials for whom they campaigned. Yet black women's discontent and frustration with white women's organizations, with the Republican party, and with a racist society in general during the 1920s translated not into an abandonment of politics but into the emergence of new leaders, alliances, and strategies.

In 1936, when the majority of black voters shifted to the Democratic party, the unswerving Republican allegiance of such leaders as Nannie Burroughs and Mary Church Terrell no longer won the applause of the black electorate. The Democratic party had shed its long-worn garb of white supremacy, its image as the party of the Solid South, segregation, and black disfranchisement. Under Franklin Roosevelt's New Deal, the Democrats came to be perceived as the party most receptive to black opportunity. Mary McLeod Bethune's visibility in the Roosevelt administration and Crystal Bird Fauset's membership on the Democratic National Committee expressed both the continuation of women's political activism and shifting opportunities for black women leaders. In 1932 Bethune sat on the Board of Counselors of the Women's Division of the Republican National Committee with such notable Republican stalwarts as Mrs. Theodore Roosevelt and Mrs. William Howard Taft. In 1936 she presided over Roosevelt's Black Cabinet.[53] Bethune's shifting allegiance symbolized the changed mood of the black electorate and, certainly not least of all, woman's prerogative to change her mind.

Notes

1   Florette Henri, *Black Migration* (Garden City, N.Y.: Anchor/Doubleday, 1975), 50–59, 68–69; Martin Kilson, "Political Change in the Negro Ghetto, 1900–1940," in *Key Issues in the Afro-American Experience,* ed. Nathan I. Huggins, Martin Kilson, and Daniel M. Fox (New York: Harcourt Brace Jovanovich, 1971), 2:175; Jacqueline Jones, *Labor of Love, Labor of Sorrow: Black Women, Work, and the Family from Slavery to the Present* (New York: Basic Books, 1985), 152–60.

2   Harold F. Gosnell, *Negro Politicians* (Chicago: University of Chicago Press, 1935), 13–92, 180–90.

3   Paul Lewinson, *Race, Class, and Party: A History of Negro Suffrage and White Politics in the South* (New York: Oxford University Press, 1932); Harold F. Gosnell, "The Negro Vote in Northern Cities," *National Municipal Review* 30 (1941): 264–67, 268; St. Clair Drake and Horace R. Cayton, *Black Metropolis* (New York: Harper and Row, 1945); James Q. Wilson, *Negro Politics: The Search for Leadership* (New York: Free Press, 1960); Kilson, "Political Change in the Negro Ghetto"; Ira Katznelson, *Black Men, White Cities* (Chicago: University of Chicago Press, 1976).

4   See, for example, Rosalyn Terborg-Penn, "Discontented Black Feminists: Prelude and Postscript to the Passage of the Nineteenth Amendment," in *Decades of Discontent: The Women's Movement, 1920–1940,* ed. Lois Scharf and Joan M. Jensen (Westport, Conn.: Greenwood Press, 1983), 261–78.

5   Aileen S. Kraditor, *The Ideas of the Woman Suffrage Movement, 1890–1920* (Garden City, N.Y.: Anchor/Doubleday, 1971), 138–71; Rosalyn Terborg-Penn, "Discrimination against Afro-American Women in the Woman's Movement, 1830–1920," in *The Afro-American Woman: Struggles and Images,* ed. Sharon Harley and Rosalyn Terborg-Penn (Port Washington, N.Y.: Kennikat Press, 1978), 17–27; Paula Giddings, *When and Where I Enter: The Impact of Black Women on Race and Sex in America* (New York: William Morrow, 1984), 129–30, 165–69, 177, 218–20.

6   "The Woman Voter Hits the Color Line," *Nation,* 6 October 1920.

7   Terborg-Penn, "Discontented Black Feminists."

8   Ida B. Wells-Barnett, *Crusade for Justice: The Autobiography of Ida B. Wells,* ed. Alfreda M. Duster (Chicago: University of Chicago Press, 1970), 345–53.

9   Henri, *Black Migration,* 52–80; Doug McAdam, *Political Process and the Development of Black Insurgency, 1930–1970* (Chicago: University of Chicago Press, 1982), 77–81; Gosnell, *Negro Politicians,* 16–19.

10   Henri, *Black Migration,* 54–55; Kilson, "Political Change in the Negro Ghetto," 170–82; Jones, *Labor of Love,* 162–80, 190, 193–94.

11   Interview with Harold F. Gosnell, 17 March 1986, Bethesda, Maryland; also see Gosnell, *Negro Politicians,* 15, 19, 374; Gosnell, *Machine Politics: Chicago Model* (Chicago: University of Chicago Press, 1968).

12   "Negro Republican Campaign Division," *Norfolk Journal and Guide,* 11 August 1928; also see press release, "Republican National Committee, for Release Thursday, 2 August 1928," Nannie Helen Burroughs Papers, Library of Congress.

13   Hanes Walton, *Invisible Politics: Black Political Behavior* (Albany: State University of New York Press, 1985), 51.

14   See the *Baltimore Afro-American* for "Equal Rights League Sends Congratulations to Women"; "Colored Woman Sits on Jury," and "Committee of Women Named—Mrs. Lethia G. Fleming of Cleveland Is Approved Chairman," 17 September 1920; "Women Hit Color Line," 8 October 1920; "Vital Meeting—Come and Hear Why We Should Stand by Our Race Candidate," 1 October 1920; "Women Spring Big Surprise," 24 September 1920; "Women Make Good," 16 October 1920.

15   Augusta T. Chissell, "A Primer for Women Voters," *Baltimore Afro-American,* 24 September 1920.

16   Ibid., 1 October 1920.

17   National Association of Colored Women, *National Notes*, April 1923, 18; Charles H. Wesley, *The History of the National Association of Colored Women's Clubs, Inc.: A Legacy of Service* (Washington, D.C.: National Association of Colored Women's Clubs, 1984), 55–100.

18   Giddings, *When and Where I Enter*, 107–9, 135–36; Evelyn Brooks, "Religion, Politics, and Gender: The Leadership of Nannie Helen Burroughs," *Journal of Religious Thought* 44 (1988): 7–22.

19   Tullia Kay Brown Hamilton, "The National Association of Colored Women" (Ph.D. diss., Emory University, 1978), 53.

20   Mary McLeod Bethune, "Biennial Report of the National Association of Colored Women, 1924–1926," *National Notes*, July and August 1926, 3–4.

21   Hallie Q. Brown, "Republican Colored Women of America," *National Notes*, December 1924, 1.

22   "Report from the Western Division and the Eastern Division," ibid. December 1924, 2–3; Wesley, *History of the National Association*, 91, 201–2.

23   "Report," *National Notes*, December 1924, 2–3.

24   Ibid., 4.

25   Ibid.

26   Gosnell notes a higher percentage of women precinct captains in the black wards. His roster showed as much as one-fourth of the captains to be women in the black Third Ward in Chicago. See Gosnell, *Machine Politics*, 61–63; "Campaign Experiences," *National Notes*, January 1925, 13–14.

27   "Campaign Experiences," *National Notes*, January 1925, 13.

28   In the southern states black disfranchisement and Democratic hegemony combined to effectively nullify any hope of amassing votes for state and local office, but posts within the Republican party as well as federal patronage positions were still available to southern Republicans by virtue of the votes they delivered at the national conventions. The influence of black Republicans and their female officeholders such as Mary Booze of Mississippi and Mamie Williams of Georgia lay largely with the ability of the black Republican organization in each southern state to achieve recognition at the Republican National Convention. Termed "black and tans," these organizations distinguished themselves from the Republican organizations with overwhelmingly white membership— "lily-whites." The influence of the black and tans was keenly felt in the presidential nominations of McKinley in 1896, Taft in 1908 and 1912, and Hoover in 1928. See Lewinson, *Race, Class, and Party*, 170–76; V. O. Key, *Southern Politics in State and Nation* (New York: Vintage Books, 1949), 286–89; and Hanes Walton, *Black Republicans: The Politics of the Black and Tans* (Metuchen, N.J.: Scarecrow Press, 1975), 133–35.

29   "Minutes of the Temporary Organization of the National League of Republican Colored Women, 7 August 1924," and "Minutes of the Subsequent Meeting of the NLRCW, 11 August 1924," Burroughs Papers.

30   "The National League of Republican Colored Women," *National Notes*, July 1928, 10.

31   Mary Church Terrell, "An Appeal to Colored Women to Vote and Do Their Duty in Politics," *National Notes*, November 1925, 1; idem, "What Colored Women Can and Should Do at the Polls," ibid., March 1926, 3.

32   Mazie Griffin to Burroughs, n.d.; Mamie Williams to Burroughs, 5 January 1925, Burroughs Papers; also see "Departments and Their Functions," *National Notes,* January 1925, 2.

33   See, for example, Frannie Givens, of the East-End Colored Women's Political Clubs, to Burroughs, 20 October 1924; Mary E. Gardiner, of the Women's Republican Club of Cambridge, to Burroughs, 21 October 1924; Susan B. Evans, state director of colored women's activities of the St. Paul, Minn., Republican State Central Committee, 22 October 1924; Elizabeth L. Gulley, of the Colored Division, Wayne County Coolidge–Groesbeck Club, Republican State Central Committee of Michigan, 29 October 1924; and Mrs. Charles W. French, Parliamentarian, Kansas State Federation of Colored Women, to Burroughs, 30 October 1924, Burroughs Papers.

34   However, the NACW's *National Notes* carried articles promoting the National League of Republican Colored Women. See "Republican Call," April 1927, 6; "The National League of Republican Colored Women," July 1928, 10.

35   "Colored Women in Politics Questionnaire," Burroughs Papers.

36   "Meeting of the Executive Committee of the National League of Republican Colored Women, Oakland, Calif., 6 August 1926"; and Burroughs to Mrs. Alvin Hert, 11 August 1926, Burroughs Papers.

37   "Summarized Report of the Conference of the Republican National Committeewomen, State Vice-Chairmen, and State Club Presidents, January 12, 13, 14, 1927," Burroughs Papers.

38   Ibid.

39   "G.O.P. Women from Twenty-three States in Session," *Afro-American* (Washington ed.), 21 May 1927.

40   Daisy Lampkin to Burroughs, 2, 17 July, 8 October 1928; Lampkin to Mrs. Paul FitzSimmons, 8 October 1928; Lampkin to Fellow Republican, 17 July 1928, Burroughs Papers.

41   Nancy J. Weiss, *Farewell to the Party of Lincoln: Black Politics in the Age of FDR* (Princeton: Princeton University Press, 1983), 3–33.

42   Gold Star Mothers were the mothers and widows of men buried in Europe who had died in active service during World War I. The U.S. government sponsored the women's passage to Europe in order to place wreaths on the graves. Black Gold Star Mothers were sent over in separate and blatantly inferior ships (ibid., 16–17).

43   Burroughs to Mrs. John Allen Dougherty, Chairman, Inaugural Charity Ball, 2 March 1929; Burroughs to Sallie Hert, 19 August 1929, 14 April 1930; Susie M. Myers to Burroughs, 3 May 1932; Burroughs to Mrs. Ellis Yost, 27 September 1932, 30 June 1934; Burroughs to Maude B. Coleman, 8 September 1936, Burroughs Papers.

44   Delilah L. Beasley, "Activities among Negroes," *Oakland Tribune,* 22 November 1925; Hettie Tilghman, "What the Study of Legislative Work Has Meant to Our Group," *National Notes,* November 1925, 3; "Miss Delilah L. Beasley," ibid., March 1928, 8; Beasley, "California Women Preparing for Biennial Convention," ibid., April 1926; Belle Sherwin to Sybil R. Burton, 31 March 1925, League of Women Voters Papers, Library of Congress (hereafter cited as LWV Papers).

45   Mrs. B. F. Bowles and Mrs. E. C. Grady, "The Colored Committee of the League of Women Voters of St. Louis: The First Nine Years"; Gladys Harrison to Ruth Siemer, 14 October 1929; Siemer to Beatrice Marsh, 30 June 1930; and Marsh to Adele Clark, 2 July

1930; also written sometime in the late 1920s but undated is Carrie Bowles, "Defends League of Women Voters," *St. Louis American;* clipping and aforementioned letters in LWV Papers; Carrie Bowles, "Women Voters' National League," *National Notes,* May 1928, 15.

46   "Mrs. Elizabeth Lindsay Davis . . . ," *National Notes,* April 1926, 1; "Illinois Federation of Colored Women's Clubs," ibid., July 1926, 24.

47   "Excerpt from letter from Florence Harrison to Miss Sherwin dated 18 June 1924" and attached page, "Sent by Mrs. Rich to B. S. 1924," LWV Papers.

48   Delilah L. Beasley to Mrs. Warren Wheaton, 23 March 1926; Wheaton to Beasley, 25 March 1926, LWV Papers.

49   Sybil R. Burton to Belle Sherwin, 27 March 1925, LWV Papers.

50   Agnes Hilton to Gladys Harrison, 9 August 1928; Anne Williams Wheaton to Hilton, 17 August 1928, LWV Papers.

51   "Special Committee on Inter-Racial Problems, 17 April 1934"; "Report of the Special Committee on Interracial Problems to the Board of Directors, December 1927"; "National League of Women Voters—Report for the Committee on Negro Problems, April 1924–April 1925"; and "Committee on Negro Problems—Chairman Mrs. Minnie Fisher Cunningham, 11 July 1924," LWV Papers.

52   See, for example, a letter written by a black woman, Eva Nichols Wright, of Washington, D.C., to Belle Sherwin: "In reply to the question 'Are colored women of your city interested as members, in the League of Women Voters or the National Woman's Party? If not, why not?' The replies with two exceptions were negative. To the question, 'To what extent do white women and colored women work together politically?' The same negative reply was received with three or four exceptions, and many expressed themselves as being discouraged." Wright to Sherwin, 25 April 1927, LWV Papers.

53   Republican National Committee, Women's Division, *Organization News,* 22 October 1932, 2, in Burroughs Papers; Weiss, *Farewell to the Party of Lincoln,* 137–48, 180–84.

From Progressive

Republican to

Independent Progressive:

The Political Career of

Charlotta A. Bass

Gerald R. Gill

Expressing his support for Charlotta A. Bass's vice-presidential campaign as the Progressive party nominee in 1952, the noted singer-activist Paul Robeson characterized Bass as "a sturdy, fighting colored woman whose life has been a forthright struggle for the rights of her people to live in peace as first-class citizens. She's a great woman, is Mrs. Bass—tried in struggle, forgiving, understanding in the fight for unity of black and white—a true Sojourner of Truth."[1] Robeson's words of praise were a fit capsulization of the life and career of Charlotta Bass. For over forty years, Bass enjoyed a public career as varied and as distinguished as that of any of her black contemporaries, male or female.

From 1910 to 1952, she was first a reporter, then managing editor, and later business manager, editor, publisher, and owner of the *California Eagle*, the oldest black newspaper on the West Coast. During these very same years, she involved herself in campaigns to abolish restrictive covenants in housing and to end job discrimination in Los Angeles County. Moreover, she was actively involved in most of the major civil rights and Pan-Africanist organizations from the heyday of the progressive era to the eve of the more active phase of the civil rights movement. Few of her contemporaries could match Bass's involvement in as many varied organizations: the Universal Negro Improvement Association, the National Association for the Advancement of Colored People (NAACP), the National Negro Congress, the International Labor Defense, the Council on African Affairs, the Civil Rights Congress, the Sojourners for Truth and Justice, and the Progressive party of the late 1940s to mid 1950s. In addition, she was a political activist on the local, state, and national level. Though her candidacy as the vice-presidential nominee of the Progressive party has been studied, there has been only fleeting examination of her political career prior to the late 1940s. In keeping with the overall theme of this book, Bass has been selected as a case study of how one black woman sought to devise new forms of black political participation in the years from 1931 to 1965. Bass should not be viewed as atypical, unusual, or particularly original in terms of her striving for political empowerment. She sought in successive stages of her journalistic and political career to mobilize black voters in Los Angeles to use the ballot "intelligently" to fight for adequate black representation in local and state government. Recognizing that one or two "black faces in high places" did not necessarily lead to overall improvement in the status of blacks, Bass then called upon black voters in Los Angeles to select candidates on the basis of their stance on issues and not on the basis of race or party affiliation exclusively. And, after having encouraged black voters to avail themselves, when and where possible, of either of the two major parties, she was not reluctant to criticize *each* or to criticize *both* for their indifference to the concerns of blacks. Thus Bass came to encourage black voters to support alternatives to the political status quo. Nothing was sacred in terms of political identification and political affiliation, she maintained, as the issues transcended the party or parties.

In spite of Bass's prominence as a journalist, community activist, and office seeker, details of her life and career before moving to Los Angeles in 1910 remain sketchy, incomplete, and often contradictory. Throughout her career Bass provided little information about her date and place of birth, her family background, her education, or her prior socialization in the East.[2] Moreover, the origins of Bass's involvement in politics differed from those of her female contemporaries such as Mary McLeod Bethune, Mary Church Terrell, Daisy Elizabeth Adams Lampkin, Elizabeth Ross Haynes, or Irene McCoy Gaines. Unlike these women who sought appointed positions in state and local governments, in presidential administrations, or in the colored or Negro divisions within the Republican or Democratic parties, or who ran for political office on their own accord, Bass's involvement in politics did not arise directly out of an involvement in the club movement activities undertaken by many black women.[3] Bass was an ardent supporter of California and national campaigns on behalf of suffrage for women, but her support was usually expressed in the pages of the *Eagle* rather than through her participation in women's organizations. Thus she played little, if any, role in local clubs and groups such as the Sojourner Truth Club (which established a home for black working women), the Women's Day Nursery Association, the Eastern Star, the Harriet Tubman Red Cross Auxiliary, the Soldiers' and Sailors' Welfare Commission, the California Colored Women's Federated Club, and the Women's Civic and Protective League.[4]

Instead, Bass, throughout her career, would involve herself in leadership positions, often outside the "female sphere." Her independence was attributable both to her unwillingness to accept a subordinate role defined by gender and to the woefully small number of black professionals in Los Angeles before World War II. Thus, by temperament, by career choice, and by her residence in a city having so few black spokespersons, she was able to be heard and to be taken seriously in ways that several of her black female contemporaries who lived in communities where leadership roles based upon gender were more fixed could not.[5]

As one of the very few black women nationwide to exercise significant editorial control over a newspaper, Bass chose to use the pages of the *Eagle* to advance strategies and policies that she perceived would benefit black males and females alike. Although the *Eagle* was never the ardent proponent of black migration from the South that the *Chicago Defender* was, Bass, upon gaining control of the paper following the death of the founder-publisher in 1912, recognized that the *Eagle* would have to become a more forceful advocate for the city's growing black population. Inasmuch as Los Angeles' black population had doubled from 7,599 in 1910 to 15,579 in 1920, the *Eagle* sought to increase the political and economic clout of black Angelenos and to combat racial discrimination throughout Los Angeles County.[6]

Although the *Eagle* was not unwilling to make use of attention-grabbing headlines to publicize abuses experienced by area blacks, neither Charlotta Bass nor her publisher husband Joseph Bass, contrary to the criticism of one of their contemporaries, made use of "irrational propaganda" and "harping on the injustices." The *Eagle* was a staunch Republican organ and implored party leaders at the state and local level to reward black loyalists through patronage and to enact legislation ensuring political and civil right for blacks. While Joseph Bass was a party stalwart, Charlotta Bass was more reform-oriented and less beholden to the established party leadership. Both Basses were enthusiastic backers of Frederick M. Roberts, who was the first black person elected to the California State Assembly in 1918 as the representative from the interracial

Central Avenue district of Los Angeles. However, Charlotta Bass was the more active supporter of women who sought elective office and a more likely supporter of progressive-era politicians who sponsored social reforms. In 1917 she endorsed the candidacy of Estelle Lawton Lindsey, a white female Republican candidate for the city council who successfully campaigned on a plank "to discourage racial and religious discrimination" and to restore honesty in city government.[7]

Although celebratory of Lindsey's victory and later success in office, Bass no doubt shared the sentiments of those "discontented black feminists" who concerned themselves more with racial issues than gender considerations in the 1920s.[8] Bass did not involve herself in efforts to organize a local chapter of the League of Women Voters, but she involved herself primarily in efforts during the 1920s and 1930s to improve the political, social, and economic status of persons of African descent throughout the diaspora. Bass was always a staunch supporter of and participant in Pan-Africanist activities. As early as 1919, following the recently concluded Pan-African Congress held in Paris, Bass was one of the two American blacks and the only woman on the five-member committee set up to make public to activists in the Americas and throughout the African continent the proceedings and recommendations of the congress.[9]

In 1920 she, along with her husband and several other prominent residents of Los Angeles, organized the city's chapter of the Universal Negro Improvement Association (UNIA). Charlotta Bass's role in the Garvey movement was not without power, as within a year she was elected "lady president" of the branch. Yet, as Theodore Vincent and Emory Tolbert maintain in their studies of the Marcus Garvey movement on the West Coast, Bass's position was that of co-equal to her male counterpart, Noah Thompson. Both Bass and Thompson made the branch's policy decisions, and in 1921, after each had become disillusioned by the news of the failure of Garvey's Black Star Line project, they made the decision for the Los Angeles branch to withdraw from the parent organization and to reconstitute itself as the Pacific Coast Negro Improvement Association.[10]

Owing in large part to Bass's and Thompson's leadership, the Los Angeles branch had always been one of the most financially supportive branches as well as one of the most independent branches of the UNIA. Although Bass was a firm adherent of the concept "Race First" in the 1920s, she would not allow her support of Garveyism to preclude cooperation and involvement with black spokespersons of differing views. She was also a member of the local branch of the NAACP and sought, however unsuccessfully, to minimize the airing of ideological differences between the NAACP and the UNIA leadership. Moreover, before her rift with the UNIA headquarters, Bass attempted to have the local branch involve itself in efforts to seek the release of Eugene Debs, the head of the Socialist party then imprisoned in a federal penitentiary for having violated the Sedition Act of 1917, and to involve itself in more general activities in support of workers, black and white. Even after her break with the national headquarters of the UNIA, Bass was not as publicly outspoken as was her husband in voicing opposition to Marcus Garvey.[11]

From the mid-to-late 1920s until the outbreak of World War II, Bass stepped up her personal involvement in local campaigns against racial discrimination and segregation and in efforts to publicize how a more independent black populace could use its growing political clout to advance its interests. For Bass, the interwar years indicate her continuing maturation in political thought. Although she was still convinced that progress for blacks in Los Angeles and throughout the nation would come from their intelligent and aggressive use of the vote, Bass on occasion would counsel her readers not to rely solely upon the Republican party. Still a registered Republican, as she would be until the late 1940s, Bass began to propose strategies of political independence. As early as 1921, Bass expressed her occasional disaffection with the policies of Republican presidential administrations. Accusing the Republicans of doing little to justify the continued overwhelming majorities that they received from eligible black voters, she poignantly indicated that "all the good men are not in the Republican party nor are all of the bad men in the Democratic party." Following her own advice for the presidential election of 1928, Bass, describing herself as "sufficiently politically mature," concluded that her fellow Californian and then secretary of commerce Herbert Hoover was not fit to be president. Instead, she endorsed Governor Al Smith of New York and "went all out" on his behalf.[12]

While criticized in some sections of black Los Angeles for her editorial support of Smith and Franklin D. Roosevelt in 1932, Bass's support of Democratic candidates was limited solely to the presidential elections. She continued to support her longtime friend and fellow Republican, Assemblyman Frederick M. Roberts, and she also supported Republican gubernatorial candidates.[13]

Bass's votes against Hoover in 1928 and 1932 were largely cast out of personal differences with the Republican nominee rather than from political or ideological differences. Thus she was not necessarily a supporter of the Roosevelt administration's first New Deal. On occasion she would comment favorably upon several New Deal initiatives that were putting many black residents of Los Angeles back to work, but her comments were intended to prod the Republican establishment in Sacramento to appoint more blacks to advisory and administrative positions in the state bureaucracy. Although Republican politicos in the state capital did not respond to her calls for patronage, Bass, following the death of her husband in 1934, sought to depict herself as ever the loyal Republican. Keenly aware of the changing sentiments and attitudes among black Angelenos, sentiments that led residents of the Sixty-second Assembly District to vote Frederick Roberts out of the office and elect Democrat Augustus Hawkins, Bass saw black support of the Democrats as short-lived. In a reversal of her earlier arguments on behalf of black political independence, she now reverted to the traditional black Republican defense that theirs was the party of Lincoln. "His [the black man's] name may be on the Democratic roll," she wrote in 1936, "but his heart, mind and conscience are with the party that gave him freedom and endowed him with the rights of a full-fledged American citizen." Indeed, she asked rhetorically in another editorial, "Can a Negro be an honest-to-goodness Democrat?"[14]

Returning to the Republican partisanship more characteristic of her late husband, Bass now eschewed her previous political pragmatism. Yet her political ambivalence and her unwillingness to acknowledge that perhaps black voters in Los Angeles, in California, and throughout the United States were looking for something more tangible than increased patronage for stalwart black Republicans were symptomatic of the attitudes of many within the black elite. Like Bass, many of these individuals had supported the Landon–Knox ticket because of their aversion to voting for a party historically beholden to white southerners.[15]

Bass had misread the mood of black voters in 1936, but her support of Wendell Willkie in 1940, while partly motivated by her class status as a member of the Los Angeles black elite, was more principled than blindly partisan. As a member of a class that was not thoroughly ravaged by the effects of the Depression, Bass could continue her crusading efforts on behalf of civil rights. Thus she remained a critic of the Roosevelt administration's inaction in terms of pursuing antilynching legislation and its overall reluctance to embrace civil rights issues as legitimate political concerns. Whether Willkie was her first choice for the Republican nomination remains unclear; however, Bass was favorably enough impressed with his statements against racial discrimination and racial violence that she accepted the position of western regional director of the Republican standard bearer's campaign.[16]

Although black voters in Los Angeles were becoming more Democratic in sentiment and allegiance in the 1930s, Bass remained personally popular with many residents of the city's central and south-central districts. Her political views notwithstanding, Bass had repeatedly shown herself to be a forceful advocate on behalf of civil rights and economic opportunities for blacks. Ever mindful of the social and economic needs of her paper's readers, Bass continued to serve as a crusader for the city's black residents. In the early 1930s she had emerged as a leading promoter of the city's "Don't Buy Where You Can't Work" campaigns. Throughout the decade she campaigned repeatedly against police brutality and segregated housing.[17]

During World War II, Bass, along with the Reverend Clayton Russell, emerged as coleaders of the Los Angeles Negro Victory Committee, a local organization that sought full participation for blacks in the defense industries. In public cooperation with Russell and in the pages of the *Eagle*, Bass championed the committee's goals. By the war's end in 1945 the committee had attained jobs for black women in the shipbuilding industry, had increased the number of accessible job training centers for black women in Los Angeles County, had attained an increased number of housing units for black workers in the defense industries, had been able to get the Fair Employment Practices Committee to hear complaints of racial discrimination in several local unions, and had won concessions from the Los Angeles Rapid Transit Company to hire black male and female conductors. In addition, Bass had taken part in successful campaigns to end job discrimination at the Los Angeles General Hospital, the Southern California Telephone Company, and the Boulder Dam construction project. And, on national civil rights issues, Bass used the editorial pages of the *Eagle* to call for the abolition of the poll tax.[18]

The World War II years were to have a considerable effect upon Charlotta Bass. Up until the mid 1940s she had been fairly conventional in terms of her political attitudes and sentiments. Though firmly convinced of the need for blacks to use the ballot to bring about improvements in their political and social station, and though supportive of protests to bring about some improvements for black workers, she nonetheless had exhibited an abiding faith in the efficacy of the two-party system. Bass was still a registered Republican, but she began to express more consistent support for Democratic candidates for local and statewide office. In part, such support stemmed from her embracing of the Roosevelt administration's handling of the war and its proposals for the postwar world. In explaining her support for Roosevelt in 1944, Bass later recollected that he "had not just advocated social, civic, and educational reforms in government, but he had started to make them real." Thus Bass organized the Republican Women for Roosevelt Committee and, along with Mary McLeod

Bethune, served as one of the leaders of the National Non-Partisan Committee for the Reelection of Roosevelt.[19]

The years from 1945 to 1954 witnessed her renewed interest in Pan-Africanist affairs as well as her fundamental transformation in political views. Ever interested in the end to colonialism in Africa, Bass became active in the Council on African Affairs. Throughout the late 1940s she served as a member of the national board, one of the very few women named to a leadership position in the organization. Bass's more striking transformation was in her political ideology and sentiments. She would abandon her faith in the two-party system and involve herself in a search for newer and more viable forms and expressions of political empowerment and political protest. Such a transformation on Bass's part, one taking place within the space of three years, would find the *Eagle* editor abandoning many of her prior beliefs and assumptions about the nature of the American political system and the roles black Americans were to play in terms of shaping their and the nation's political destiny.

Bass, like black political activists throughout the North, the Midwest, and the West, sought to mobilize the growing clout of black voters in urban centers and in industrial states in 1945. Knowing that Los Angeles' black population had nearly doubled during the war years and was still largely confined to the central district, she and her allies tried to invigorate a "critical mass" of black voters to make use of their political potential. Supportive of nearly all efforts by black males to pursue elective office in Los Angeles, in January of 1945 she was herself selected to run for a district seat on the city council. Perhaps emboldened by the successful efforts by first Adam Clayton Powell, Jr., and later Benjamin J. Davis, Jr., in winning council seats in New York City, she attempted to replicate their strategies. Bass made use of her long-established contacts with black religious leaders, civil rights activists, labor organizers, and businesspersons to fashion an alliance supportive of her candidacy. In her campaign against the incumbent Carl Rasmussen, she stressed the need for the local government to address the concerns of job security, adequate wages for workers, construction of homes, construction of additional health and recreational facilities, lowering of utility rates for consumers, and better delivery of public services. Enjoying endorsements from most of the district's black ministers and by several black women's organizations—the Women's Political Study Club, the Sojourner Truth Club, and Alpha Kappa Alpha sorority—Bass, "the people's champion for jobs and security," forced Rasmussen into a runoff. Although she was optimistic of victory, she was defeated in the runoff.[20]

Bass masked her disappointment behind the terse assessment: a campaign of "such a rosy beginning and such a sad ending." While Bass looked to the successful campaigns of Powell and Davis in Manhattan and to those waged by black insurgents in Chicago as models, her campaign was doomed in part by the nature of Los Angeles politics. She could not depend upon a system of proportional representation, a system that aided each of the two black candidates in New York. And, despite relying upon friends and erstwhile supporters in the district, Bass's candidacy was hampered by the historic absence of precinct or ward-by-ward organizing that characterized urban districts elsewhere.[21] Others, however, attributed Bass's defeat to her willingness to work with black and white Communists, and her advocacy of postwar proposals deemed radical. To the *Los Angeles Sentinel*, which supported the Bass campaign, the "Communist slant" was key and was "a test-worthy question in the minds of the Negro electorate." *The Los Angeles Tribune*, a more conservative black newspaper, had been a longtime critic of the editor of its journalistic rival. The newspaper described Bass as "the pawn of vested interests" and "a party liner, and it does not seem to matter which party—Republican, Democratic, or Communist."[22]

Undaunted by such criticism of her allies or her positions, Bass, nevertheless, was clearly troubled by the direction of American domestic and foreign policy during the early years of the Truman administration. It seemed to Bass that the unelected president was making decisions in direct contradiction to those Franklin Roosevelt would have pursued. Thus editorials in the *Eagle* were harshly critical of both the Truman administration's policies toward the Soviet Union and its support of the major imperialist powers.[23]

Such concerns led Bass to consider supporting candidates in terms of their stands on issues, not in terms of race or ethnicity, and caused her to reassess her previously held view of black political solidarity on behalf of any black candidate, particularly one running against a white candidate. Although Charlotta Bass had supported former Republican assemblyman Frederick M. Roberts in all of his previous campaigns for office, she could not support his 1946 effort to unseat liberal Democratic congresswoman Helen Gahagan Douglas. Douglas had compiled a domestic record, particularly in terms of working on behalf of blacks in her district and of speaking out on national civil rights issues, that Bass found impressive. Furthermore, the *Eagle* editor viewed the Democratic incumbent as someone equally as distrustful as she of the Truman administration's foreign policy. Repeatedly, Bass stressed that Douglas was more "progressive and forward-looking" than Roberts, that the challenger was "an unwitting Republican puppet," and that blacks should display a political sophistication in which they viewed candidates in terms of their stands on the issues.[24]

Owing in some part to the *Eagle*'s urging, black residents of the district gave their support to Douglas. But other black commentators, supportive of Roberts, chided those black Democrats who either deferred automatically to white office seekers or who were "more loyal to a political party than to [themselves]." And, in a thinly veiled reference to Bass, one *Sentinel* analyst wrote that Roberts's defeat "will stand forever as a monument of shame to a people who constantly clamor for equal opportunities, but fail too often to take advantage of such opportunities when offered."[25] The *Tribune* was more biting in terms of its assessment of Bass's support of Douglas. With no love for Bass, the *Tribune* intoned:

> There is a great similarity between Mrs. Bass and Representative Douglas. They were both suspected of getting their convictions by mimeographed dispatch weekly from one of the lesser hierarchy of Stalin. . . . Mrs. Bass, as we know, is a political chameleon who already appears to have a pink tinge at present because she is fairly blushing with popularity. Mrs. Bass shifts her loyalties on an average of once every four years and she is never known to give any logical reasons for her actions. First, Hoover the Republican; then Roosevelt the Democrat; later Langdon [*sic*], Republican, and Stalin-Whatchamacallit.[26]

In spite of the *Tribune*'s "Red-baiting," Bass's support of Douglas—certainly no Stalinist—led her to reject any call that blacks refrain from associating politically with persons deemed "soft on communism" or Communists themselves. Following the exacerbation of tensions between the United States and the Soviet Union throughout 1947, Bass became more disillusioned with the status of the two-party system. With politicians such as Douglas now supporting the administration's initiatives, Bass severed her remaining ties with both Democrats and Republicans. Neither party, she contended, should be seen as articulating the interest of blacks in terms of civil rights and the interests of Americans in general in terms of a less belligerent foreign policy. Thus Bass rejected the concept of black voters serving as the "balance of power" in campaigns between Democrats and Republicans. Instead, she came to support strategies of black political independence in which black voters and would-be office seekers would participate in the establishing of viable alternatives to the two-party system.[27]

Such sentiments led Bass to support Henry Wallace's campaign for the presidency on the Progressive party ticket in 1948 and to pursue elective office herself as Progressive party candidate in 1950 and 1952. For Bass, the insurgent Wallace was a natural—a former vice-president during Franklin Roosevelt's third administration who had also become disenchanted with the Truman presidency. Thus she involved herself in efforts to ensure that Wallace would appear on the California ballot in 1948 and used the office of the *Eagle* to register prospective voters.[28]

Throughout 1948 Bass wrote and spoke on behalf of Wallace and the newly established Independent Progressive party (IPP) of California. "The Wallace platform," she wrote in one *Eagle* editorial, "is a solid platform upon which the people of America can stand unafraid." Fully supportive of the party's calls for increased cooperation between the two leading superpowers and unwavering support for civil rights and civil liberties at home, Bass was a national committeeperson from California, cochair of the national Women for Wallace organization, and secretary of the credentials committee for the 1948 convention. Ever the political optimist, Bass was not dismayed by Wallace's poor showing in the general election. Finding many hopeful signs in the national and statewide campaigns, Bass, like other party stalwarts, "decided to dig in harder than ever, and to force the Democrats, again in power, to keep the promises made in the campaign, and to work harder than ever for victory in 1950 and '52."[29]

With renewed fervor, Bass, having resigned from the Republican party in 1947, devoted herself to Progressive party activities. She served as first vice-chair of the Los Angeles County Central Committee of the IPP, member of the California Central Committee of the party and chair of the southern California branch of the party. She continued to speak out on behalf of civil rights and the need for legislation mandating fair employment practices. Once the Korean War broke out in late June of 1950, Bass emerged as one of the foremost black critics of American involvement in what she perceived to be a civil war. And Bass was most critical of Henry Wallace's support of the Truman administration's decision to send troops to the Korean peninsula.[30]

The question of American participation in the Korean War badly divided the Progressive party, a split from which it never recovered. Nevertheless, Bass still perceived the party as the only political party committed to peace and justice and once again sought elective office. In 1950, she secured the party's nomination as its candidate for the Fourteenth Congressional District seat, the seat being vacated by Bass's former ally Helen Gahagan Douglas in her unsuccessful campaign against Richard Nixon for the United States Senate seat in California. Bass, as always, campaigned vigorously on a platform of full civil rights for blacks, the repeal of the Taft–Hartley Act, the McCarran Act, a negotiated end to the Korean War, and the beginning of negotiations between the heads of both the United States and the Soviet Union.[31]

Bass clearly recognized that she did not have the widespread support from black voters she had enjoyed five years earlier in her campaign for city council. Yet, in constant appeals to district voters, Bass maintained that she, not her Democratic rival Sam Yorty, could accomplish more "to bring to fruition your desires for peace and security." And, while putting forth her position on the issues, she also resorted to a tactic that she herself had rejected in 1946—her candidacy as a black person. On election day 1950, Bass stated to district voters, "You will have an opportunity to do what you have said for a long time you want to do—send a Negro to Congress." Bass did not see her position in 1950 as antithetical to her 1946 position. District voters in 1950 could choose between a true progressive concerned with the welfare of blacks and working people or a Democrat who would take their concerns for granted. The issues in 1946 and in 1950 were similar, Bass reasoned, and voters should choose the "progressive candidate," not the candidate beholden to the political status quo. Although her assembly district voted "almost solidly" for her, Bass was swamped in other parts of the congressional district. Nevertheless, Bass could write, "I shall continue my fight for decent living conditions and for all the little plain people in the city and in the United States of America."[32]

True to her words, Bass continued to "fight." As the Korean War continued with no apparent resolution in 1951 and 1952 and as the public mood turned hostile toward the Truman administration, the Progressive party sought to offer an alternative to the policies of the Democrats and Republicans in 1952. Charlotta Bass was not the first choice for the vice-presidential nomination by many black and white male leaders and spokesmen within the party. However, she quickly emerged as an acceptable choice as the running mate for the presidential nominee, Vincent Hallinan. Whereas Hallinan as a labor lawyer might attract workers and civil libertarians disenchanted by the administration's failure to overturn the Taft–Hartley Act and the McCarran Act, party leaders hoped Bass might attract votes from civil rights proponents and from blacks and women in general.[33]

As was her campaigning style, Bass was an energetic and spirited spokesperson for the Progressive party. Stressing the unique opportunity that voters had in electing a black woman to national office, Bass emphatically called for an end to the Korean War, for "peaceful understanding and peaceful relations" among the superpowers, for American recognition of the People's Republic of China, and she criticized the continued American support of oppressive and imperialist regimes. She ardently endorsed the party's domestic plank, one calling for an extension of the Truman administration proposals for a national housing program, a national health insurance plan, increased spending for public schools, and repeal of the Taft–Hartley Act. Throughout her campaign Bass stressed those domestic issues in which the Progressive party was far in advance of either the Republican party or the Democratic party—full civil rights for blacks, equal employment opportunities for blacks and other minorities, equal pay for women, an increased minimum wage for workers, and repeal of the Smith, McCarran, and McCarran–Walter acts.[34]

In spite of the dismal showing nationwide by the Hallinan–Bass ticket (0.2 percent of the popular vote), Bass could find a silver lining. As in the 1948 and 1950 campaigns, the Progressive party in 1952, Bass stressed, had committed itself to those principles and issues that would improve the quality of life of all Americans and that would lead to a more peaceful and more just world. Both the Republicans and Democrats, Bass always maintained, would have to address the ever-consistent principles of the Progressive party, "Peace and Equality."[35]

Bass's vice-presidential campaign would effectively conclude her political career. Having sold the *California Eagle* in 1951, Bass retired from the national limelight. However, she continued to involve herself in the California branch of the Independent Progressive party and in the activities of the Civil Rights Congress until her advanced age and declining health in the early 1960s prevented any further active involvement on her part.[36]

Over the course of her journalistic, civic, and political career, Charlotta Bass was an outspoken advocate on behalf of civil rights, economic opportunity, and social justice at home and on behalf of self-determination for and peaceful relations among the world's people. Throughout most of her career, Bass had maintained a strong and abiding faith in the American two-party system. Abuses could be redressed and more positive changes could come about, she reasoned, if restraints against blacks of voting age were lifted and if black voters used their ballots to reward friends and to ensure their empowerment. At the same time Bass recognized that electoral politics was not the only means to empowerment. Through protest and through tireless advocacy, she strove for equality and increased opportunities for blacks in Los Angeles and throughout the United States. Ever the crusader, she constantly encouraged her supporters to continue the struggle: "You can't win by giving up."[37]

Though her critics would chastise her as opportunistic, inconsistent, or manipulative in politics, Bass viewed herself as a pragmatist in her early career and an idealist in her later career. Yet such shifts, she maintained, were not duplicitous ones. To Bass, the issues of equality and justice were paramount, and their attainment transcended permanent party allegiances. Whether as a registered Republican, an occasional supporter of Democratic party candidates, or as a Progressive party stalwart, she did show the capability to evolve and to mature as a political activist as the circumstances and situations warranted. However, though her affiliation with political institutions changed and her commitment to the two-party system was fundamentally altered, Bass never wavered in her basic commitment as a journalist and political activist to help "shape the destiny of a community, a race and a nation."[38]

Notes

1 "Address at the National Convention of the Progressive Party, Chicago, July 4, 1952," in *Paul Robeson Speaks: Writings, Speeches, Interviews, 1918–1974*, ed. Philip S. Foner (Secaucus, N.J.: Citadel Press, 1978), 322–23.

2 Biographical information on the early years of Charlotta Bass is scarce. In her autobiography, *Forty Years: Memoirs from the Pages of a Newspaper* (Los Angeles: Charlotta A. Bass, 1960), she does not give her date and place of birth and mentions in all-too-brief passing that she lived on the East Coast and migrated to California for health reasons. Her biographical entry in the 1928–29 edition of *Who's Who in Colored America* likewise contains no mention of date and place of birth but does mention that she was educated at Brown University, Pembroke Hall; Columbia University; and the University of California (Joseph J. Boris, *Who's Who in Colored America: A Biographical Dictionary of Notable Living Persons of African Descent in America, 1928–1929*, 2d ed. [New York: Who's Who in Colored America Corporation, 1929], 23). Her profile was not included in the editions for 1930–32, 1943–44, and 1950.

During her 1952 campaign for the vice-presidency, Bass indicated that she was born in Little Compton, Rhode Island, and was sixty-two years old. Federal Bureau of Investigation reports on Bass, maintained from 1944 until her death in 1969, cited the records of the registrar of voters for the city of Los Angeles, which indicated that she was approximately ten to twelve years older than she professed. However, FBI agents were never able to ascertain her place of birth as the Rhode Island Public Health Department had "no birth data" concerning Bass (FBI Reports, 5 April 1944, 100–20874, 21 May 1953, 100–20874; reports in author's possession). Her obituary in the *Los Angeles Sentinel*, 17 April 1969, gave only fleeting reference to a Rhode Island place of birth and gave her age at death as ninety-four, suggesting an 1874 or 1875 date of birth. In their profile of Bass, Andrew Buni and Carol Hurd Green write that Bass was born in Sumter, South Carolina, and suggest an October 1880 birth date; although they write that Bass moved to Rhode Island before 1900, they provide no more information about her schooling (*Notable American Women: The Modern Period*, s.v. "Bass").

3 See the biographies of Bethune, Terrell, Lampkin, Haynes, and Gaines in *Notable American Women: The Modern Period*.

4 Delilah L. Beasley, *The Negro Trailblazers of California* (1919; rpt., New York: Negro Universities Press, 1969), chap. 18.

5   James Q. Wilson, *Negro Politics: The Search for Leadership* (New York: Free Press, 1960), 108.

6   Bass, *Forty Years*, 27, 28, 63; Lawrence B. de Graaf, *Negro Migration to Los Angeles* (San Francisco: R and E Research Associates, 1974), 10, 20–21.

7   Octavia B. Vivian, *The Story of the Negro in Los Angeles County* (1936; rpt., San Francisco: R and E Research Associates, 1970), 16–17; Bass, *Forty Years,* 39, 42, 63.

8   Rosalyn Terborg-Penn, "Discontented Black Feminists: Prelude and Postscript to the Passage of the Nineteenth Amendment," in *Decades of Discontent: The Women's Movement, 1920–1940,* ed. Lois Scharf and Joan M. Jensen (Boston: Northeastern University Press, 1987), 261–78.

9   Theodore G. Vincent, *Black Power and the Garvey Movement* (San Francisco: Ramparts Press, 1972), 56.

10 Ibid., 130, 198; Emory J. Tolbert, *The UNIA and Black Los Angeles* (Los Angeles: UCLA Center for Afro-American Studies, 1980), 51, 75–76.

11 Tolbert, *The UNIA,* 75, 92, 94; Vincent, *Black Power and the Garvey Movement,* 159–70.

12 James Adolphus Fisher, "A History of the Political and Social Development of the Black Community in California, 1850–1950" (Ph.D. diss., State University of New York at Stony Brook, 1972), 207–8, 221; Bass, *Forty Years,* 174–75.

13 Bass, *Forty Years,* 174–75.

14 Cited, as is, in Fisher, "Black Community in California," 230–34.

15 Nancy J. Weiss, *Farewell to the Party of Lincoln: Black Politics in the Age of FDR* (Princeton: Princeton University Press, 1983), 217–18.

16 Ibid.; Gerald R. Gill, "Win or Lose—We Win: The 1952 Vice-Presidential Campaign of Charlotta A. Bass," in *The Afro-American Woman: Struggles and Images,* ed. Sharon Harley and Rosalyn Terborg-Penn (Port Washington, N.Y.: Kennikat Press, 1978), 110.

17 Gill, "Win Or Lose—We Win," 110.

18 E. Frederick Anderson, *The Development of Leadership and Organization Building in the Black Community of Los Angeles from 1900 through World War II* (Saratoga, Calif.: Century Twenty-one Publishing, 1980), 85–104; Fisher, "Black Community in California," 248–49; *California Eagle,* 12 November, 2 December 1942.

19 Bass, *Forty Years,* 174–75; *California Eagle,* 28 September, 12 October 1944.

20 Fisher, "Black Community in California," 237, 240; Bass, *Forty Years,* 132, 174–75; *California Eagle,* 18 January, 8 March 1945.

21 Wilson, *Negro Politics,* 27, 108.

22 Bass, *Forty Years,* 133; FBI Files—Charlotta A. Bass, FBI Report, 6 July 1945, 100–20874.

23 FBI Files—Bass, FBI Report, 25 November 1946, 100–20874.

24 Fisher, "Black Community in California," 258–60; Helen Gahagan Douglas, *A Full Life* (Garden City, N.Y.: Doubleday, 1982), 242; Colleen M. O'Connor, "Imagine the Unimaginable: Helen Gahagan Douglas, Women, and the Bomb," *Southern California Quarterly* 67 (Spring 1985): 40–43.

25 Cited in Fisher, "Black Community in California," 261.

26 *Tribune* article, 6 April 1946, cited in FBI Files—Bass, FBI Report, 25 November 1946.

27 Bass, *Forty Years,* 141–42.

28 Ibid.

29 Ibid.; Fisher, "Black Community in California," 267–70; Curtis D. MacDougall, *Gideon's*

Army: The Decision and the Organization (New York: Marzani and Munsell, 1965), 2:451, 459.

30   FBI Files—Bass, FBI Report, 3 November 1950, 100–20874.

31   Bass, *Forty Years*, 173–75.

32   Ibid.

33   Gill, "Win or Lose—We Win," 111.

34   Ibid.

35   Ibid., 118.

36   Office memorandum, A. H. Belmont to D. H. Ladd, 25 May 1951, FBI Files, 100–297187–32; FBI Reports, 3 October 1955, 100–297187, 19 May 1964, 100–20874. Even after Charlotta Bass suffered a stroke in 1967, FBI agents continued to monitor her physical condition (FBI Report, 3 July 1967, 100–297187).

37   *Los Angeles Sentinel*, 24 April 1969.

38   Bass, *Forty Years*, 196.

Shining in the Dark:

Black Women and the

Struggle for the Vote,

1955–1965

Martha Prescod Norman

When disfranchised southern black women won the right to vote in the mid 1960s, it was the first time in the history of America that such women had voted. By 1960 the right of women to vote had been recognized for almost half a century, and at least two generations of southern black men had participated in the franchise beginning slightly less than 100 years earlier. Still, these southern black women had to engage in a serious and hard-fought battle in order to exercise this right.[1]

Southern black women waged this battle in a context where the franchise was a part of a larger struggle to topple the system of racial oppression dominating southern life. They struggled hand in hand with their male counterparts, who were also unable to vote and suffering under the same yoke of racial oppression.

On one hand, this struggle was an attempt to claim basic American citizenship. On the other hand, this effort was part of a radical social movement that modified certain overall notions of the suffrage and influenced the ways in which American women of all racial backgrounds thought about themselves. Most importantly, this movement demonstrated that people with grievances, but with little conventional power, could move to change the social and political terms on which their lives were based. It showed that efforts to bring about social change could be successful.

The nature of the struggle black women waged for the franchise in the South is encapsulated in the story of two women's attempts to register to vote. The first woman, Mrs. Georgia Mae Turner, a resident of Fayette County, Tennessee, went to register at the end of the summer of 1960. She had been considering this step all summer and had decided it was best to wait until she received her last sharecropping check in August. Her landlord, Mrs. Ethel McNamee, must also have given some thought to timing, because she waited to evict Mrs. Turner until a snowfall the following winter.[2]

That winter, Turner left the home she had lived in for thirty-eight years. Unable to find another place to live or work, she was among 700 other share-croppers evicted from farms in her home county of Fayette and the neighboring county of Haywood because they had registered to vote. Many of those evicted established a tent city on a black farmer's land in Fayette County, where they eked out a marginal existence throughout 1960 and 1961. They relied heavily on private support efforts to provide their basic needs. And they were occasionally harassed by nightriders shooting into their tents.[3]

The second woman, Mrs. Fannie Lou Hamer, is better known. Like Mrs. Turner, she was a lifelong sharecropper. In the summer of 1962, Mrs. Hamer was one of the first and among the few people in Sunflower County, Mississippi, to become involved in early civil rights activities there. On 31 August she traveled with seventeen other local residents to the registrar's office in Indianola, Mississippi, and applied to become a registered voter. She immediately found herself evicted from the Marlowe plantation where she and her husband had lived for eighteen years. Ten days later nightriders fired sixteen times into the Tucker home in Ruleville, Mississippi, where the Hamer family had moved temporarily. No one was injured in this shooting, but that same evening shots were also fired into the home of the McDonald family, injuring their daughter. The McDonalds regularly sheltered members of the Student Nonviolent Coordinating Committee (SNCC) who were engaged in civil rights organizing in Ruleville.

The Hamer family moved in with a relative in Tallahatchie County, but the nighttime harassment continued, so they returned to Ruleville, renting a home from a black woman. In December Mrs. Hamer traveled to Indianola to take the literacy test again. After identifying herself, Mrs. Hamer remembers telling the circuit clerk, "Now, you cain't have me fired 'cause I'm already fired, and I won't have to move now, because I'm not living in no white man's house. . . . [And] I'll be here every thirty days until I become a registered voter." Evidently the clerk did not relish the thought of repeated visits from Mrs. Hamer. This second application was successful, and she did indeed become a registered voter. However, neither she nor her husband, Pap Hamer, could find work or escape continued harassment. She commented:

> I passed that second test, but it made us become like criminals. We would have to have our lights out before dark. It was cars passing that house all times of the night, driving real slow with guns, and pickups with white mens in it, and they'd pass that house just as slow as they could pass it . . . three guns lined up in the back. All of that. This was the kind of stuff. Pap couldn't get nothin[g] to do.[4]

From childhood both Mrs. Hamer and Mrs. Turner had experienced the stringent life of southern Black Belt sharecroppers. Fannie Lou Hamer was the last child born into a family of twenty children during World War I. This large family enjoyed only a brief period of economic adequacy and independence as tenants when Fannie Lou was twelve years old. Otherwise, they lived as share-croppers. At one point, the family made their living by scavenging through already picked fields for scrap pieces of cotton. They were so poor that they could not afford to buy shoes and did this work with their feet wrapped in rags. At night, the young Fannie Lou slept on a cotton sack stuffed with dried grass.[5]

Mrs. Hamer's family struggled partly because there were so many members, Mrs. Turner's because there were so few. During World War I, Mrs. Turner's family was decimated by what she termed "typhoid-malaria." Mrs. Turner recalled, "We lost all of our peoples. Lost five brothers. All the brothers I had. . . . The fever left me, my mother and three other womenfolk." This female family lived a truly hardscrabble existence. Mrs. Turner remembers living without lights, plumbing, or adequate heating arrangements. She had neither sufficient clothing nor shoes for school, for inclement weather, or for colder temperatures. Her heavy-set mother sometimes loaned her own oversize dresses to her daughter to wear to school or made the girl dresses from the rough woven sacks used for gathering cotton.[6]

Almost all their lives, both women worked in the fields performing all of the most laborious tasks connected with farming. Mrs. Hamer began picking cot-ton with her family at the age of six, working twelve to fourteen hours a day. Mrs. Turner described similar hours of labor and other working conditions reminiscent of slavery. In words that echo Sojourner Truth, Mrs. Turner stated:

> I started working in the fields when I was eight. I been working fifty years. I chopped sorghum, corn, cotton, chopped anything. And I picked. When I first started picking cotton, I couldn't pick but fifty pounds a day,

but I kept inching up higher. I started plowing when I was fourteen years old 'cause we didn't have no man. I had to do all that plowing and that rough work to make a living. I have taken an axe and cut wood from about seven o'clock in the morning until it gets dark in the evening. You oughta see the logs that I've hauled.

I could hear the bell ring every morning at five o'clock for you to get up and go feed your mules. I'd be cooking breakfast when that bell rang. Then they ring it a second time and you go to the fields. You better be there at that hour. Then they'd ring the bell at twelve o'clock for you to come in to dinner and ring the bell at one to go back. You didn't need nobody to ring it for you in the evening.

My mother did all she could. Some days we had something to eat, some days we didn't. I remember on many days we have went to the blackberry bushes and picked berries off the bushes and taken them berries and washed them and mashed them up and get some corn bread and crumble them up in a bowl, eat them for dinner. Then go back to the field. Plow a mule until sundown.

Sometimes I would be sick and if you was sick you had to work just the same. You go to them for a doctor. "Unh-uh, I can't furnish you with no doctor. I can't furnish you with no doctor." You had to be just as low as you could be to get a doctor. Now that's the truth.[7]

Both women were quite conscious of the disparity between their material condition and that of their respective landowners. After describing her own life and home, Mrs. Turner spoke about the size and luxuriousness of her "boss-lady's" home, the house where only the owner, Ethel McNamee, and her daughter lived. Mrs. McNamee had taken Mrs. Turner on a tour of the house, displaying, in Mrs. Turner's words, "all her pretty what-she-haves." Mrs. McNamee also bought a new car every year and never allowed her black tenants to ride in it, even if they were sick and willing to bear the expense of being taken to a doctor. Mrs. Turner remarked, "She [Mrs. McNamee] told me she had the prettiest car on the road. She took me out there and showed it to me, got inside of it, just showing it, making light of me."[8]

Mrs. Hamer lived in a home in which the landlord had refused to make the plumbing operative. One day she was cleaning a functioning bathroom in the owner's home and was told that this particular bathroom was reserved for the family dog's use. She not only noted the unfairness of the situation but also recognized her family's contribution to the owner's life style. Concealing her anger until she arrived home, Mrs. Hamer told her husband, "Now they got a dog higher'n us. We workin' and got them settin' down. They settin' down off what we've done for them."[9]

Their gender did not protect these women from the hardest kind of living or the hardest kind of work. Further, their daily interactions brought them face to face with the hard realities of the social inequities present in their situations. Far from defeating them, however, the harshness of their lives seemed, in general, to strengthen them and, in particular, to prepare them for political struggle. Mrs. Turner explained how the difficulty of her everyday life eased her decision to take the risk of registering. She was not at all deterred when people told her she would have a hard time if she registered. "Well," she said, "I had a hard time before I registered. Hard times, you could have named me that—Georgia Mae Hard Times."[10]

Hard times didn't scare off Mrs. Hamer either; after she registered she worked all over Sunflower County doing citizenship education preparing others to register to vote. Then, early in the summer of 1963, on her way back from a voter registration workshop held in South Carolina, she and several younger women were arrested for entering the white side of the bus station at a rest stop in Winona, Mississippi. Her companions, Euvester Simpson, June Johnson, and Annelle Ponder, were all badly beaten in the Winona jail, as was Lawrence Guyot, when he went to find out what their bail was.[11]

Mrs. Hamer received a particularly savage going-over. After the jailers in Winona got information about her voting activities from Ruleville authorities, they forced her to lie face down on a bed while two male prisoners hit her with a wide piece of leather weighted with rock or lead. The first prisoner beat her until he was tired, and then the second took his turn while the first sat on her feet. They beat her, she recalled, until "my hands [which she had placed behind her back for protection] were as navy blue as anything you've ever seen . . . that blood, I guess and then beatin' it 'til it just turned black." Afterward, she noted, "I had been beat 'til I was real hard just like a piece of wood or somethin'. A person don't know what can happen to they body if they beat with something like I was beat with." The police had ordered the beating saying, "You, bitch, you we gon' make you wish you was dead." Remembering that day, Mrs. Hamer said, "And let me tell you, before they stopped beating me I wish they could have hit me one more lick that could have ended the misery that they had me in."[12]

Mrs. Hamer was undaunted, though permanently injured by this beating. Obviously familiar with the kinds of threats and intimidation that would follow, knowing also that her friend Medger Evers had just been killed for his civil rights activism, Mrs. Hamer left jail and took some time to recover partially from her injuries. She then returned to Ruleville and continued her involvement in voter registration and other civil rights activities as a field secretary for SNCC. Asked at this time how long she intended to keep doing this kind of work, Mrs. Hamer affirmed a lifelong commitment by putting words into a church/freedom song, saying, "if they ever miss me from the movement and couldn't find me nowhere, come on over to the graveyard, and I'll be buried over there."[13]

Why do this? Mrs. Turner's words again offer an explanation: "The reason I registered, because I want to be a citizen. . . . I registered so that my children could get their freedom. I don't figure it would do me no good." Then, capturing the entire system of southern racial oppression in an everyday social interaction, Mrs. Turner continued:

> I registered for my children so they won't have to stand at the back door like I stood in the rain and cold and Mrs. McNamee sat in the front until she got ready to come to the back to see what I wanted. I'd stand there and look up. Sometimes I'd be so cold, I'd be shivering and sometimes she would come there and talk to me through the screen and I would still be in the cold. I come over hard times; I come over hills and mountains. I wouldn't want none of my children, none of my friends to have to come through it—run, rocking and rolling over the hills and mountains that I come over.

After making this statement, Mrs. Turner demonstrated the depth of her level of commitment. James Forman tells us that Mrs. Turner "leaned over her grandson and stroked his head. 'I tell you child,' she whispered. 'I done made up my mind. I'm ready to go down right here on this tent ground. Not for my sake. I'm too old. . . . But for yours. I'm ready to go down, down right here on this tent ground. For you, Little Man.' "[14]

Concern for future generations and a willingness to risk life and limb were also touchstones of Mrs. Hamer's activism. The opposition she and other Mississippi activists encountered from the white community did not shake her determination to go on. Explaining why she felt no fear when she decided to apply to become a registered voter, Mrs. Hamer stated, "The only thing they could do to me was kill me and they'd been trying to do that a little bit at a time ever since I could remember." Later, Mrs. Hamer spoke at a Greenwood, Mississippi, mass meeting after brutal police attacks on civil rights demonstrators there. She questioned the intensity of white hatred, especially in light of that community's privileged position and the beneficial relationship that had existed between white and black Mississippians. She had made a similar observation to her husband on this relationship (quoted earlier in this essay). At the end of her speech she expressed her and her fellow activists' intention to keep on fighting:

> Why do they hate us so bad—and we've been working for them all of our lives? They go on riding in the fine cars while our children go to school barefoot and never got no automobile and we're not able to pay for one. Why do they try to just keep us down? We're not ready to stay down now and we're ready to fight. Amen.[15]

Mrs. Turner was the first in her family to register to vote. Other family members followed her to the registrar's office and then to tent city. After Mrs. Turner's daughter's tent was shot up by nightriders seeking to frighten the camp's inhabitants and after her son-in-law received a flesh wound in his shoulder from one of the bullets, Mrs. Turner revealed the source of her determination, what she thought of the white people who tried to intimidate her, and how she was able to withstand their threats. Using religious imagery, she stated:

> I'm [de]pending on the Lord. White people think they got all the power, but they haven't. . . . You know, people like that—they can't turn me around. You can drown this old body but you can't harm my soul. I['ve] gone too far. I'm too old. I come down too many roads and I dug deep. You know what I got? I got gold. It shines in dark places.[16]

The level at which these two women struggled, the obstacles they faced, and the sacrifices they made certainly represent the most striking characteristics of this contemporary struggle for the franchise. Obviously, other black women by the thousands joined Mrs. Hamer and Mrs. Turner in making the same decision to risk everything—their homes, their livelihoods, their lives—to face bombings, burnings, and physical assaults in their attempt to register to vote.

If we keep these images and Mrs. Turner's words on our minds, we can form a more accurate image of women's contribution to the civil rights movement. To begin with, we ought to focus on these community women like Mrs. Turner and Mrs. Hamer, who by their sheer numbers made up a significant proportion of movement participants. We see them in film clips of demonstrations and still pictures of movement activities—waving pledges in an Albany, Georgia, church and being beaten on the Edmund Pettus Bridge in Selma, Alabama. We've heard their voices raising songs and giving testimony in recordings of Mississippi mass meetings. Yet I don't think that as historians we have given them their due.[17]

Our first error is that we speak of the early civil rights years as a time of "awakening" in the black community. This, of course, implies that before this time the community was quiescent, passive, and unaware. It is then hard to imagine that such a community had much to offer to a dangerous, activist struggle. The logic of this "awakening" view suggests that in a movement situation the community would be propelled along by an outside force rather than the movement being generated by, or receiving anything of value from within, the community.[18]

Mrs. Hamer made clear that her decision to participate in the civil rights movement represented nothing new for her—no sudden awakening, no overall change in her activities or level of awareness. Even trying to become a registered voter, which was something she had not really thought about before, was, as she said in response to a query, "no bolt out of the blue." Before the sixties movement, Mrs. Hamer said, "I would get out in the fields and I was always talkin[g] to folks about conditions." Then, making reference to a white southern tendency to characterize black people who were open in their opposition to the existing racial order as crazy, Mrs. Hamer continued, "And I was the one that they say didn't have real good sense."

Mrs. Hamer further suggests that her own situation of being poor and black in Mississippi did not allow her to be at ease or to think everything was all right. Again responding to a white southern notion, this time that outside agitators were responsible for civil rights activity, Mrs. Hamer stressed visible racial inequities, as she frequently did when speaking, and pointed out:

> You know they said outsiders was coming in and beginning to get the people stirred up because they've always been satisfied. Well, as long as I can remember, I've never been satisfied. It was twenty of us, six girls and fourteen boys, and we just barely was making it. You know I could see the whites was going to school at a time when we would be out of school . . . and most of the time we didn't have anything to wear. I knew something was wrong.[19]

The awakening view, with its corresponding notions of passivity and quiescence, can overlook this kind of preexisting consciousness, awareness, and restlessness in community women. In addition, such an appraisal does a further disservice to these women who, like Mrs. Hamer and Mrs. Turner, brought something of extraordinary value to the movement—their familiarity with hard times.

For coping with hard times had created tough, struggle-oriented women long before the 1960s came along. A lifetime of daily struggle against the harshest forms of racism had prepared them for a political struggle to change such conditions. Mrs. Turner's words about hard times and indestructible souls along with her images of hard traveling, wealth, and light do hit the mark. From these women's familiarity with hard times was born an ability to struggle unceasingly and an unconquerable spirit, exactly the things that fueled the civil rights movement and kept it going through dark days of intimidation and repression and in areas of the country long darkened by the shadow of racial oppression. Whatever the physical toll from hard work, deprivation, and punishment had been, these women had endured; and their souls were strong and indeed unharmed. Tested and tried by life experiences, these women had great inner resources. They were rich in the fundamental skills and attitudes necessary for struggle. They did bring gold to the movement and made it shine in dark places.[20]

It stands to reason that these tough, struggle-oriented women played tough activist roles in the civil rights movement; yet if they are remembered at all in our histories they are frequently recalled as "Movement Mamas"—ladies who sheltered, fed, and protected civil right workers. This they did, and it took a great deal of courage. As we have already seen, homes that contained civil rights activists were subject to violent attack. These women are described in strong activist terms that refer to premovement lives similar to those of Mrs. Hamer and Mrs. Turner. Charles Sherrod, director of the SNCC project in southwest Georgia in the early sixties, stated, "There is always a 'mama.' She is usually a militant woman in the community, outspoken, understanding, and *willing to catch hell, having already caught her share*" (emphasis added). These "Mamas" took militant steps to protect their young movement charges. For example, activists who stayed in Lee County, Georgia, remember Mama Dolly Raines spending nights sitting on her porch with a rifle across her lap to ensure the safety of her SNCC children sleeping inside.[21]

But obviously these community ladies did a lot of civil rights work outside their own homes. They were enthusiastic demonstrators, picketers, and organizers and were among those who filled southern jails. They were activists, people who pushed aggressively for their rights. When we see their numbers, the sheer weight of their constant presence in all of the movement activities during this period, it seems inappropriate to ask what was their role or their place, for they did not play just a certain part in the movement or give just a certain thing to the movement. They were not just the backbone, or the spine, of the movement. They were not a specified part, something distinct, or something that can be compartmentalized. Rather, they were such an integral part of the movement that they permeated every aspect, every nook and cranny.[22] They should be viewed by history as synonymous with the movement itself and then treated accordingly.

Remembering the level at which southern black women struggled and the nature of their involvement, we should not base our inquiries on the assumption that they took a back seat to anyone or settled for second place within the movement. Nor should we assume that holding a title or being a national spokesperson established leadership or greater influence within the movement. These were indeed front-line circumstances where all participants were risking the most precious thing they had, their lives. That reality fostered a certain equality in stature and influence.[23]

This sense of equality was demonstrated to me during the 1964 Democratic party convention in Atlantic City, when the Mississippi Freedom Democratic party (MFDP) delegates discussed the compromise arrangement offered by the Democratic party. The women delegates in particular were quite vocal in their opposition. Secure in their movement experiences and trusting their judgment, the women rejected the direct, in-person pleas to accept the compromise made by top male civil rights leaders like Martin Luther King and Bayard Rustin as well as the pleas of very important political figures like United States Senator Wayne Morse and United Auto Workers general counsel Joseph Rauh, who was also a confidant of the vice-president, Hubert Humphrey. At the same time these women felt free to instruct these men on the nature of democracy.

My recollection of a portion of Mrs. Hamer's response was that she emphasized the word "democratic" in her explanation of why she disliked the Democratic party's proposed compromise. She acknowledged that, even though she might not have had as much education as the men recommending acceptance, she thought she had a better understanding of what was democratic and what was not. She knew that in a democratic arrangement people got to choose their own representatives, yet the compromise dictated which two MFDP members would be accepted as delegates. Further, she argued, in a democracy there was supposed to be equal representation, and how could roughly half the population of Mississippi, those the MFDP stood for, be represented by only two delegates and the other half, whom the existing Democratic delegates stood for, require sixty-eight?[24]

We also need to ask not just what these community women did and how they acted but what they thought about what they were doing, what they believed, if they had a philosophy, ideology, or at least a point of view. There is also the question of why they acted when they did. I suspect that, just as the most public and powerful civil rights figures did, these community women made some judgment of historical and social conditions, of movement strategies and tactics, before putting their lives on the line. Yet we don't know these things, not even about the best-known female civil rights figure, Mrs. Rosa Parks. What has lasted instead is the image of a lady simply too tired to give up her seat. While we are establishing these ladies as doers, we ought to allow for the possibility that they were thinkers as well.

Finally, we might ask if their civil rights activism in any way changed the personal or collective sense of women's roles in their homes and in their communities. I wonder if it made any difference at all or every difference in the world. Then there is the other side of this question: whether there were specific skills, connections, or experiences that these women brought from their personal and social lives that benefited the movement and which of these skills were found primarily or exclusively among women in these communities. I would like to see these issues raised in our interviews and research to round out our picture of women's participation in this effort.[25]

Once we have focused on southern black community women, then we need to give some attention to the interaction, the joining of these women and the student activists who were also part of the movement. This connection did not have to be made. Granted, both groups wanted to fight for equality; but the students might have come with a philosophy or program or set of attitudes that gained, at best, a lukewarm response from the community. It was perhaps the greatest strength, the greatest triumph, of the black student movement that the students turned to the community and moved about these communities in such a way that they helped foster the growth of a serious mass-based movement for social change.

What was it that eased this joining? To begin with, perhaps it was clear from the sit-ins, the freedom rides, and the students' decision to leave promising academic careers to devote full time to civil rights work that these young activists were willing to struggle at the same serious level as women like Mrs. Turner and Mrs. Hamer.

The students also had developed a strategy of organization that said it was necessary to focus the civil rights struggle on the rural southern Black Belt where these ladies resided. Previous to this, most civil rights groups had worked from the assumption that it was best to focus attention on more moderate areas first, thus isolating the hard-core South. This strategy was still visible, to a degree, in the Southern Christian Leadership Conference (SCLC) choice of the industrial city of Birmingham as a stage for protest and Dr. King's expectation of some support from moderates within that community.[26]

But the students argued that it was necessary to concentrate attention where racial oppression was at its worst. They felt this strategy would make the civil rights movement more comprehensive, more radical, and more successful. The movement would become more comprehensive by addressing the needs of the most racially oppressed black people; more radical in that, once their needs were included, the movement would by definition become more radicalized; and more successful because there was a sufficient concentration of black people in the targeted rural counties to create the possibility of mass involvement, of greater power.[27]

This potential for power was especially clear in the area of suffrage. In the rural southern Black Belt counties where black people faced the most stringent racial oppression in the country, black residents made up the overwhelming majority of people of voting age and thus could look forward to controlling local politics once they gained the ability to vote. Their participation in politics also carried with it the possibility of facilitating the liberalization of American politics on a national level by undercutting the power of the hidebound conservative southern Democrats, elected to the House and the Senate on the basis of the white vote from these same rural Black Belt counties. These southerners chaired many Senate and House committees in the early sixties and were in a position to block significant liberal legislation. There was a decision, then, to focus movement attention on voting because of the political potential involved. At the same time, civil rights activists were aware that a country projecting itself as the model democracy throughout the world would have no basis for denying the right to vote to any of its citizens.[28]

In their focus on the franchise, the students quickly abandoned the past civil rights custom of insisting on equal application of voting restrictions—that is, if there were a literacy test (and there was in all Deep Southern states), requesting that this test be applied to black citizens in the same manner as it was to white applicants. And, of course, that had not been the practice. Blacks with doctoral degrees might find themselves unable to pass a literacy or understanding test, whereas white citizens with less than a third-grade education might pass such a test and be included in the voting rolls. Now, the students essentially demanded that the franchise be granted without restriction. It should come with citizenship. Occasionally we made the corollary argument that to insist upon literacy in an age when many people got most of their political information from electronic media was absurd.

At mass meetings, in affidavits, African American Black Belt residents established the length of time they had lived in a given area and what lasting contributions they'd made to these places, mostly in the area of work, to buttress their claim for full citizenship. They argued that it was double jeopardy to establish poor schools for black people and then deny them the right to vote on the basis that they were illiterate. This argument was heard by the framers of the 1965 Voting Rights Act, who suspended all literacy tests. It is hoped that these Black Belt citizens have laid the notion to rest that there need be any qualifications for voting other than citizenship. They may have established for all of us that exercising the franchise is a basic American right, not a privilege.[29]

Student activists felt that it was important not only to involve rural southern black people in the civil rights struggle but also to do so in such a manner that the local people controlled their movement, dictated its terms, plotted its strategy, and decided what actions to take. "Let the people decide" was a motto of student organizing. (Not that this was a new way to organize, for it was brought to the students' attention by longtime organizer Miss Ella Baker.) The students tried to foster local leadership that would be limited, lightly exercised, and widespread so that many people could assume a leadership role.[30] What matters here, I think, is that it is difficult to imagine that women like Mrs. Hamer and Mrs. Turner would have been attracted to a movement that offered them anything less than full participation and full control. Student activists were able to tap this precious community resource by directing their organizational efforts toward that community and by doing so in terms acceptable to that community.

We should also explore whether or not the presence of young black women among the student organizers was a factor in encouraging local women's cooperation and vice versa. Then we need to understand what the relationship was. I'm not sure there was a sense, even among those of us who had no direct geographical ties or genealogical links to the rural black South, of coming full circle as Paula Giddings suggests, because I am not sure there was as much sense of separation from rural southern culture as she suggests. How can you come back to something you never left or, more precisely, that never left you? Few black people grew up in America without knowing something of struggle, even fewer without being deeply rooted in a general African American culture.

This culture linked us together—northern, southern, rural, urban—and was itself based in the black community's historical and ongoing struggle for survival and advancement within a hostile social, political, and economic environment. In sharing this general culture with community women, we shared some sense of struggle, as well as all the other things, great and small, that people from the same culture share: values, rules of courtesy, as well as the words and music of common songs. It was perhaps this similar cultural foundation, along with the mutual desire for freedom that Giddings mentions, that allowed us to join together in the somewhat different activity of building a movement for social change.[31]

The way that historians approach and characterize the history of the civil rights movement also affects our assessment of community women's contribution to this struggle. Whatever the nature of that connection between the students and community folk discussed above, the results are obvious: constant activism and creative programs, involving large numbers of people in many different areas. As we weigh the achievements of the civil rights movement, we should see this activity itself as a success. Historians make a serious error of sorts when they ask whether the McComb project or the Albany movement was a success or a failure and then make a judgment based on the specific gains made in these specific places. Being able to sustain repeated and continuous civil rights activity in the repressive and terrorist Black Belt South in the 1960s represented a tremendous success in and of itself.[32]

Further, it was the adding up of these local movements, which stayed in motion and kept happening all over the South, that created a situation in which change had to be made. These activities need to be judged in terms of their contribution to the civil rights movement as a whole. Did they add to the movement's momentum? Did they heighten the level of struggle? Did they provide models for others to follow, add strategies or tactics? To ask whether this project or this city accomplished particular stated goals as a way to judge its significance should not be the only way to analyze the history of this movement. For our purposes it detracts from the very real accomplishments of these local women activists, and it undervalues the weight of their achievement by deeming successes, failures. For example, I am somewhat surprised that we have a body of historical literature that dismisses the Albany movement as a failure, even though it kept some kind of civil rights activity in the forefront in the early 1960s, served as a model of citywide multiissue demonstrations for the entire civil rights movement, and showed the possibility of mass involvement on the serious level of facing jail and physical injury in the rural southern Black Belt.[33]

Similarly, historians have sometimes described the organizing work undertaken during these years in terms that suggest it was done in an anarchic, unstructured, and undisciplined fashion. Yet activity after activity kept taking place under the most difficult of circumstances. All these activities required planning, preparations, constant effort, and often a lot of creativity in order to hold the public's attention and to sustain local movements. How did all that happen, given the few material resources available to rural southern movements, if not with some significant level of organization and discipline? Not only young activists but community people like Mrs. Hamer and Mrs. Turner participated in this work. Watching the movement function on a close-up, day-to-day basis, would community women choose to risk everything they had, to struggle alongside a bunch of antiauthoritarian, individualistic, rebellious activists?[34] Did community women themselves operate on a similar basis? To do justice to their judgment and their history, we need to take another look at how the movement was put together—how various projects and activities were designed and carried out.

Similarly, we need to examine the decision-making processes without assuming that consensus was not a useful form of decision making. At present, it seems to be treated as some kind of inappropriate holdover from pacifism. Again, if we keep in mind that people were indeed risking their lives and making tremendous economic sacrifices to be a part of the struggle, we might see some basic sense in arriving at decisions through consensus. Everyone involved here was a volunteer. Who can decide for someone else how to risk his or her life? To act as a group under such circumstances, it is necessary to seek consensus and group understanding. However unwieldy it might seem in theory, in these circumstances it might be quite practical. It is difficult to imagine strong, militant women like Mrs. Turner and Mrs. Hamer accepting any other procedure.[35]

SNCC workers' insistence on the political importance of rural southern community people, coupled with their commitment to developing grass-roots leadership as well as organizing along democratic lines, led to respectful treatment of community women. It is this treatment that the women remembered—the philosophy in action. A respectful approach may have represented a break from the past and may have formed the bond that underlay movement activities. Mrs. Hamer, for example, noted that other civil rights groups had not thought rural black folk important, and in commenting on class arrogance within the black community, she remarked that SNCC workers were different:

> Nobody ever came out into the country and talked to real farmers and things . . . because this is the next thing this country has done: it divided

us into classes, and if you hadn't arrived at a certain level, you wasn't treated no better by the blacks than you was by the whites. And it was these kids what broke a lot of this down. They treated us like we were special and we loved [th]em. . . . We didn't feel uneasy about our language might not be right or something. We just felt like we could talk to [th]em. We trusted [th]em.[36]

After examining community women's participation in the movement and their interaction with civil rights workers and their organizing philosophies, we should also turn our attention to the question of sexism in the movement. Did it exist? At what level? Was it something that altered or affected community women's participation? Were they aware of it? Did they experience it? Any discussion of sexism in the movement should include the experiences of community women.

Without dealing with this question of sexism in the movement as a whole, I would like to make a brief response from my own experience to a few of the issues raised in this discussion. My own experiences and attitudes may be unique, but in that they differ from the existing picture, there is the suggestion that, as we cast our net wider, a very different synthesis might emerge.

Since the discussion of sexism has become intertwined with racial issues, I would like to approach it by making some comments about relationships between white and black women activists, between black and white staffers, and between black male and female activists. To date, the little that's been written— by Sara Evans and Paula Giddings, for example—might suggest that the main emotion transmitted back and forth between women of different races was black women's jealousy of white women because of black men's preoccupation with and preference for white women.[37]

This framework overlooks some of the strong feelings of solidarity that passed back and forth between women of both races and indeed among activists of varying organizations and ideologies. We were all there facing those bombs and bullets together and for that reason had a kind of fundamental respect and admiration for each other. Casey Hayden, for example, was a friend and activist role model for me, just as she was for Mary King.[38] I admire Casey for her courage, her seriousness, her making good sense out of things, and her ability to remain warm and nurturing at the same time she exercised her strength and her skills. There are other white women whom I met when I was a field secretary or a fund raiser for SNCC that I remain in touch with today.

Second, in a more general sense, the racial issues in the movement, SNCC in particular, were not always based on a one-way flow of negative emotions from black people to white. Yet this is often the way the whole issue of deciding to ask white staff to leave black communities or to advocate black power has been discussed by historians. That is, black staff, due to feelings of racial insecurity and historical anger, settled on an approach of racial exclusivity. This interpretation neglects all the serious political and rational issues involved, such as the effectiveness and the logic of white organizers in a movement based on black self-control—or how it may have been important to reflect the militant tone and genuine desires of the black community. It also does not address the deep racial chauvinism embedded in our society that was reflected in many white civil rights workers' attitudes toward their black counterparts, or how limited white support became during this period. All this needs to be remembered in our history.[39]

I have spoken before about how I, as a young woman, experienced the movement as an open and supportive environment. I see some of the same sense in Sara Evans's book of being encouraged not just to do what you could but to expand and develop your abilities and skills in the movement context.[40] What I'd like to add is how I appreciated SNCC men's "macho." I'm reluctant to take that away from them—primarily because I can't imagine anything more legitimately macho than putting your life on the line for your community's rights. Though I want to keep the macho, I'd like to get rid of the notion of a SNCC mystique, because there ought to be nothing mysterious or unexplained here, just that these men acted with a great deal of courageousness and that's a fact plain and simple. In addition, it seemed to me that this "macho" and courage did not detract from our strength but reinforced our own toughness as women and contributed to our ability to stand fast against southern racism.[41]

In conclusion, I would like to reemphasize that black community women's struggle for the franchise in the sixties was waged on the highest level of commitment and for the highest of goals. These women came into the movement tough and struggle-ready, and they conducted a militant and dedicated fight. There was nothing stereotypically feminine in their approach to that struggle. Driven by their own internal decisions and desires, they entered the fray without hesitation, often in advance of other members of their families and communities. They certainly did not seek to avoid confrontational situations. Their gender in no way limited their participation in all kinds of movement activities both inside and outside of their homes; nor did it protect them from the worst kinds of racist retaliation and violence.

I think that if we keep these facts in mind as we approach the history of this voting rights struggle we will be able to better appreciate the role community women played and more accurately reflect the realities of the movement years in our work. Further, when we see the alacrity with which southern black women seized the historical opportunity to launch a full-scale attack on racial oppression as well as the level of sacrifice and suffering they endured to carry this attack through, we can be sure it wasn't some ordinary political tool, political office, or even full citizenship they sought. We must know they were acting out of the most fundamental human yearnings for justice and freedom. If we listen to them, that will be clear.

When southern black women like Georgia Mae Turner spoke of registering, in the next breath they spoke of freedom. When they stood on voter registration lines, they didn't sing about the vote. Instead, they reached back over a hundred years into their own history and chose a song that expressed their level of commitment and their ultimate goal. They sang, "O Freedom, O Freedom, O Freedom over me / and before I'll be a slave, I'll be buried in my grave / and go home to my Lord and be free."[42]

Notes

1   It is difficult to define by area—rural, urban, Deep South, upper South—which southern black women (and men) were without the franchise in the 1960s. Although there might be a few individual exceptions, African American residents of Deep Southern, rural Black Belt counties could not vote. The Student Nonviolent Coordinating Committee (SNCC) directed most of its voter registration activity toward such counties. Yet Black Belt conditions might exist outside these states, such as in Haywood and Fayette counties in Tennessee, examples used in this essay. Voting restrictions and racial discrimination tended to be lighter in the upper southern states; still, SNCC workers found areas— certain counties in rural Maryland, e.g.—where black people did not exercise the franchise. In urban areas voting participation might be related to class. SNCC worker Julian Bond has pointed out in conversations with me that middle-class black people in areas such as Atlanta and Birmingham exercised the franchise, but poorer black residents of these cities tended not to vote. Bond, who lived in Atlanta and worked on voter registration there, explained that simply filling out the voter registration form was a literacy test in itself because the person registering was expected to write his or her name and address as well as sign the form. He felt this requirement discouraged a number of less affluent, black urban residents, along with their habit of avoiding white officials and officialdom of any kind.

2   James Forman, *The Making of Black Revolutionaries* (New York: Macmillan, 1972), 116, 124–25. According to Mrs. Turner, her landowner gave her until January to move but would not give her any food money as was customary during the winter. According to her testimony, she was forced to move in the snow, and Forman notes that she moved into the tent city two days before Christmas of 1960. Shortly after Mrs. Turner moved

into the tent city, Forman interviewed her twice and included the transcript in one of his chapters on the tent city. This interview is a powerful piece in its entirety. It is further enhanced by Forman's description of Mrs. Turner as she is telling her life story as well as by his description of the circumstances in the tent city at the time. I remembered Mrs. Turner's story when I was thinking about this essay because of an earlier general discussion with John Bracey about the valuable interviews included in Forman's book.

3   Forman, *Revolutionaries,* 126–27, 130–31. The story of the Fayette/Haywood struggle is often left out of civil rights chronologies of this period, yet it was significant both in raising the consciousness of activists and in opening up possibilities for the movement as a whole. It was an organizational training ground for black student activists like Jim Forman and Sterling Stuckey (Forman, *Revolutionaries,* 130–45). This may be the first community struggle where SNCC members offered direct and indirect support. See Clayborne Carson, *In Struggle: SNCC and the Black Awakening of the 1960s* (Cambridge, Mass.: Harvard University Press, 1981), 30. Members of the fledgling Students for a Democratic Society (SDS) chapters also came in contact with this tent city through various campus relief efforts. When I arrived on Ann Arbor's campus in the fall of 1961, it seemed that most of the core members of the SDS chapter there had participated in some efforts for, if not visited, tent city. In Tom Hayden's autobiography, *Reunion* (New York: Random House, 1988), he mentions that his introduction to the rural South and community civil rights efforts was in Fayette County (46–47). Perhaps more important, the actions of Fayette farmers opened up possibilities and new directions for the civil rights struggle as a whole. These farmers showed that African American residents of rural, southern Black Belt counties were ready for activism and willing to struggle at a high level of risk, thus making possible a whole range of civil rights programs and strategies in this part of the oppressive South.

4   Mr. Hamer had lived and worked on the Marlowe plantation for thirty years. Howell Raines, *My Soul Is Rested* (New York: Bantam Books, 1977), 275, 271–75. As the sources show, both of these women's stories have been readily accessible in published literature for some time. In one sense their stories are atypical for most southern rural black women during this time period, because Mrs. Hamer and Mrs. Turner actually were registered to vote. Most people who attempted to register to vote were not put on the voting rolls. A good portion of civil rights activity in the early sixties was geared toward showing that there were large numbers of southern black citizens interested in exercising the franchise. Jim Forman, Ella Baker, and Bob Moses, for example, mention this aspect of Mississippi voting rights efforts. See Forman, *Revolutionaries,* 354; Miss Baker is quoted in Ellen Cantarow, with Susan Gushee O'Malley and Sharon Horton Strom, *Moving the Mountain* (Old Westbury, N.Y.: Feminist Press, 1980), 90; Bob Moses in Howard Zinn, *SNCC: The New Abolitionists* (Boston: Beacon Press, 1964), 100–101.

5   Mrs. Hamer's family was reduced to scavenging as punishment for their brief period away from their landowner. Their more comfortable lives as tenants were cut short by someone among their white neighbors who poisoned the black family's stock. Susan Kling, *Fannie Lou Hamer* (Chicago: Women for Racial and Economic Equality, 1979), 11–13.

6   Forman, *Revolutionaries,* 117–21, 123. As adults, both Mrs. Hamer and Mrs. Turner took care of their invalid mothers for at least a decade (Kling, *Hamer,* 14; Forman, *Revolutionaries,* 119–20).

7   For Mrs. Hamer, see Kling, *Hamer,* 11–12, and Paula Giddings, *When and Where I Enter* (New York: Bantam Books, 1984), 288. In Giddings, Mrs. Hamer speaks more of her mother's hard work—cutting trees with an axe, for instance—than her own. For Mrs. Turner, see Forman, *Revolutionaries,* 117.

8   Forman, *Revolutionaries,* 123.

9   Raines, *My Soul,* 279–80.

10   Forman, *Revolutionaries,* 126.

11   Zinn, *SNCC,* 94–95; Raines, *My Soul,* 276–77.

12   Raines, *My Soul,* 277–78.

13   Zinn, *SNCC,* 96, and see also p. 95; Raines, *My Soul,* 275. Mrs. Hamer recuperated away from home to avoid having her family see the condition she was in (Raines, 278); Kling, *Hamer,* 23–24. Working as a SNCC field secretary was essentially a volunteer job; basic pay for field staff was ten dollars a week. See Zinn, *SNCC,* 13; Carson, *In Struggle,* 71.

14   Forman, *Revolutionaries,* 126.

15   On future generations, see Kling, *Hamer,* 29, 37, 45; Carson, *In Struggle,* 73–74. The first quotation is also in Carson, 73; the second is in *The Story of Greenwood Mississippi,* recorded and produced by Guy Carawan for Folkways Records, 1965.

16   Forman, *Revolutionaries,* 129–30. The first part of the quotation was actually spoken directly to a man accompanying an FBI investigator visiting Mrs. Turner's tent. She identified this man as a "mean man," referring to the manner in which he addressed her. This man, like the sheriff before him, seemed intent on proving that the shots were fired from within the tent. In addition, he was suggesting that blanks, not real bullets, were fired (129–29). On Mrs. Turner being the first in her family to register, see p. 124.

17   The ladies waving pledges in Albany are in the cover picture for Aldon Morris's book, *The Origins of the Civil Rights Movement* (New York: Macmillan, 1984). The film clips of Bloody Sunday in Selma, which used to be shown occasionally on various television productions, are now included in "Bridge to Freedom," *Eyes on the Prize* I, no. 6 (Boston: Blackside, 1986). Several Mississippi women activists are included in Carawan's recording, *Story of Greenwood.*

18   Even very sensitive historians and researchers seem to use the term "awakening" automatically when talking about this period. For example, the first segment of the *Eyes on the Prize* series is entitled "Awakenings." Carson chose for the subtitle of his book on the SNCC, *SNCC and the Black Awakening of the 1960s.* Terms such as "dormant" and "passive" are used to describe local communities before the advent of the civil rights movement in the sixties. See Carson, *In Struggle,* 56, 63; Sara Evans, *Personal Politics* (New York: Vintage Books, 1979), 65–66; Morris, *Origins,* 77, 96; Zinn, *SNCC,* 122, 123.

A number of civil rights workers do describe overcoming fear as one of their major focuses (see, e.g., Forman, *Revolutionaries,* 248; Charles Sherrod, quoted in Zinn, *SNCC,* 125), which may be what forms the basis of this concept of awakening. But the fear the workers are discussing I believe is not one which has a life of its own within the community's psyche but one based on the very real and present dangers inherent in civil rights activism in the Deep South in the 1960s. At the same time, no less a civil rights personage than Martin Luther King, early in his civil rights career, like the historians mentioned above, also viewed a good portion of the 1950s southern black population as apathetic and passive. In *Stride toward Freedom* (New York: Harper and Row, 1958), King defined "the passivity of the uneducated" as one of the factors inhibiting social reform in Montgomery (21–22). This awakening view, of course, overlooks the very rich and long-term history of various forms of activism in which southern blacks had participated long before the sixties civil rights movement began. It can represent a rather chauvinistic view of poor and oppressed people and thus minimize their role in determining the nature and course of this struggle.

19   Raines, *My Soul*, 279, 280; Zinn, *SNCC*, 95. Evidently Hamer did not limit her political conversations to black people or to issues with only local implications. In her premovement life, she recalls telling her plantation owner that she didn't see any reason why black men from Mississippi should fight for the United States. For, "when they come back home, if they say anything, they['re] killed, they['re] lynched, they['re] murdered" (Giddings, *When and Where I Enter*, 289).

20   As can be seen in following the quotations and endnotes in this essay, SNCC workers' sense of community women in general often emphasized these ladies' toughness and strength. There is no overall description of Mrs. Turner offered by Forman, but he does characterize Mrs. Hamer in terms that would support this notion of being made strong through daily struggle. Mrs. Hamer, he states, was "a worldwide symbol of black heroism . . . a warm and always human symbol of the power of people to struggle against hardship, adversity, terror—the living realities of the Mississippi Delta" (291). The description of Mrs. Hamer by another SNCC worker, Mary King, even more clearly emphasizes the idea of strength, both physical and spiritual: "Everything about her suggested strength of character as well as physical stamina, and the more you knew her the more you felt her vitality, warmth, and spiritual strength." See Mary King, *Freedom Song* (New York: William Morrow, 1987), 141.

21   The quotation is from Sherrod's 20 September 1962 field report. The complete report can be found in Forman, *Revolutionaries*, 275–77. In this part of the report, Sherrod is describing a shooting at the home of Terrell County Movement Mama Mrs. Carolyn Daniels (276–77). Giddings also uses this same quotation to describe Movement Mamas. In addition, she identifies other Mamas who were not mentioned in Sherrod's report (*When and Where I Enter*, 284–85). These women are also mentioned in Zinn, *SNCC*, 12, 103, 139, 145–46; and Evans, *Personal Politics*, 51–52, 75–76. Evans suggests that these ladies were new and different models of womanhood for the early white female workers in SNCC and the later Mississippi Summer volunteers. The image of Mama Dolly and her rifle is one I remember from movement lore. I recently confirmed my recollection in conversations with Charles Sherrod and Faith Holsaert, one of the first white female field secretaries to work in Albany and the surrounding counties. In the field report mentioned above, Sherrod describes Mama Dolly as "a gray-haired old lady of about seventy who can pick more cotton, 'slop more pigs,' plow more ground, chop more wood, and do a hundred more things better than the best [male] farmer in the area" (Forman, *Revolutionaries*, 276).

22   Zinn does mention that these women participated in demonstrations (*SNCC*, 12), Evans that they were active in local movements. Zinn also offers a description of an early activist, brave enough to endure two months in the notorious Parchman Penitentiary under horrible conditions in 1963, a story that helped to form my notion of the kinds of people who went to jail for civil rights. Mother Perkins, an Itta Bena, Mississippi, resident, was

"fragile and small, seventy-five years old at the time" (*SNCC*, 98). The backbone images that I'm using negatively here initially stuck in my mind for the opposite reason, that they furnished positive assessments of women's activities. Evans states that the Movement Mamas "furnished the backbone of leadership in local movements" (*Personal Politics*, 76). Giddings points out that in Montgomery "Women, who made up a large part of the black passengers who rode the city buses . . . proved to be a firm spine for the boycott" (*When and Where I Enter*, 266). Former SCLC lieutenant Andrew Young used both images of women, the latter at Mrs. Hamer's funeral (in King, *Freedom Song*, 11, 469–70). Giddings, relying on a quotation from Ella Baker, also suggests that far more women than men were involved in SNCC organizing efforts (*When and Where I Enter*, 284). SNCC worker Lawrence Guyot agrees, stating that, in early SNCC work in Mississippi, "It's no secret that young people and women led organizationally" (Raines, *My Soul*, 261). At the same time, I remember SNCC organizing efforts such as farmers' cooperatives and trade union organizing which involved mostly men.

23   These community women were preceded by other female civil rights activists who played public and prominent roles in earlier civil rights history. There were women like Daisy Bates, Constance Baker Motley, and Rosa Parks as well as all the young women involved in school desegregation efforts, Autherine Lucy and Charlene Hunter in particular. It is likely that some, if not all, of these public figures were known to southern community women. Perhaps these national figures served as role models and reinforced local women's sense that they as women could be important in the civil rights struggle. Some of these early activists were inspirational figures for male SNCC worker Cleve Sellers; see his *River of No Return* (New York: William Morrow, 1973), 16–17. It would seem that they would be even more salient models for other black women. Although these early activists are included in Giddings, who of course is concentrating on the history of black women, and in *Eyes on the Prize*, to a large extent they are not consistently included in movement histories, nor is the full weight of their historical contribution recognized. We need to ensure that the names of these women and their stories become a familiar part of civil rights history, so that the significance and implications of their activities will not be forgotten.

24   In addition to my personal recollections, on several occasions I have heard MFDP delegate Victoria Gray tell how she and other women were especially vocal in their opposition to the compromise and instrumental in persuading the male delegates to reject it. Unita Blackwell's reaction to Dr. King's plea to accept the compromise suggests that she also felt she understood the circumstances better than he did. She explained, "Of course, he didn't understand. . . . We got a lot of people who is big fish so-called, but it look like they don't seem to understand the trick that they be put in, for them to come in and use their own people." She was even more scathing in her criticism of NAACP head Roy Wilkins and MFDP cochair Aaron Henry, who was also her brother-in-law (Giddings, *When and Where I Enter*, 294–95). On the Mississippi Challenge and this meeting, see Forman, *Revolutionaries*, 357, 386–96; Len Holt, *The Summer that Didn't End* (New York: William Morrow, 1965), 155, 165, 170, 175–76; and Sellers, *No Return*, 108–10. All three of these authors were movement activists present at the meeting. Like myself, all of them also saw Mrs. Hamer's response to the compromise as significant. Forman suggests that her direct comment, "We didn't come all this way for no two seats" summarized the

feeling of the MFDP delegates (*Revolutionaries*, 395). Holt includes Mrs. Hamer's statement rejecting the compromise, made outside the meeting, to show the militancy of the
delegation. Here, Mrs. Hamer likened the compromise to Mississippi traditions of racial
injustice. "It's a token of rights on the back row that we get in Mississippi. We didn't
come all this way for that mess again" (Holt, *Summer*, 174). Sellers emphasizes the
thoughtfulness and the emotional impact of Mrs. Hamer's talk. He recalls that she "was
the last person to address the meeting. Speaking slowly with great clarity, she brought it
all home. She told the delegates that she had come to Atlantic City to unseat the regular
delegation. Addressing the liberals, she said she understood why they believed two seats
were better than none. Then she told them why they were wrong. She was on the verge of
tears when she finished. Some of the rest of us were too" (*No Return*, 109).

25   At present, I am not aware of any discussion of the effect of the movement on community women's roles, though some SNCC staffers have thought about the special contributions of women to movement activity. Speaking of organizing efforts in Lowndes
County, Alabama, SNCC field secretary Stokely Carmichael (now Kwame Ture) mentioned that community women played an important role in these efforts because they
"knew the community well and were well known. . . . They had considerable influence
in the black community, being staunch church members, for example." He also mentions that both men and women learned political skills which they brought to the
movement as members of the various organizations in the county. See Stokely Carmichael and Charles V. Hamilton, *Black Power* (New York: Vintage Books, 1967), 102–3,
101. I have heard another SNCC worker, Bernice Johnson Reagon, speak of the role that
community women who were song leaders traditionally played in church and subsequently in the movement. These women would raise the intensity and height of the
meeting through their selection and rendering of songs. This essay, of course, does not
suggest that or even ask if this struggle readiness described in Mrs. Hamer and Mrs.
Turner was a particularly female characteristic.

26   Cities in the South, even in the Deep South, had a reputation for being less oppressive
and rigid on racial matters than the rural Black Belt. At the same time that King describes
Birmingham as a strictly segregated city, he indicates that he thought some white support a possibility, particularly from the religious and industrial community. Martin
Luther King, *Why We Can't Wait* (New York: Mentor Books, 1963), 90, 113.

27   From the first SNCC meeting I attended in the spring of 1962, this is what I understood
to be the basic rationale for directing SNCC's organizational efforts toward the southern
Black Belt—this and our own kind of domino theory, that if we could find a way to
topple racially oppressive structures in places like Mississippi where they were strongest,
doing so elsewhere would be easy. We talked about being social action "catalysts," helping to build lasting organizational "vehicles of power" in these areas. I believe that this
rationale was so generally accepted and agreed upon that it wasn't often mentioned
in recorded SNCC meetings (or later, when activists wrote about their experiences),
though part of it would be used occasionally as a point of reference. See, for example,
Courtland Cox on SNCC's purpose (in Forman, *Revolutionaries*, 400); Forman on
SNCC characteristics (385, 397, 416, 430); Ivanhoe Donaldson on early SNCC beliefs (in
Carson, *In Struggle*, 201); and Stokely Carmichael on what was radical (in Carson, 154).

Although historians recognize SNCC's desire to build a mass movement and make social change, they tend to see SNCC's focus in less pragmatic terms. See Zinn, *SNCC*, 61, 124; Evans, *Personal Politics*, 41–42; Carson, *In Struggle*, 249, 154, 211. Whether SNCC's goals were achieved or not, I think it is important in understanding and evaluating SNCC's work and its relationship to the communities where it had projects to know that the notion of building lasting organizational structures was a part of its efforts. Similarly, we should understand that the focus on the Black Belt was formed from an analysis of historical/political possibilities, not out of some sense of bravado, sympathy, or paternalism but out of a sense of political necessity. When SNCC workers Michael Thelwell and Lawrence Guyot wrote about the MFDP in Mississippi, they emphasized the effort to build a solid, effective, and by implication lasting political organization and entitled their essay, "The Politics of Necessity and Survival in Mississippi." This article is now available in a collection of Thelwell's essays and some fiction entitled *Duties, Pleasures, and Conflicts* (Amherst: University of Massachusetts Press, 1987), 88–89, 98–99, 105, 106–7. Incorporated in all of this was the idea that in these counties lay the potential strength to effect social reform for black people all over the country, and that was why some of us left the North and went south.

28   Stokely Carmichael points out that the early SNCC was concerned with black people's "potential political power [and so] SNCC had Black Power in mind long before the phrase was used" (Carmichael and Hamilton, *Black Power*, 78). For liberalization of national politics, see Tim Jenkins, in Raines, *My Soul*, 245, and Carson, *In Struggle*, 41; Forman, *Revolutionaries*, 264–69. Jenkins's comments emphasize the possibility of administration support in this task of "smashing the southern block." Forman points out that organizing in the areas SNCC chose represented something more radical than either the administration or the NAACP desired. Charlie Cobb's description of his work as a SNCC field secretary shows how a consciousness of this issue affected day-to-day choices in early organizing efforts. Once a beachhead in Greenwood was established, SNCC workers next targeted Sunflower County, where Mrs. Hamer lived, "the reason being," Cobb explains, it was "Jim Eastland's home county." Raines identifies Eastland as the senior Democrat in the U.S. Senate (*My Soul*, 265–66).

29   See Bob Moses's remarks at the April 1963 staff meeting, quoted in Forman, *Revolutionaries*, 305–6, and Moses's May 1963 testimony on Kennedy's civil rights proposal in JoAnn Grant, *Black Protest* (New York: Fawcett, 1968), 300–301, and described in Carson, *In Struggle*, 89; *Story of Greenwood*, side 1. *Gomillion v. Lightfoot*, the most noted case of a well-educated Negro not passing the literacy test, involved a Tuskegee sociology professor. The 1965 Voting Rights Act, which did suspend literacy tests, is a temporary measure requiring renewal; its principles may stand, or they may not. See David Garrow, *Protest at Selma* (New Haven: Yale University Press, 1978), 64, 68. Perhaps a stronger and more lasting measure could have been passed in 1965. The administration considered a constitutional amendment that would restrict voter registration requirements to age and residency (Garrow, *Protest at Selma*, 37, 41–42, 63). SNCC initially argued that there was a need not for new legislation but for the enforcement of already existing measures (Zinn, *SNCC*, 191–215, esp. 206–7). Once additional legislation was being considered, SNCC activists unsuccessfully pushed for the inclusion of provisions that would protect those registering as well as those helping others to register from physical and economic reprisals (Holt, *Summer*, 61–75).

30   For Miss Baker, see Cantarow, *Moving the Mountain,* 84; Carmichael and Hamilton, *Black Power,* 88; Carson, *In Struggle,* 55, 142, 177; Evans, *Personal Politics,* 4; Forman, *Revolutionaries,* 419: Amzie Moore in Raines, *My Soul,* 255; Sellers, *No Return,* 117; Thelwell, *Duties, Pleasures, and Conflicts,* 106, 117. Carson emphasizes the development of local leadership as a characteristic of SNCC's organizing. SNCC people talk more about assisting in the development of the power of local people as a whole and of a leadership that would be quite limited and valid only in that it represented these people.

31   Giddings seems to be using this term to express coming back to one's roots. At the same time she suggests that there was a vast distance between the "young urban students" and "rural folk of the South," peering "at each other across the generations and a gulf of life-experience" (*When and Where I Enter,* 285–86; see also 282). Even though I had no family roots in the South, I didn't have this sense of difference. (In this paper, I am both exploring my personal experiences and looking for the factors that facilitated movement building in general.)

32   For the most part, movement victory or success seems to be judged on the basis of certain kinds of outcomes—how many facilities were desegregated; how many people registered to vote; whether or not federal intervention or federal legislation resulted from a specific activity. But other things may matter more in understanding and assessing a movement for social change. In Albany, for instance, whether the movement was actually able to desegregate facilities or fill the jails may matter less than the level of risk people were willing to take in order to participate in movement activities or whether a change in the local social/political dynamics took place. The level of risk determined whether or not the movement could exist at all. Once Albany's black citizens went into motion, then throughout the overall course of the movement they became the actors. Chief Pritchett lost his determining control and became the reactor. Even in that reaction, in light of circumstances created by the movement, Pritchett knew he should not use the more vicious responses in a southern police chief's traditional arsenal of racial repression. If we use a yardstick of federal intervention, we will think Pritchett is in charge (see, for example, "No Easy Walk," *Eyes on the Prize* I, no. 4). If we look at these other kinds of things, we'll see a different picture. And if we ask what brought these things about we will have to learn more about the thinking and motivations of community women and men.

        This, in turn, might lead us to look at the specifics as well as the generalities of movement building rather than to treat it as something more or less destined to happen and to happen as it did. Our histories might place more emphasis on the step-by-step process of bringing it into being. (For example, early civil rights organizers in the repressive South had first to establish that they could and would stay in communities, then that they could organize there. See Sam Block in Forman, *Revolutionaries,* 283; Cobb in Raines, *My Soul,* 268, Moses in Zinn, *SNCC,* 89; Thelwell, *Duties, Pleasures, and Conflicts,* 93.) We might also ask the more difficult question of historical possibilities and judge the movement in those terms. Did these activities make the most of these possibilities or the least? All these kinds of assessments are necessary to understand fully the significance of community women's participation in civil rights activities.

33   Zinn assesses the Albany movement in a positive light, using a yardstick similar to that used in this essay (*SNCC,* 123). A fairly negative assessment of the Albany movement

characterized the presentations made by almost all the scholars invited to be a part of a twenty-year reunion of the movement, held in Albany during August of 1981. Only Vincent Harding, who was closely connected with the movement, offered a generally positive assessment. Seeing the confusion and disbelief of the local movement veterans, who had made so many sacrifices for their activism, on being told, essentially, that their efforts had not made any positive contribution to the civil rights movement as a whole reinforced for me how important is the way we judge movement activities. Some of the Movement Mamas like Mama Dolly were present, along with most of the women from Albany who had been in the core group of regular activists. Marion King was not present, but her story was very much on my mind. During the movement she had gone to visit her husband and other movement prisoners in the Camilla jail. Although visibly pregnant, she was knocked unconscious by the deputy sheriff, resulting, we believed, in the death of her baby (Zinn, *SNCC*, 135). Martin Luther King himself spoke of the Albany movement in fairly negative terms, but at the same time he refused to acknowledge it as a defeat; see *Why We Can't Wait*, 43–44. Most scholars writing about Albany generally characterize the movement as a defeat or setback, though some acknowledge that some important movement lessons were learned there. See Garrow, *Protest at Selma*, 221; David Lewis, *King: A Critical Biography* (New York: Praeger, 1976); and Morris, *Origins*, 242–50. Carson is more balanced in his assessment, suggesting that the setbacks were of an immediate nature and seeing Albany's importance as a model for other movements as well as a training ground for SNCC workers (*In Struggle*, 62–63, 65).

34   Carson, in particular, characterizes SNCC workers in such terms. SNCC workers' organizing efforts, to Carson, represented a kind of "youthful, impulsive activism" (*In Struggle*, 133), which was accompanied by "individualistic forms of rebelliousness" (173) as well as a reluctance "to accept the constraints of institutional roles and political pragmatism" (16). Carson, taking his cue, I think, from an early SNCC conference invitation that defined one of the movement goals as "individual freedom and personhood" (28), repeatedly uses the term "individualistic," already quoted in one context above, to describe SNCC workers' underlying motivation (4, 17, 149, 154). He also suggests that SNCC staff was antiauthoritarian and undisciplined (13, 169, 149, 159, 169). Overall, his description gives the impression of a kind of anarchic, unplanned, and unstructured activism, somewhat removed from everyday political realities. Some SNCC workers used terms similar to Carson's to describe certain groupings of staff people (Forman, *Revolutionaries*, 413–14, 421–23, 425, 433–37, 439–40; Sellers, *No Return*, 130–34). But they are describing a period late in the organization's history and referring to certain groups, not the staff as a whole. Sellers does describe SNCC's origins as "anarchistic." On the projects where I worked, my experience was that most staff worked hard, worked regularly, worked long hours, seven days a week. My sense of my coworkers' motivations and values was not that they were acting out of some kind of generalized individualistic, antiauthoritarian rebelliousness but that these organizers were ready to sacrifice everything they had on the chance of securing some measure of progress for black people. Political concerns and political effectiveness therefore were more or less our whole purpose in being there.

35   Evans's description of SNCC meetings, for example, suggests that they were a little impractical: "Early SNCC meetings developed a pattern of anarchic democracy. Without

order, agenda, or acknowledged leadership, staffers would go on and on into the night focusing on whatever problems seemed most pressing until a consensus could be reached" (*Personal Politics*, 42). I think we need to look at these meetings less in terms of their immediate results and ask, Were they a help or a hindrance in building a social movement? I mean this in terms of their order, flow, and inclusiveness as well as the topics discussed. How did our community women relate to these meetings? It seems to me that the main topic always on the floor in these meetings, national or local, large or small, was how to think about and go about building a movement for social change. Were there signs of growth and development in the ways we thought about these things? I wonder if some of SNCC's vitality—its ability to launch all kinds of creative programs and projects, to support and articulate various political viewpoints and causes—had its base in the open-ended discussions that took place in these meetings as well as in crowded jail cells, rickety freedom houses, and fast-moving cars. At the same time, we need to look at the mass meetings held during this period. Discussions were held there. Decisions were made there too, and often large numbers of community people were present and/or were key actors in these meetings. That you can't tell a volunteer how to risk his or her life is something I remember Bob Moses saying.

36   Raines, *My Soul*, 251. Another Mississippi community activist, Mrs. Unita Blackwell, made a similar statement, which is quoted in Giddings, *When and Where I Enter*, 286. Describing SNCC workers, Mrs. Blackwell states: "We were all excited about these young people, because they was educated and they treated us so nice. All the educated folk we had known looked at us like we were fools and didn't know nothing, and these here talked to us like we was educating them."

37   On this subject, Giddings relies heavily on Evans (Evans, *Personal Politics*, 78, 79–82, 88–89; Giddings, *When and Where I Enter*, 301–2).

38   Mary King describes her close relationship with Casey mostly in personal terms, but she does mention Casey as her mentor. I assume this was in things political. See Mary King, *Freedom Song*, 74–78. On the other hand, Zinn's work on the early SNCC so emphasizes a sense of interracial unity within the organization and a commitment to interracialism in general that it might not give sufficient weight to feelings of race consciousness and race pride among black workers at this time (*SNCC*, 167, 170–71, 173–74, 181, 185–89).

39   Rising nationalism, decisions for racial exclusivity, and/or the adoption of black power are usually described in negative emotional terms. And it is usually black people with the negative emotions. Discussing interracial tensions in SNCC following Mississippi Summer, for example, Carson mentions "Racial hostilities," "anti-white anger," and "black frustrations" (*In Struggle*, 144). Evans carefully limits the role of emotion, stating that "The anger of black women toward white women was only one element in the rising spirit of black nationalism" (*Personal Politics*, 89; see also 81, 88). She also describes the attitudes of the post-1964 staff—growing more deeply nationalist—in emotional terms such as "bitter and disillusioned" (90), "hopes crushed repeatedly" (91), and she includes psychiatrist Robert Coles's description of staff members suffering from "a syndrome of weariness, depression and guilt" (92–93). Meier and Rudwick use similar emotional terms to explain the rise of black power in both CORE and SNCC; August Meier and Elliot Rudwick, *CORE* (Urbana: University of Illinois Press, 1973), 413, 415.

40   Speech at conference, "The Sixties Speak to the Eighties," October 1993, University of

Massachusetts at Amherst, sponsored by the Department of Afro-American Studies, Women's Studies Program, and Social Thought and Political Economy Program. Evans, *Personal Politics*, 67, 70, 73, 108. Sometime after presenting this paper, I was on a panel with Casey Hayden. In her presentation, Casey reiterated a characterization of the movement which I had heard her make informally many years earlier and which became part of my understanding of SNCC. She described the movement as a nurturing, feminine space that encouraged each participant's growth. Her paper was titled "Women's Consciousness and the Nonviolent Movement against Segregation, 1960–1965: A Personal History" and was presented at the Carter G. Woodson Institute's Center for the Study of Civil Rights conference on the Roles of Women in the Civil Rights Movement held at the University of Virginia in 1989.

41 I do not like the term "macho" itself because of its clear implication that these kinds of characteristics are limited to the male gender. The term, however, is used in such a negative way in the general discussion of interpersonal relationships within SNCC (see, e.g., Evans, *Personal Politics*, 77) that the real contribution courage made to the building of the movement is almost lost, as well as the real empowerment that being part of that movement gave to each participant. Thinking of both these notions, sometimes when I talk about these years and what it felt like to be a part of SNCC I have appropriated the term, saying that when I worked as a SNCC field secretary I felt macho. "Mystique" is another term that is readily connected to SNCC (see, e.g., Meier and Rudwick, *CORE*, 168). SNCC people sometimes used the term to poke fun at themselves. Michael Thelwell wrote a paper about certain staff attitudes in the midsixties which he remembers calling "Mississippi's Metaphysical Mystics: An Enigma Wrapped in a Mystique." (Forman quotes the title as "Mississippi: A Metaphysic Wrapped in a Mystique" [*Revolutionaries*, 422].)

42 The song can be found in Guy and Candie Carawan, *We Shall Overcome: Songs of the Southern Freedom Movement* (New York: Oak Press, 1963), 72–73.

Directions for

Scholarship

Bettina Aptheker

The Jamaica-born novelist and poet Michelle Cliff offers us a wonderful description of the kind of history writing so evident in the preceding essays:

> It is a marble building—but like a cave inside. In the basement—against granite—a woman sits in plain sight. She is black: and old. "Are you a jazz singer?" someone asks. "No—a historian." . . . She is writing a history of incarceration. Here is where black women congregate—against granite. This is their headquarters; where they write history. Around tables they exchange facts—details of the unwritten past. Like the women who came before them—the women they are restoring to their work/space—the historians are skilled at unraveling lies; are adept at detecting the reality beneath the erasure.[1]

In 1979 the National Council of Negro Women—and Bettye Collier-Thomas had a lot to do with this—organized the first National Scholarly Conference on black women's history. In reflecting upon the inspiring works presented here in this book, I thought about the direction African American women's history scholarship has taken in the last eight years. Visioning the ancestors has been a process of reclamation and empowerment, a source of political vitalization.

In an essay she titled "What It Is I Think I'm Doing Anyhow," Toni Cade Bambara described what happened to her when she went to live in a new community:

> Some years ago when I returned south, my picture in the paper prompted several neighbors to come visit. "You a writer? What all you write?" Before I could begin the catalogue, one old gent interrupted with—"Ya know Miz Mary down the block? She need a writer to help her send off a letter to her grandson overseas." So I began a career as the neighborhood scribe— letters to relatives, snarling letters to the traffic chief about the promised stop sign, nasty letters to the utilities, angry letters to the principal about that confederate flag hanging in front of the school.[2]

Analogous to Bambara's experience, I thought about what it would be like to move into a community and have someone say, "What do you do?" And you would say, "I'm a historian." Yes, well, but would do you *do?* The essential thing about women's history and African American women's history is that it is a source of empowerment; that the visioning and re-visioning of the collective story is a way of valuing the lives of black women. It is a source of self-esteem, of pride, of beauty, of a precious legacy. That this history has been distorted, so filled with stereotypes and myths about mammies, sapphires, and matriarchs, that people, women in particular, have been robbed of their history, is part of the way in which racism, sexism, and class oppression have been perpetuated; as if people, as if women, ordinary, working-class black women, have no history, came from nowhere.

I look at many of the young people, eighteen and nineteen years old, in my classes. I mention to them, say, the civil rights movement, and I realize that they don't really know what I'm talking about because it has not been part of their personal experience. If it has been taught to them at all in the public schools, it has seemed remote. I realize that the words "civil rights movement" simply do not resonate in them the way they do in me, the way they do in those of us who lived through it, in those whose lives were forever changed by it, however partial its victories. We are severed, one generation from another. Part of our task as historians is to reconnect the generations, to reconnect the women to each other; it is to make this history a story, accessible to younger people and to the community so that people know their legacy.

When thinking about these essays and the work that has gone on and the new directions for scholarship, I thought a great deal about what it means to place African American women at the center of our thinking, of our interpretation, of our analysis. In doing this, the paradigms of traditional historical analysis are unraveled. For example, I was so moved by Martha Norman's analysis of black women and the struggle for the vote, 1955–65, "Shining in the Dark." African American women are at the center of her interpretation; they are at the emotional center, at the intellectual center.

Norman's understanding of the experiences, strategies, choices of these black women informs her telling; it *is* the interpretative center. She does not try to take this experience and "fit it" into a preexisting theory, thereby making it something other than itself. It is this *process* that gives her historical vision such a radical potency. Her essay also spoke to the fact that we as scholars are ourselves engaged in a political struggle within the institutions to which we are affiliated, especially in African American women's history and in women's studies. It is a struggle to get people to recognize the legitimacy of this history. We are constantly having to justify our subject, the kinds of questions we ask, our research methods, the use of oral as well as written records of "archives" embodied in quilts and gardens, recipes, and folk wisdom. One is continually reminded of the extent to which the traditional history of so many of our white colleagues is still taught as though we didn't exist. Norman also modeled for us the way in which activism and scholarship can be combined. Her knowledge is as much a product of her knowing women like Georgia Mae Turner and Fannie Lou Hamer, of her own deeply intuitive understanding of the movement from the inside out, as it is a product of meticulous research and documentation.

Another theme evidenced in many of the essays, and made explicit in the work of Elsa Barkley Brown, is that the model of pluralist democracy as a way of history writing is not only not helpful to us but obscures the real and significant differences that highlight the historical experiences of women and men, African American women and Euro-American women, and so forth. The pluralist model adds a little of this or that people or culture, but Euro-American men, and usually from the most privileged classes, still remain at the center of the periodization and the designation of what is "important" in any particular historical period. Pluralism doesn't change the historical paradigms. It doesn't allow black women to be at the center of anything because they are, by definition, always marginalized by the previously designated categories of what is important.

I have been thinking about this problem for several years because it has come up continually in my teaching and in my writing. Once we place "women" at the center, we still have a crucial problem because "women" are not one category. Women are multifaceted. Women are an ensemble of the social relations in which they have existed in all the diversity of culture and race and class and religion and sexual preference, and so on. Women cannot be universalized.

To deal with this problem I've developed an approach that I call "pivoting the center." The idea is that you focus on *a* center to begin. Let's say African American women are your center. You gather as much information as you can. You use models of historical research that are socially, aesthetically, politically compatible with the experiences of African American women. You allow the experiences of the women to define the categories, to designate what's important. This is one center. Then, you may pivot your attention to another people, say to Native Americans (and often you will need to designate nation or tribe), to Asian Americans (and you will need to designate countries of origin), to Chicana, Puerto Rican, to various ethnic groups, such as Arlene Avakian's work on Armenian American women, or work that is being done on Jewish American women and the history of antisemitism.[3] In each case you replicate the process of cultural, aesthetic, political, religious, and class designations appropriate to the women, generated by the women themselves out of their life experiences, their ways of knowing. The women in this sense are both the informants (to use the anthropological jargon) and their own ethnographers; they become the subjects of their own experience; as scholar-activists we work to dissolve the boundaries between "subject" and "object"; we seek to interpret and know from their experience.[4] You have women at the center, but the focus of the race and the culture and the class may shift.

We gather this information. I don't mean necessarily each one of us as individuals, but I mean this as a process, as a method of work in women's studies, in women's history. This becomes a way of thinking, and the focus pivots. You don't then have to change one people in order to accommodate to another's sense of what is important. With this process you can allow each of the women, in the words of Alice Walker's wonderful poem about revolutionary petunias, to bloom "Gloriously for its Self."[5] Now, one of the problems we have in allowing each to bloom in this way is that we have been trained in masculinized, Europeanized modes of theory, the essential function of which is to form patterns of causality or probability, a pattern that connects and shapes a way of knowing. If an experience, an event, or a people doesn't fit that pattern, it is excluded from the purview of what is defined as knowing. I am proposing that we change the conception of how theory is done and of how paradigms of historical analysis are generated. This has been done very effectively in many of the essays in this book. We do not have to abandon causality, but we do have to change the ways in which we have thought about it.

Pivoting the center of our thinking about women clears a space in which difference provides meaning. It provides a way of knowing how we are connected. The point is not whether this connection is always positive or progressive. Very often it isn't. The point is simply to know the attributes, tensions, dimensions, depths of connection, to reconnoiter and to step carefully from there so that you can walk in the garden and you can see each flower, if I can continue to use the metaphor, "for its Self." You can't try to make it into something else in order to fit a theoretical generalization.

We have experienced some important shifts of paradigm in doing African American women's history. When we began we were doing what might be called primarily a contributory or compensatory history. We maintained the basic paradigms of the profession as to what history was, how it was documented, and what events were important, and so on. Then we inserted women—African American women—into those paradigms. But what has become so clear in these essays, again, is that those paradigms do not in fact contain the real heart, the fuller scope of the experience of African American women. In breaking those old paradigms we're creating a whole new way of doing history. I want to give a few examples from the papers presented.

In her introductory overview, Rosalyn Terborg-Penn pointed out that many white women's historians have argued that black women perceived themselves as having to choose between race and sex in the struggles in which they were engaged. Faced with this dichotomy, "race versus sex," these historians argued, black women invariably chose race as the more pressing issue. Terborg-Penn argues, however, that you can't make a paradigm out of particular historical moments, such as the moment in which support for the Fifteenth Amendment was debated. In reconstructing the dailiness of African American women's lives over time, and attending to the numerous struggles initiated by black women, we see, Terborg-Penn suggests, the simultaneity of struggles around race, sex, and class.[6] Many of the essays presented here illustrate this observation. For example, Janice Sumler-Edmond's discussion of black women litigants, 1867–90, shows the extent to which racial discrimination in transportation, public accommodations, and education was challenged by black women because racism so insulted and degraded their womanhood. In other situations, black women have made tactical and strategic decisions about shifting priorities in a particular moment in accord with the way in which the power structure has forced the priorities, as in the debate around the Fifteenth Amendment. When this has happened it has not been a function of what the women have wanted; it has been a function of a male power structure that has imposed that decision upon them. It has certainly also not come from a lack of consciousness about sexism on the part of black women, which is often the (unspoken) accusation of white-centered historians, as if black women somehow had a lesser consciousness of political reality than their white counterparts.

Another paradigm shift is dramatically illustrated in the essay by Elsa Barkley Brown. In redefining personhood and citizenship from the perspective of newly emancipated African women, Brown moves away from the model of representative government as the norm to one she defines as peoplehood and community. Similarly, she moves from the notion of bourgeois individualism to what she calls an "ethos of mutuality." I see this essay as a brilliant continuation of work begun by Filomina Steady, Sharon Harley, and Rosalyn Terborg-Penn in developing a concept of Africanist feminism and in exploring cross-cultural perspectives of African women in the diaspora.[7]

The central theoretical tension in Barkley Brown's paper is in defining African and Western cosmologies and describing the ways in which African American women have balanced these two systems of cultural reality for themselves, synthesizing, adapting, inventing. The struggle of African American women in the Richmond, Virginia, of the late 1860s in enacting their own definitions of citizenship and personhood is made visible for the first time, and in ways that may revolutionize our understanding of Reconstruction itself.[8]

A cross-cultural, diasporic perspective is extremely valuable as a central paradigm in African American women's history. It has also been a useful model for other women's histories. For example, in interpreting the oral histories of Jewish, Greek, or Armenian elders, it makes much more sense to locate the women first in their cultures of origin and then to follow their process of synthesis and adaptation, to understand the choices these women have made, rather than forcing a comparative model in which the dominant Anglo culture is presumed to be both normative and "normal."

A third shift can be seen in changing the traditional definition of politics. This is crucial to understanding the actual political power wielded by African American women. It is misleading to look at politics exclusively or primarily from the point of view of representative democracy, of elections, and legislative actions when assessing the historical role of black women because the whole point of masculinist, white tradition has been their exclusion. If we focus on the exclusion we do two things. First, we tend to focus on victimization rather than on survival and resistance. Second, we obscure the actual history of struggle, ingenuity, and skill in the face of overwhelming odds.

For example, women's historians who focused on the Euro-American experience have tended to see suffrage as the central issue in the women's rights movement of the nineteenth century. Though universal suffrage was certainly endorsed by black women and was a significant part of their concern about emancipation, it was by no means the only focus of political activism. Papers by Sharon Harley, Janice Sumler-Edmond, and Cynthia Neverdon-Morton, for example, amply illustrate the independent initiatives by black women toward establishing a power base in the community from which to assert greater influence and control over issues crucial to their daily lives. These issues included civil rights, antilynching, education, land claims, community health, adequate child care for working mothers, care for the aged and the indigent, and so on. Likewise, when participating in the struggle for woman suffrage, black women had often to do battle with white suffragists over the race issue.

In each of these instances we see the ways in which African American women, synthesizing African, European, and distinctly American inventions, enacted their own concept of political democracy, "to catch the vision of freedom," in Elsa Barkley Brown's memorable phrase. They did these things because they were *both* black and female, and they used tactics most suitable to the particularity of their circumstances. For example, as Barkley Brown shows, black women assumed their right to influence as coequals the vote their husbands would cast in the Reconstruction South, actualizing their belief that the ballot was collectively owned rather than individually exercised, and that the franchise should be cast in the best interests of the community as a whole. Barkley Brown records that "These black women assumed the political rights that came with being a member of the community even though they were not granted the political rights they thought would come with being citizens of the state."

Similarly, the ways in which personal issues inspired political struggle are well illustrated by Janice Sumler-Edmond's discussion of the ways in which women challenged Jim Crow laws. A lot of the initiative for these challenges came from the feeling of personal effrontery when forced to ride in segregated smoking cars, with men, and the sexual degradation that implied. Indeed, the struggles of African American women to undo two and a half centuries of institutionalized rape could form the basis of a much deeper feminist understanding of what constitutes a *women's* politics.

This shift in the traditional boundaries of political theory, and in the traditional definitions of politics—that is, challenging the assumption of representative democracy and individualism, challenging the assumption of what is political and what is personal—illuminates the ways in which black women have been a "force in history," walking purposefully in and out of the front door of their lives.

Another paradigm shift related to this process of changing traditional definitions of politics is the perception of nurturing as a form of resistance. This is evident, for example, in the essay some years ago by Bernice Johnson Reagon in which she describes the women in her childhood, from her mother, grandmother, aunts, and kin to her first-grade teacher, to all the women in her community who created for her a web of life in which she could be nurtured. This nurturance was the foundation for her political activism in the sixties.[9] This theme is historically evidenced in the work of Deborah White as she describes matrifocality in the enslaved communities, and the mother/tribe bond.[10] Jacqueline Jones makes a similar point about the nurturing work of black women when she poses the dynamic tension of priorities between family and work as a motive force of resistance in the lives of black women.[11] For a people to go on, the children have to know who they are, they must be endowed with culture, and history, and pride. That endowment is a form of nurturance. When it's done collectively, over time, it becomes a measure of historically defined resistance.

African American women have been about the business of defining their own agenda, however constricted their apparent choices. Our history writing has increasingly drawn from these experiences, and for this reason it has become an increasingly authentic record, upsetting—indeed, frequently overturning—the received wisdom of the historical canon.

I would like to conclude with a few thoughts about future work. New directions for research and thinking need not be limited to the traditional boundaries of history itself, as a discipline. Historians can be so narrow! People's lives are so complicated. We are so often trained to do research in one particular area sandwiched between "significant" dates. We might begin to think in broader and more interdisciplinary ways, in more conceptual and, if you will, more artistic terms. Feminist research has greatly influenced the field of social history, and I urge us to expand these boundaries so that oral, literary, poetic, musical, theatrical productions by African American women—both those accorded professional recognition and those induced by ordinary life—may become a source of knowing.

Recently, for example, I have been studying the lives and works of African American women artists. The works of Edmonia Lewis, Meta Warrick Fuller, and Augusta Savage provide an astonishing visual, historical record. Fuller's work, in particular, conveys an interiority of slavery, of suffering and redemption that is—if I may use the popular expression—awesome.

I think also of the work of Elizabeth Catlett, graphic artist and sculptor.[12] She did this wonderful work in 1968 in tribute to the black women of the civil rights movement, and it was called "Homage to My Young Black Sisters." It is a tall figure, carved in wood, with an upraised fist, and in the center there is a hollowed, empty space. In antiquity, figures of the goddess often displayed such an empty space where the womb is. In antiquity, this was believed to have symbolized the goddess representing the concept of birth as "the ceaseless generation from infinite space." *The ceaseless generation from infinite space.* I think about that sculpture, and about Martha Norman's essay, and about all the labors of African American women this history reveals. It has been, it is, a ceaseless generation from infinite space.

Notes

This is an edited and revised version of a transcript of my comments during the round-table discussion at the conference "Afro-American Women and the Vote, 1837–1965." I attempted to maintain the informal flavor while providing adequate coherence and context. I added reference notes for the convenience of readers.

1   Michelle Cliff, "Against Granite," in Cliff, *The Land of Look Behind: Prose and Poetry* (New York: Firebrand Books, 1985), 33.

2   Toni Cade Bambara, "What It Is I Think I'm Doing Anyhow," in *The Writer on Her Work,* ed. Janet Sternburg (New York: W. W. Norton, 1980), 167.

3   See, for example, Arlene Avakian, "Armenian-American Women: The First Word . . . ," in *Transforming the Curriculum: Ethnic Studies and Women's Studies,* ed. Johnnella Butler and John Walter (Albany: State University of New York Press, 1991), 271–301.

4   A very useful article that explores the idea of women as their own ethnographers, and authority, is Alvina Quintana, "Women: Prisoners of the Word," in *Chicana Voices: Intersections of Class, Race, and Gender,* ed. Teresa Cordova et al. (Austin: Center for Mexican American Studies, University of Texas, 1986), esp. 209–10.

5   Alice Walker, "The Nature of This Flower Is to Bloom," in Walker, *Revolutionary Petunias & Other Poems* (New York: Harcourt Brace Jovanovich, 1973), 70.

6   It is useful also to see that the concept of simultaneity is one of the particular contributions black feminists have made to the women's liberation movement. See, for example, "The Combahee River Collective Statement, 1974," in *Home Girls: A Black Feminist Anthology,* ed. Barbara Smith (New York: Kitchen Table Press, 1983), 272–82.

7   See, for example, Filomina S. Steady, ed., *The Black Woman Cross-Culturally* (Cambridge, Mass.: Schenkman, 1981), and Rosalyn Terborg-Penn, Sharon Harley, and Andrea Benton Rushing, eds., *Women in Africa and the African Diaspora* (Washington, D.C.: Howard University Press, 1987).

8   See also the more recent, generative essay by Elsa Barkley Brown, "African-American Women's Quilting: A Framework for Conceptualizing and Teaching African-American Women's History," *Signs: Journal of Women in Culture and Society* (Summer 1989): 921–29.

9   Bernice Johnson Reagon, "My Black Mothers and Sisters; or, On Beginning a Cultural Autobiography," *Feminist Studies* 8 (Spring 1982): 85–86.

10   See Deborah Gray White, *Ar'n't I a Woman? Female Slaves in the Plantation South* (New York: W. W. Norton, 1985).

11   Jacqueline Jones, *Labor of Love, Labor of Sorrow: Black Women, Work, and the Family from Slavery to the Present* (New York: Vintage, 1985).

12   See the beautiful retrospective by Samella Lewis, *The Art of Elizabeth Catlett,* published in collaboration with the Museum of African American Art, Los Angeles (Claremont, Calif.: Hancraft Studios, 1984).

Suggestions for Further Reading

Alexander, Adele Logan. *Ambiguous Lives: Free Women of Color in Rural Georgia, 1789–1879.* Fayetteville: University of Arkansas Press, 1991.

Andrews, William L., ed. *Sisters of the Spirit: Three Black Women's Autobiographies of the Nineteenth Century.* Bloomington: Indiana University Press, 1986.

Aptheker, Bettina. *Woman's Legacy: Essays on Race, Sex and Class in American History.* Amherst: University of Massachusetts Press, 1982.

Barnett, Ida B. Wells. *Crusade for Justice: The Autobiography of Ida B. Wells,* edited by Alfreda M. Duster. Chicago: University of Chicago Press, 1970.

Berkeley, Kathleen C. "'Colored Ladies Also Contributed': Black Women's Activities from Benevolence to Social Welfare, 1866–1896." In *The Web of Southern Social Relations: Women, Family, and Education,* edited by Walter J. Fraser, Jr., R. Frank Saunders, Jr., and Jon L. Wakelyn. Athens: University of Georgia Press, 1985.

Berry, Mary Frances. "Judging Morality: Sexual Behavior and Legal Consequences in the Late Nineteenth-Century South." *Journal of American History* 78 (December 1991): 835–56.

Brooks, Evelyn. "Religion, Politics, and Gender: The Leadership of Nannie Helen Burroughs." *Journal of Religious Thought* 44 (1988): 7–22.

Brown, Elsa Barkley. "Negotiating and Transforming the Public Sphere: African American Political Life in the Transition from Slavery to Freedom." *Public Culture* 7 (Fall 1994): 107–46.

Buhle, Mari Jo, and Paul Buhle, eds. *The Concise History of Woman Suffrage: Selections from the Classic Work of Stanton, Anthony, Gage, and Harper.* Urbana: University of Illinois Press, 1978.

Byrd, Richard W. "Interracial Cooperation in a Decade of Conflict: The Denton (Texas) Christian Women's Inter-racial Fellowship." *Oral History Review* 19 (Spring-Fall 1991): 31–54.

Carby, Hazel V. *Reconstructing Womanhood: The Emergence of the Afro-American Woman Novelist.* New York: Oxford University Press, 1987.

Cashman, Sean Dennis. *African-Americans and the Quest for Civil Rights, 1900–1990.* New York: New York University Press, 1991.

Crawford, Vicki L. *Women in the Civil Rights Movement: Trailblazers and Torchbearers.* Brooklyn, N.Y.: Carlson Publishing, 1990.

Flexner, Eleanor. *Century of Struggle: The Woman's Rights Movement in the United States.* New York: Atheneum, 1973.

Giddings, Paula. *When and Where I Enter: The Impact of Black Women on Race and Sex in America.* New York: Morrow, 1984.

Gordon, Linda. "Black and White Visions of Welfare: Women's Welfare Activism, 1890–1945." *Journal of American History* 78 (September 1991): 559–90.

Hall, Jacquelyn Dowd. *Revolt against Chivalry: Jessie Daniel Ames and the Women's Campaign against Lynching.* New York: Columbia University Press, 1979.

Higginbotham, Evelyn Brooks. *Righteous Discontent: The Women's Movement in the Black Baptist Church.* Cambridge, Mass.: Harvard University Press, 1993.

Hine, Darlene Clark, Elsa Barkley Brown, and Rosalyn Terborg-Penn, eds. *Black Women in America: An Historical Encyclopedia.* 2 vols. Brooklyn, N.Y.: Carlson Publishing, 1993.

Jones, Jacqueline. *Labor of Love, Labor of Sorrow: Black Women, Work, and the Family from Slavery to the Present.* New York: Vintage, 1985.

——. "The Political Implications of Black and White Women's Work in the South, 1890–1965." In *Women, Politics, and Change,* edited by Louise A. Tilly and Patricia Gurin, 108–29. New York: Russell Sage Foundation, 1990.

King, Richard. *Civil Rights and the Idea of Freedom.* New York: Oxford University Press, 1992.

Kling, Susan. *Fannie Lou Hamer.* Chicago: Women for Racial and Economic Equality, 1979.

Kraditor, Aileen S. *The Ideas of the Woman Suffrage Movement, 1890–1920.* Garden City, N.Y.: Anchor/Doubleday, 1971.

Lawson, Steven F. "Freedom Then, Freedom Now: The Historiography of the Civil Rights Movement." *American Historical Review* 96 (April 1991): 456–71.

——. *Running for Freedom: Civil Rights and Black Politics in America Since 1941.* Philadelphia: Temple University Press, 1991.

Lerner, Gerda, ed. *Black Women in White America: A Documentary History.* New York: Vintage, 1972.

Lewis, Janice Sumler. "The Forten-Purvis Women of Philadelphia and the American Antislavery Crusade." *Journal of Negro History* 66 (Winter 1981–82): 281–88.

Locke, Mamie E. "The Role of African-American Women in the Civil Rights and Women's Movements in Hinds County and Sunflower County, Mississippi." *Journal of Mississippi History* 53 (August 1991): 229–39.

McAdam, Doug. "Gender as a Mediator of the Activist Experience: The Case of Freedom Summer." *American Journal of Sociology* 97 (March 1992): 1211–40.

McPherson, James M. *The Struggle for Equality: Abolitionists and the Negro in the Civil War and Reconstruction.* Princeton, N.J.: Princeton University Press, 1964.

Malson, Micheline, et al., eds. *Black Women in America: Social Science Perspectives.* Chicago: University of Chicago Press, 1988.

Neverdon-Morton, Cynthia. "Afro-American Women in Baltimore: Activists for Change and Progress, 1904–1925." In *Maryland: Unity in Diversity. Essays on Maryland Life and Culture*, edited by A. Franklin Parks and John B. Wiseman. Dubuque, Iowa: Kendall and Hunt, 1990.

——. *Afro-American Women of the South and the Advancement of the Race, 1895–1925.* Knoxville: University of Tennessee Press, 1989.

——. "The Black Woman's Struggle for Equality in the South, 1895–1925." In *The Afro-American Woman: Struggles and Images*, edited by Sharon Harley and Rosalyn Terborg-Penn. Port Washington, N.Y.: Kennikat Press, 1978.

Quarles, Benjamin. "Frederick Douglass and the Woman's Rights Movement." *Journal of Negro History* 25 (January 1940): 35–44.

Ripley, C. Peter, et al., eds. *The Black Abolitionist Papers.* 5 vols. Chapel Hill: University of North Carolina Press, 1985–1992.

Robinson, Armstead L., and Patricia Sullivan, eds. *New Directions in Civil Rights Studies.* Charlottesville: University Press of Virginia, 1991.

Sawyer, Mary R. "Black Religion and Social Change: Women in Leadership Roles." *Journal of Religious Thought* 47 (Winter/Spring 1990–1991): 16–29.

Scott, Anne Firor. "Most Invisible of All: Black Women's Voluntary Associations." *Journal of Southern History* 56 (February 1990).

Shaw, Stephanie J. "Black Club Women and the Creation of the National Association of Colored Women." *Journal of Women's History* 3 (Fall 1991).

Sterling, Dorothy, ed. *We Are Your Sisters: Black Women in the Nineteenth Century.* New York: W. W. Norton, 1984.

Stewart, Maria. *Maria W. Stewart, America's First Black Woman Political Writer: Essays and Speeches*, edited by Marilyn Richardson. Bloomington: Indiana University Press, 1987.

Terborg-Penn, Rosalyn. "Discontented Black Feminists: Prelude and Postscript to the Passage of the Nineteenth Amendment." In *Decades of Discontent: The Women's Movement, 1920–1940*, edited by Lois Scharf and Joan M. Jensen. Boston: Northeastern University Press, 1987.

——. "Discrimination against Afro-American Women in the Woman's Movement 1830–1920." In *The Afro-American Woman: Struggles and Images*, edited by Sharon Harley and Rosalyn Terborg-Penn. Port Washington, N.Y.: Kennikat Press, 1978.

Thomas, Mary Martha, ed. *Stepping Out of the Shadows: Alabama Women, 1819–1990.* Tuscaloosa: The University of Alabama Press, 1995.

Tilly, Louise A., and Patricia Gurin, eds. *Women, Politics and Change.* New York: Russell Sage Foundation, 1990.

White, Deborah Gray. "The Cost of Club Work, The Price of Black Feminism." In *Visible Women: New Essays on American Activism*, edited by Nancy A. Hewitt and Suzanne Lebsock. Urbana: University of Illinois Press, 1993.

Vaz, Kim Marie, ed. *Black Women in America.* Thousand Oaks, Calif.: Sage Publications, 1995.

Wright, Michelle D. "African American Sisterhood: The Impact of the Female Slave Population on American Political Movements." *Western Journal of Black Studies* 15 (Spring 1991): 32–45.

214 Suggestions for Further Reading

Yee, Shirley J. *Black Women Abolitionists: A Study in Activism, 1828–1860*. Knoxville: University of Tennessee Press, 1992.

Yellin, Jean Fagan. *Women & Sisters: The Antislavery Feminists in American Culture*. New Haven: Yale University Press, 1989.

Notes on Contributors

Editors

Ann D. Gordon
Editor, Papers of Elizabeth Cady Stanton and Susan B. Anthony, and Associate Research Professor of the Department of History, Rutgers University, New Brunswick, New Jersey.

Bettye Collier-Thomas
Director, Center for African-American History and Culture, and Associate Professor, History Department, Temple University, Philadelphia.

Arlene Avakian
Associate Professor, Women's Studies Program, University of Massachusetts, Amherst. Avakian is the author of *Lion Woman's Legacy: An Armenian-American Memoir* (1992) and editor of *Through the Kitchen Windows: Feminists Write about Food* (1997).

Joyce Berkman
Professor, History Department, University of Massachusetts, Amherst. Berkman is the author of *The Healing Imagination of Olive Schreiner: Beyond South African Colonialism* (1989).

John Bracey
Professor, W.E.B. Du Bois Department of Afro-American Studies, University of Massachusetts, Amherst. Bracey is the coeditor of the Black Studies Research Resources microfilm

series (University Publications of America), which includes "Records of the National Association of Colored Women's Clubs," "Mary McLeod Bethune Papers," and "Records of the Ladies Auxiliary of the Brotherhood of Sleeping Car Porters."

Contributors

Bettina Aptheker
Professor, Women's Studies Program, Kresge College, University of California, Santa Cruz. Aptheker is the author of *Woman's Legacy: Essays on Race, Sex, and Class in American History* (1982) and *Tapestries of Life: Women's Work, Women's Consciousness, and the Meaning of Daily Experience* (1989).

Elsa Barkley Brown
Assistant Professor, Center for Afro-American and African Studies and Department of History, University of Michigan, Ann Arbor. Barkley Brown is associate editor of the two-volume *Black Women in America: An Historical Encyclopedia* (1993).

Willi Coleman
Associate Professor, Department of History, University of Vermont, Burlington.

Gerald R. Gill
Associate Professor, Department of History, Tufts University, Medford, Massachusetts. Gill is the author of *Meanness Mania: The Changed Mood* (1980), and with John E. Fleming and David H. Swinton of *The Case for Affirmative Action for Blacks in Higher Education* (1978), and coeditor of *The Eyes on the Prize Civil Rights Reader* (1991).

Evelyn Brooks Higginbotham
Professor, Afro-American Studies Department, Harvard University, Cambridge. Higginbotham is the author of *Righteous Discontent: The Women's Movement in the Black Baptist Church* (1993).

Cynthia Neverdon-Morton
Professor, History Department, Coppin State College, Baltimore. Neverdon-Morton is the author of *Afro-American Women of the South and the Advancement of the Race, 1895–1925* (1989).

Martha Prescod Norman
Graduate student, Department of History, University of Michigan, Ann Arbor. Norman is a former field secretary and fund raiser for the Student Nonviolent Coordinating Committee.

Janice Sumler-Edmond
Sumler-Edmond is a practicing attorney. She also serves as an associate professor and chairperson of the Department of History at Clark Atlanta University in Atlanta, Georgia.

Rosalyn Terborg-Penn
Professor and Coordinator of Graduate Programs, History Department, Morgan State Uni-

versity, Baltimore. Terborg-Penn is the editor of two collections of original essays: *The Afro-American Woman: Struggles and Images*, with Sharon Harley (1978), and *Women in Africa and the African Diaspora*, with Sharon Harley and Andrea Benton Rushing (1987). She is also the editor of *Black Women in America: An Historical Encyclopedia*, with Darlene Clark Hine and Elsa Barkley Brown (1993).